The New Female Sexuality

The sexual practices and experiences of social nudists, "potential" nudists, and lesbians

The New
Female Sexuality

MANFRED F. DeMARTINO

Foreword by Albert Ellis

✳✳

THE JULIAN PRESS, Inc., Publishers • New York 10011
1969

Dedicated to all those altruistic and
        courageous persons who made this book possible

Also by Manfred F. DeMartino

Dreams and Personality Dynamics *(editor and contributor)*

Counseling and Psychotherapy with the Mentally Retarded *(co-editor and contributor)*

Understanding Human Motivation *(co-editor)*

Sexual Behavior and Personality Characteristics *(editor and contributor)*

CONTENTS

FOREWORD

Considering how important the realm of sexual behavior is, it is amazing how few full-fledged research studies have been done in this area. Everyone knows, of course, about the Kinsey and the Masters-Johnson reports; but how many other first-hand investigations of this nature can the average reader name? Even most social scientists, I am afraid, would be hard-pressed to recall more than a few.

Manfred F. DeMartino's *The New Female Sexuality* is not only a genuine research study in the field of human sexuality, but it is also a happy exception to the rule that such studies are wont to be filled with endless statistical tables, written in deliberately obscurantist terms, and only a little less boring than a school catalogue. It has one feature that might well be expected in most studies of sexual responsiveness but that actually is quite rare: namely, the inclusion of the verbatim responses of many of Mr. DeMartino's female subjects to just about all the important questions that he asked. The perusing of these verbatim responses gives the book's reader a feeling of really entering into the heart of the study; and it also gives him an insight into the sexual attitudes and reactions of what largely appear to be quite healthy American women which he would often fail to get in many other sex books.

DeMartino's research is of course not perfect and (like the Kinsey reports) it will probably be criticized for many aspects of sex, love, and marriage in regard to which it does not query its subjects. It does, however, have several notable assets: (a) It is an up-to-date study of American females, about whom we still know relatively little. (b) It is a pioneering investigation of female nudists, who up to now have been much discussed but practically never scientifically explored. (c)

It not only compares the responses of its main experimental group, female nudists, with those of an adequate control group, females who are potential nudists but who have not as yet actively practiced nudism, but it also includes data on two other interesting groups: first, a number of potential nudists who are also lesbians and second, a number of female members of Mensa (an organization which includes only individuals with unusually high intelligence-test scores). (d) It employs certain psychological tests, especially Maslow's self-esteem and security-insecurity scales. (e) It takes a highly objective, non-moralistic attitude toward its subjects and their responses while at the same time including a distinctly humanistic outlook toward them and their behavior.

As a result of his recent researches with the groups of women reported in this book, as well as other studies in which he has been engaged in recent years, DeMartino concludes that women really are sexually freer today than they tended to be a decade or so ago and that although we may not have had a true sex revolution during this decade, as far as the average male's outlook and behavior is concerned, we may well have had and still be having one on the female side. Do I disagree with the author in this respect? Most certainly not: for I am delighted to have him affirm what I have been saying in this respect on many American campuses and in various other public talks and workshops which I have given since the mid-sixties. While the term *revolution* may be quibbled with, I heartily maintain that literally millions of American females are today having more premarital sex relations than their counterparts in our land ever had before, are much less guilty and upset than they previously would have been about having such relations, and are considerably more liberal and permissive in regard to the sex lives of other women than almost any social thinker would have dreamed they would be in the now almost dim and forgotten 1950's.

In the realm of marital sexuality, our current sex practices are almost certainly even more "revolutionary" in character. For whereas the average wife of the first half of this century largely restricted her relations with her husband to straight sexual intercourse and frequently solely in the time-honored "missionary position" (with the male surmounting the female) at that, today's matron usually experiments with several kinds of noncoital sex acts as well and often looks upon herself as limited and "frigid" when she does not. If anyone thinks that DeMartino's descriptions of the fairly wide-ranging and pluralistic sex lives of the nudist and potentially nudist females which he cites in this volume are only typical of the women in these two fairly permissive types of groups, he'd better give the matter more thought. For I think it is hard to find even highly religious and sexually nonpermissive females today who, in their marital relations with their legal spouses, do not try a reasonably wide range of sexual acts including many that their grandmothers and even mothers would have insisted were "abnormal," "unnatural," and "perverse."

Two other points are nicely confirmed by DeMartino's data: (a) Women, not startlingly different from men, frequently have varietistic leanings. Even when they are highly monogamous in their actual sex and love lives, their fantasies range far afield and they often imagine doing what they do not as yet overtly practice. When, moreover, their imaginings are encouraged rather than discouraged by their husbands, actual adultery and other forms of pluralism tend to become common. (b) Human sex differences are enormous. Where one woman will be completely cold another will be equally impassioned about almost any sex act one can name; and where one woman's range of sex interest is extremely narrow, another's will be exceptionally wide. As I have noted in several of my own sex books, the first law of sexuality and of psychology tends to be the law of widespread individual differences. The information included in *The New Female Sexuality* amply confirms this hypothesis.

It is easy to see why I am delighted with so much of DeMartino's book. Aside from my own biases, however, I am certain that many other readers will find its scholarship, its humanness, and its wealth of fascinating information most informative and instructive.

ALBERT ELLIS

New York, 1969

PREFACE

This book is the first to be published in what it is hoped will be a series dealing with the relationships between the sexual behavior patterns of different types of females and certain personality characteristics. Female social nudists and "potential" nudists with whom this book is mainly concerned comprise one segment of the writer's large sample of females on which data relating to sexuality have been gathered. The total group of subjects consists of females from various walks of life, e.g. housewives, lesbians, TV performers, "exotic" dancers, prostitutes, college students, those of very high intelligence, etc.

As will be seen in the ensuing chapters, this is the first volume ever to report detailed information, based on objective scientific research, concerning the sexual attitudes, desires, practices, and experiences of female social nudists and "potential" nudists, as related to feelings of self-esteem and security. Even A. C. Kinsey, W. B. Pomeroy, C. E. Martin, and P. H. Gebhard in their monumental study did not investigate the sexual practices, etc., of female nudists. The hitherto lack of scientific data pertaining to the sexual activities of female social nudists has been due to a number of factors, including the fact that it is *extremely* difficult to ascertain such information. As a group, for a variety of reasons (especially their frequent experiences of unfair harassment and persecution by the general public and various legal authorities), female nudists (as well as most nudists), are very reluctant to reveal any intimate aspects of their sexual lives, even when requested to do so in a completely anonymous manner. It was only because of the writer's dogged determination and the very gracious help of a number of prominent male and female nudists, along with many other people, that the data presented in this book were obtained. In this regard, the writer would like to express his deepest gratitude to the following persons,[1] most of whom the writer has never had the pleasure of meeting: Brooking P. Tatum, for his help in getting the nudist study underway; Rose Holyrod, Executive Director of the American Sunbathing Association (national association of social nudists), for her very valuable support and for having helped distribute the research forms to female nudists; Dr. Forrest Emerson, Past President of the American Sunbathing Association, for his kind cooperation and understanding, for having been instrumental in getting a number of persons to help the writer acquire nudist subjects, and for making it possible for notices of the nudist study to appear in *The Bulletin* of the American Sunbathing Association; Charles Cropsey, Public Relations Director of the A.S.A. and Executive Editor of *Nude Living* and *Nudist Adventure,* for the time and effort he expended in behalf of this study, for having distributed the research materials to various female nudists, and for having placed a notice of the study in *The Bulletin* of the A.S.A.; June Lange, former Editor of *Nude Living* and *Nudist Adventure,* for having placed a notice of the research project in *Nude Living,* and for having helped obtain subjects; Iris Bancroft, a well-known photographer and one of the editors of *Nudism Today,* for having written an article in *The Bulletin* of the A.S.A. in support of this writer's study, and for encouraging female nudists to participate in the project; Blanche Noir, for having placed a notice of the nudist study in her publication *The Continental Spectator;* Professor William E. Hartman[2] and Marilyn Fithian of the Sociology Department at California State College (Long Beach, California), for having obtained the cooperation of female nudists and having distributed the writer's research materials to subjects; Carolyn Symonds, for her very valuable and enthusiastic assistance in securing the cooperation of a number of subjects; Zelda Suplee, for having distributed the research forms to female nudists; Rey Anthony, for having helped obtain subjects; Robert Novick, formerly an Assistant Professor of Psychology at the State University of New York at Oswego, for having encouraged female students and others to participate in the writer's general study; Dr. William F. Anderson, Jr., a well-known psychologist at Syracuse University, for having made it possible for the writer to include in his overall study of female sexuality a goodly number of subjects who were

---

[1] Because of the limitation of space it is not possible to name all the people who assisted the writer in some way.

[2] See: Hartman, W. E., and Fithian, M. *Nudism in America: A Social Psychological Study,* to be published.

students (some at the graduate level) at Syracuse University; The Research Committee of Mensa (an international organization comprised of individuals of very high intelligence) for having encouraged its female members to take part in the writer's general study; and The Research Committee of the Daughters of Bilitis (a national women's organization whose aim is to promote "the integration of the homosexual into society"), for having distributed the writer's research materials to *Ladder* subscribers. (*The Ladder*, which is published monthly, is a Lesbian Review.)

Most of all, the writer would like to thank his long-time faithful friend and former teacher, the internationally renowned psychologist, Dr. A. H. Maslow, former Chairman of the Psychology Department at Brandeis University, and Past President of The American Psychological Association, for having encouraged the writer to undertake this research project and for having been of immeasurable help in many ways.

MANFRED F. DeMARTINO

Syracuse, New York
April, 1969

The New Female Sexuality

######## 1 ###

INTRODUCTION

While psychologists, sociologists, and anthropologists have studied a wide variety of primitive societies, cultures, subcultures, and cults, the one cult or subculture which has received only scant professional attention is that one which has as its main mode of distinction social nudism. Because of the extreme paucity of scientific data on social nudists, very little is actually known about the sexual attitudes, desires, experiences, motivations, or personality characteristics of such people. Nevertheless, however, females who practice nudism in the presence of nude males are generally regarded by the average uninformed citizen in our society as being exhibitionists, somewhat peculiar and brazen. Then, too, since heterosexual social nudism is contrary to our society's mores and customs, most Americans tend to assume that *all* female nudists are completely uninhibited sexually and engage in all sorts of weird, immoral, and "abnormal" sexual acts. Moreover, the stereotyped conception of a nudist camp (or park) is that it is a place where sexual indiscretions occur constantly. As will be seen in this chapter (and others), however, many of the existing notions concerning the activities of female nudists while they are at nudist parks simply are not supported by the present and previously reported research.

Before turning to an evaluation of the specific sexual practices, experiences, etc., reported by female nudists, it seems in order that some comments be made concerning the history of social nudism, the number of social nudists, the nature of nudist camps or parks (the concept nudist "colony" is incorrect), and nudist magazines.

Historical background of social nudism

For an excellent detailed review of the history of social nudism, the reader is referred to a book by Ilfeld and Lauer, entitled *Social*

2 | THE NEW FEMALE SEXUALITY

Nudism in America. These authors point out that ". . . social nudism as practiced today had its origins in Germany at about the turn of the century. The practice was brought to America in 1929 by Kurt Barthel. Originally under the leadership of Illsley Boone, the movement has expanded until now there are well over one hundred recognized camps in twenty-six states. These are under the direction of three national organizations, the American Sunbathing Association (A.S.A.), the National Nudist Council (N.N.C.), and the Central Sunbathing Association (C.S.A.). The history of the American movement has been seen as characterized by limited facilities, rigid rules, legal battles, internal conflicts, and a pre-occupation with health and naturalness. . . . The European nudist sought health by bathing in the curative rays of the sun. He was a vegetarian and neither smoked nor drank alcohol. Exercise was indulged in regularly. Nudism to him was of moral as well as physical benefit. Removing his clothes put him into 'a natural state.' However, although such physical health may be verbally stressed in American nudism, no such health practices predominate as are encountered in Europe. American social nudism now accents relaxation and sociability as major benefits more than physical health. American nudism, as practiced at present, has changed from its earlier days in that the rigid rules have been somewhat modified."[1]

It is important to point out that like most organized social movements there is not complete unanimity among social nudists concerning the values, ideational philosophy, and attitudes which should be stressed and promoted by social nudism. While the more conservative element still is pretty much in control of things, during the past several years a trend toward increased maturity and liberalism, particularly in regard to sexuality, has been discerned from a number of different quarters. (See for instance: *Nude Living* and *Nudist Adventure*[2] and *Eden Quarterly*).[3] This trend, it appears, is a healthy one, in that it is more consistent with basic human nature.

Since there are many social nudists who are not directly affiliated with any official nudist organization, it is difficult to determine the exact number of social nudists that exist in America and Canada at present. In terms of various reports, however, it would seem that a reasonable estimate would be somewhere around 25,000.

[1] Ilfeld, F. Jr., and Lauer, R., *Social Nudism in America* (New Haven, Connecticut College and University Press 1964), pp. 39–40. By permission of the publisher. For a history of social nudism see also: Johnson, D., *The Nudists.* (Spokane, Washington: Outdoor American Corporation, 1959).

[2] Both of these magazines are published by Elysium, Inc., 5436 Fernwood Avenue, Los Angeles, California, 90027.

[3] *Eden Quarterly* is published by the Outdoor American Corporation, Eden, P.O. Box 7069, Spokane, Washington, 99209.

Nudist camps

Although nudist camps or parks, like nudists, are not all the same, the great majority of them in America impose many restrictions on the behavior patterns of their members. Among other sanctions, as a rule only the first names of the members are used in social conversation, no alcoholic beverages are permitted on the camp grounds, no profanity, "dirty" jokes, or suggestive stories are tolerated, nor is any discussion of religion or politics allowed. Furthermore, no extensive bodily contact is permitted between adult males and females, and nude dancing is prohibited. It is interesting to note that because of the many rigid regulations of nudist camps, some female (and male) nudists prefer to stay away from nudist camps and practice nudism around their homes or in social situations (small groups) which are much less restrictive.

The predominant activities at nudist camps include swimming, sunbathing, playing volley ball, shuffle board, badminton, and tennis. Beauty contests also take place from time to time during which a king and queen are usually chosen. Attendance at the camps is largest on weekends, and to become a member, in addition to meeting a number of "moral" requirements, it is generally necessary that the husband and wife both join. A limited number of single males and females are also accepted as members in many camps. Once a year a national convention is held by the American Sunbathing Association, and sectional conventions are also convened by the Eastern Sunbathing Association, Midwest Sunbathing Association, Northwest Sunbathing Association, and Western Sunbathing Association.

Dr. Albert Ellis, who, by all standards, has to be regarded as one of America's most prominent psychologists in the area of human sexual behavior, has commented as follows with respect to the social nudist movement and nudist parks: "Over the last decade I have had very cordial relations with some of the leaders of the nudist movement in the United States, including Dr. Illsley Boone, June and Ed Lange, and Brooking Tatum—all of whom I have found to be exceptionally enlightened individuals. Sexual liberalism, however, is by no means prevalent among all nudists, as I discovered when I gave a talk to the National Nudist Council Annual Convention at May's Landing, New Jersey, several years ago.

"In fact, if a few of the puritanical nudists who were present had their way at the time, I would have been unceremoniously run off the grounds (in my birthday suit no doubt!) and the likes of me never again invited to sully the pristine chastity of the dyed-in-the-flesh nudists. Fortunately, however, the more than bare (pun intended) majority upheld my right to free speech, and everything went off (no pun intended) quite well. . . .

"Although the American public tends to think of nudists as satyrs and nymphomaniacs, and of nudist camps as "free love" colonies, this picture of nudist life is so far from becoming true that it is not merely a caricature: it comes perilously close to being a contrariety. If anything, nudist communities are much more in danger of being distilleries of antisexualism than factories of rampant sexuality.

"I say this as one who is not a nudist, and who has only spent one full weekend at a nudist park. But I do—as years of psychotherapeutic practice and much clinical research will attest—know a thing or two about sex. And through my patients, friends, and correspondents, I have been in fairly close contact with the American nudist movement for the last two decades.

"Why does nudism perilously border on the fringe of antisexualism? For several reasons:

"1. Nudists have for so many years been unjustly accused of being sunworshipping lechers that they have frequently leaned over backward in the puritan direction, in order to prove their essential pure— and I mean *pure*—heartedness. Most nudist parks strongly favor married couples and their children; and although they do not rigorously ban unaccompanied unmarried individuals who are looking for sex-love mates, or married persons whose mates are not themselves nudists, they subtly discourage or screen such individuals and make many of them feel that they are *personae non gratae*.

"2. Nudists are frequently faddists . . . who are much more interested in *depriving* themselves for various 'healthful' causes—such as vegetarianism, anti-drinking, and anti-smoking—than they are in leading a full, and perhaps a bit sinful, life. Healthy-blooded prosexualists just do not thrive well in this kind of abstemious atmosphere and tend to wind up at non-nudist resorts where the going is smoother and sexier.

"3. . . . Nudists play mixed games together, but are not supposed to touch each other while playing. They go for walks in the woods— but in groups rather than heterosexual twosomes. They engage in social dancing—but in the evening, when they are clothed. Sex, in all this, is not literally proscribed. But, at least by implication, it is often rendered neutral or nonexistent.

"4. Nudists rarely directly face the fact of the erection of the male genitalia. At first I was told, when I questioned young and older nudists about this matter during my stay at a well-known park, that such phenomena just do not occur at nudist gatherings. Further careful questioning brought out the fact, however, that they definitely do occur—but that the 'afflicted' male almost invariably covers himself with a towel, turns his stomach toward the ground, or otherwise hides his impassioned state. This, to me, sounds like the same kind of hypocritical, let's-never-squarely-face-the-issue view of sex that is prevalent in our general society, and that helps keep honest sexuality a secret, shameful thing.

"5. For reasons such as the foregoing ones, it seems clear to me that many confirmed nudists are in the inhibited and low-sexed part of the sexual spectrum. The more fully released, higher-sexed candidates often get eliminated somewhere along the way, while the sexual conservatives hang on for years and years. Quite probably, many or most of the privately practicing nudists in the United States are just as sexually vigorous as any group in the country. But the publicly practicing ones—well, I wonder. . . .

"Fortunately, however, all is not quite lost. Although I have not had the opportunity to make a first-hand survey of the newer nudist groups in this country, my impression from reading their literature and talking to some of their most ardent members, is that puritanism among American nudists is somewhat on the wane. Many more young, single people seem to be taking up nudism than ever before; and fewer of these seem to be of the vegetarian-fruitarian crackpot variety so common to the clan in previous decades. Abstinence and abstention are apparently less stressed in the nudist credos and rule books; and joyous, healthy *living* seems to get the more modern stress."[4]

Some personal observations

In order to observe firsthand the nature of a nudist camp and nudists, this writer visited on two occasions (one was a very special day when nudists from a number of other camps were also present) what is regarded to be the largest nudist camp in New York State, namely, "Empire Haven." This camp is located in a very secluded area a short distance from Moravia, New York, and has approximately eighty members. The overall facilities while not elaborate are adequate and among other things consist of a swimming pool, volley ball court, canteen, all-purpose building, a few small cottages, a number of trailers and small privately constructed living quarters, and ample grounds. "Empire Haven" is run by a very congenial middle-aged couple by the name of Mr. and Mrs. George Robinson, and unlike some other nudist camps

[4] Ellis, A., *If This Be Sexual Heresy.* (New York: Tower Publications, 1966), pp. 66–69. By permission of Dr. Albert Ellis.

(based on various reports), the internal atmosphere of this camp seemed to be essentially one of relaxation and flexibility. While this camp has certain rules and regulations, they are kept at a minimum and as far as could be determined from observation and talking with the Robinsons, they are not the rigid or puritanical kind characteristic of certain other nudist parks. For instance, there is no marked attempt to conceal one's last name, there are no stringent restrictions concerning topics of conversation (while I was there a jovial and good-natured reference was made to a female in regard to my sex-research project[5]— also during a volley ball game in which this writer participated some minor profanity was expressed), nor is there any taboo concerning the touching of a member of the opposite sex; also single persons, including males, are accepted as members. All in all, "Empire Haven" appeared to be a nudist camp where an individual could relax and enjoy himself or herself, provided he or she behaved with a certain amount of decorum and emotional maturity.

From a psychological viewpoint this writer was particularly impressed (introspectively) by the ease and quickness with which the sight of nude females of various ages took on the quality of "commonplace," "naturalness," and "normalcy." In part this was felt to be due to the factor of mental set. Since it was expected and anticipated that nude females would be seen, there was a psychological preparedness present which greatly minimized any possibility of surprise. What was somewhat startling to this writer was the number of females who were extremely overweight and obese. In terms of the kinds of bodily types that one might imagine present at a nudist camp, there were enough so contrary to my anticipated image that I responded somewhat with a sense of amazement. As was expected, there were several females who were quite attractive physically, but for the most part they were more or less average in terms of physical structure.[6] The body builds of the males varied and included several that were definitely obese. While no great amount of physical activity on the part of the adult

[5] In neither of this writer's visits to "Empire Haven" was any major attempt made personally and directly by the writer to obtain subjects. This possibility was discussed with the owners of the camp, who were very understanding, but it was mutually agreed upon that such an undertaking in all probability would prove extremely difficult and unsuccessful. One married female (mentioned above) who was young, friendly, very outgoing, and attractive, however, was approached by the writer in this regard; but she stated that she would first have to ask her husband. Before departing (and never returning) she did say that she became a nudist at the urging of her husband, who frequently expressed a strong visual interest in attractive females, even while driving.

[6] See also: Ilfeld, F. Jr., and Lauer, R. *Social Nudism in America.* (New Haven, Connecticut: College and University Press, 1964), p. 47.

nudists (many children were also present), nor very much group so-cializing was witnessed, it was obvious that the photographing of at-tractive females (with their consent) by *males* was a much-indulged-in pastime. (Based on various reports in nudist magazines, this seems to be a rather prevalent activity among male nudists.) Other than pic-ture-taking, this observer did not notice any *overt* signs of sexual curiosity or sensuality on the part of either the males or females. The camp members simply moved about the grounds in a more or less non-chalant manner and the overall environment took on an air of what may be termed asexuality.[7]

Nudist magazines

During the past few years this writer has had ample opportunity to become familiar with several leading nudist magazines associated with the American Sunbathing Association. Since such magazines have received much criticism on moral grounds from various civic groups and organizations over the past years, a brief discussion of the contents and quality of these magazines seems warranted. Certainly from a structural viewpoint, i.e. the quality of the paper used, photographs (especially those in color), and typography, these magazines have to be regarded as being of very high grade. With respect to the nature (or intent) of the photographs, in this writer's opinion only a small per cent of them have any significant erotic qualities. The great major-ity of the pictures are of rather young and attractive females portrayed in innocent and nonprovoking circumstances. There are also photo-graphs of males and children of various ages, as well as many pictures of complete family units, e.g. mother, father, and children.

By comparison, not only are the leading "sexy" commercial mag-azines which feature *seminude* females far more provocative and titillating than most nudist magazines, but so are many of the ad-vertisements that appear in our most respectable magazines and daily newspapers. (Observe, for instance, some of the advertisements de-signed to sell various female undergarments and cosmetics.) The main objection to nudist magazines is that, unlike most other commercial magazines, they present photographs of adult females and males *com-pletely* nude and include the pubic regions. Many people in our so-ciety, therefore, *imagine* that such photographs are highly erotic and thus obscene. Actually, however, while the novelty of such pictures may at first produce some degree of "shock" on the part of certain viewers, it is felt that in the case of even relatively mature persons,

[7] During my two visits I did not notice the presence of any Negroes.

a desensitizing process occurs rather quickly and observance of the pubic area tends to lose much of its initial sensuality. (This is not to imply that photos of totally nude females come to be viewed without interest. On the contrary, a truly attractive female remains so whether she is completely clothed or nude.)

The articles contained in the magazines usually are written with the essential aim of emphasizing the naturalness of nudity and the wholesomeness of the naked human body. Arguments are presented which support the social nudist movement in all of its ramifications, and often articles appear which have been written by important people in different literary and professional fields. In general, the writings are informative, interesting, and of high quality.

Contemporary developments in social nudism

Presently in our American society there is being witnessed an unparalleled movement which is characterized by a marked tendency toward exposure of the human body (nudity). Evidence of this movement is exemplified by such events as the widespread employment of topless waitresses and the like in restaurants and night clubs throughout the country; the clothing fashions of females, e.g. mini and ultra-mini skirts and dresses, transparent blouses and dresses, the non-wearing of brassieres, the universal acceptance of bikinis; the increasing number of appearances of top Hollywood stars in nude American movie scenes; the frequent and blatant displays of nudity in all sorts of advertisements; the many references to nudity made by TV performers; and most dramatically by the recent rash of Broadway plays in which not only do the actors appear totally nude, but members of the audience also join in and disrobe completely.

Then too, on the psychological scene there has been a resurgence[8] of nudity, particularly in regard to psychotherapy. This resurgence has been especially prominent in California, as manifested in the work of Paul Bindrim, M.A. (certified psychologist), who has been conducting nude group-therapy marathon sessions with much success.[9]

The reasons for this national movement toward increased nudity (aside from the obvious commercial aspects) are complex and varied, and in all likelihood any adequate explanation of this cultural develop-

[8] The word resurgence is used because of the fact that over the years certain psychoanalysts have had their patients remove all of their clothes at the outset of the therapeutic session.

[9] See: Bindrim, P., "A Report on a Nude Marathon: The Effect of Physical Nudity upon the Practice of Interaction in the Marathon Group." Presented at the Forum for Humanistic Psychology, Los Angeles, July 13, 1967.

ment would need to include the following: a) That in part it is an expression of protest against the "establishment" as well as previously adhered-to moralistic, puritanical, and hypocritical traditions, b) That it represents an attempt at a more honest and realistic acceptance of sexuality and the human body, and c) That it symbolizes a desire for a greater feeling, both psychological and physical, of freedom and independence. One very important point that should be highlighted in connection with this nudist cultural movement is that although social nudism is definitely on the rise on the part of society at large, *organized* social nudism in terms of nudist camp membership and the like, is not. The significant aspect here is that the increased acceptance and exhibition of nudity in the United States appears to be much more of a spontaneous and independent than of an organized or formal nature.

What the future modes of dress and behavior will be are always extremely difficult to predict. Nevertheless, one thing seems quite certain, and that is that our American society is moving more and more toward what may be termed "an age of nudity."

2

NATURE OF THE SAMPLE AND SOURCES OF DATA

Introduction

Although every attempt possible was made to obtain a representative sample of female social nudists (see Preface), it is questionable that this was accomplished. The findings reported in this book, therefore, which pertain to the sexual desires, practices, and experiences of social nudists, should be viewed as being based on a somewhat select group of female nudists. The female nudists who in all likelihood are least adequately represented herein (as is true of almost all studies that deal with intimate aspects of sexual behavior) are those who may be described as being "ultraconservative." In this regard, it should be emphasized that female nudists constitute a heterogeneous rather than a homogeneous group. That is, they all do not have similar attitudes or desires with respect to matters relating to sex, etc. Some are quite liberal, accepting and understanding, while others are highly conventional, puritanical, and reactionary. These latter individuals, (the "ultraconservative" group) are the ones who, as indicated above, in all probability are most poorly represented in the present study. In this connection, it is important to point out that from time to time reports were channeled back to this writer to the effect that certain high-ranking nudist leaders, as well as nudist members (both males and females), were "shocked" by the nature of some of the sexual questions included in my questionnaire and thus they refused to support the study or participate in it. This is a reaction which this writer has never been able to fully understand, inasmuch as the anonymity of the respondents was assured. In an attempt to explain the dynamics underlying this emotional response, a few of the more sophisticated and liberal female nudists have suggested, in essence, that while some

10

social nudists are able to accept nudity in a physical sense, they are unable to do so in a *psychological* sense.

Since female social nudists are still rather rare (percentage-wise) in America, it was felt that it would be also of value to include in our presentation the findings based on "potential" nudists. This group consisted of females who indicated either that they *would* like to join a nudist group, *might* like to join a group, or were *undecided* about the possibility of becoming a member of a nudist group. In analyzing and reporting the results of the overall study, as will be noted, "potential" nudists are dealt with separately. Included among the "potential" nudists is a small subgroup which is referred to as lesbians. These subjects, almost all of whom are lesbians essentially, were obtained mainly from my national study of lesbians in which the Daughters of Bilitis organization was most helpful in securing participants. The present study was started during the summer of 1964 and concluded in 1967.

Plan of approach

Each subject was supplied with an eight-page mimeographed questionnaire which dealt with different aspects of sexuality, e.g. attitudes, desires, practices, experiences,[1] etc., two self-administering personality inventories, namely the Maslow Security-Insecurity Inventory (a test which measures feelings of security), and Maslow Social Personality Inventory for College Women, (a test of self-esteem or dominance-feeling), and an addressed (to the writer) and stamped (first-class) envelope. Participants were instructed to answer the questionnaire in as much detail as possible, respond to the inventories, and return everything directly to the writer. While certain identifying information was requested on the questionnaire, such as age, marital status, religious affiliation (and strength of such, in terms of Devout, Moderate, Nonpracticing), education level, and I.Q., the subject's name was *not* asked for. The personality inventories provided space for similar and additional information, including occupation, height, and weight.

As was stated in the Preface to this book, the nature of the study and an appeal for subjects was brought to the attention of female nudists primarily through the personal efforts of certain interested and benevolent people as well as through notices placed in *The Bulletin of the American Sunbathing Association, Nude Living* (a top-grade

[1] The "potential" nudists (lesbians), who were obtained through the assistance of the Daughters of Bilitis organization, responded to a questionnaire which was designed especially for lesbians. The questions asked of these subjects dealt mainly with their *homosexual* (rather than heterosexual) practices, experiences, desires, etc.

nudist magazine), and *The Continental Spectator*. While a number of female nudists wrote directly to the writer and indicated a willingness to participate in the project, many of the subjects were given or sent the research materials by individuals who assisted the writer. A supply of the research forms were sent to these latter persons (assistants) and they in turn distributed them either personally or by mail to interested female nudists. Several of the nudist subjects and most of the "potential" nudists were obtained from college (Brandeis University, Syracuse University, and Onondaga Community College) and noncollege samples, as well as through the cooperative efforts of Mensa,[2] and The Daughters of Bilitis.

Number of subjects and age range

Through the combined efforts of a number of people living in different parts of the United States, over a span of almost three years data was collected on 102 female nudists and 73 "potential" nudists. The nudists ranged in age from 17 to 62 years and had an average age of 34.7 years. The age range of the "potential" nudists was from 17 to 52 years. Their average age was 26.9 years.

Marital status

The great majority (80 per cent) of the nudist subjects were married; eight of whom were married for a second time. A small per cent (9) were divorced, three were separated, two were widows, and five were single.

In the case of the "potential" nudists, 41 per cent were married (several for a second time), 45 per cent were single, and 8 per cent had been divorced. One of the subjects had her marriage annulled, two were separated, and one was a widow.

Religious affiliation

The nudists were comprised mainly of Protestants (50 per cent), and there was an equal number of Catholics (11 per cent) and Jews (11 per cent). That these subjects were not deeply religious in the conventional sense was made apparent by a number of factors including the fact that only two of the Protestants and Catholics respectively

[2] As was indicated in the Preface, Mensa is an international organization which consists of persons who have very high I.Q.'s.

described themselves as being devout, while none of the Jews did so.[3] Although 36 per cent of the Protestants and 33 per cent of the Catholics indicated that they were not practicing their religions, in both instances, however, a greater number of the subjects viewed themselves as being moderate with respect to their religious affiliations. (Protestants = 50 per cent, Catholics = 50 per cent).[4] A few of the responses were not scorable with respect to degree of Protestant affiliation. In the case of the Jewish female nudists, the picture was quite different, in that only two subjects described themselves as being moderate while the rest of them (83 per cent) reported that they were not practicing their religion. Other nudist responses in regard to religious affiliation were as follows: Agnostic (7 per cent), Humanist (3 per cent), "Belief in God" (1 per cent), Atheist (1 per cent), and None (4 per cent). A few of the responses were not scorable.

Of the "potential" nudists, 36 per cent were Protestants, 15 per cent were Catholics, 16 per cent were Jews, 5 per cent were Agnostics, 8 per cent were of no religious affiliation, and 8 per cent were Atheists. Other religious affiliations noted were: Greek Orthodox, Quaker, Scientology, and Zen Buddhist. In a few instances the responses were not scorable.

As a group, like the nudists, the "potential" nudists did not give the impression of being very "religious." For while 37 per cent of the Protestants, 54 per cent of the Catholics, and 20 per cent of the Jews characterized themselves as being of moderate affiliation, 51 per cent of the Protestants, 36 per cent of the Catholics, and 69 per cent of the Jews reported that they did not practice their religions. Moreover, only a very few of the subjects employed the term devout in reference to their religious allegiance.

Educational level

In general, it may be said that the nudists constituted a very well-educated group.[5] This was denoted by the fact that 32 per cent of

[3] See also: a) Ilfeld, F. Jr., and Lauer, R. *Social Nudism in America* (New Haven, Connecticut: College and University Press, 1964), pp. 71–72 and 77. b) Casler, L., "Some Sociopsychological Observations in a Nudist Camp: A Preliminary Study," *Journal of Social Psychology*, 1964. *64*, p. 316. c) Weinberg, M.S., "The Nudist Camp: Way of Life and Social Structure," *Human Organization*, 1967, *26*, p. 94.

[4] The various percentages noted in this study were calculated without any reference to decimal places.

[5] See also: a) Ilfeld, F. Jr., and Lauer, R. *Social Nudism in America* (New Haven, Connecticut: College and University Press, 1964), pp. 69–70. b) Weinberg, M.S. "The Nudist Camp: Way of Life and Social Structure," *Human Organization*, 1967, *26*, p. 94.

them were high school graduates, 37 per cent had received some college education, 16 per cent held college degrees, and 5 per cent possessed advanced degrees (Master of Arts degrees in various fields). Only seven of the nudists did not complete their high school education. One participant did not disclose her educational level.

The "potential" nudists, too, were quite well-educated. High school graduates comprised 23 per cent of the group, while 49 per cent had attended college for a period of time, and 17 per cent had completed college. Six (8 per cent) held Master of Arts degrees and one subject had a Ph.D. degree. There was not any member in this sample who did not at least complete high school. It may be of some significance to observe that, as a group, the "lesbians" were especially well-educated.

Occupations of subjects

The occupations reported by the nudists were as follows: advertising designer, artist, "Beatnik," beautician, chemical analyst, clerk (various kinds), computer programmer, dental assistant, editor, editor (magazine), editor (magazine) and photographer, factory worker, figure model, housewife (this was the most frequently indicated occupation), lab technician, librarian, machine operator and welder, manager of editorial office, medical technologist, psychiatric social worker, peripatologist (mobility instructor of blind persons), punch-press operator, real estate sales, saleswoman, school nurse for a college, schoolteacher, secretary (various kinds), social case worker, student (college), and voice teacher.

The "potential" nudists disclosed the following occupations: accounting, artist, artist's model, bookkeeper, clerk, college student (this was the most prevalently stated occupation), dental technician, domestic, editor, housewife, librarian, minister (in church of Scientology), nursery-school teacher, office worker, psychoanalyst, public relations, real estate saleswoman, registered nurse, secretary, social worker, teacher, technician in electronics lab, and writer.[6]

[6] Although our subjects were not asked any questions relating to their race, there is every reason to believe that practically all of them were Caucasians (white). One nudist indicated that she was a Negress. See also: a) Casler, L., "Some Sociopsychological Observations in a Nudist Camp: A Preliminary Study." *Journal of Social Psychology*, 1964, *64*, pp. 309 and 321. b) Ilfeld, F. Jr., and Lauer, R. *Social Nudism in America.* (New Haven, Connecticut: College and University Press, 1964), p. 47.

Geographic locations of subjects

Since the subjects were not asked to indicate their place of residence, their geographical locations (other than in instances in which the writer sent materials directly to subjects) could be determined only from noting the postmarks on the envelopes in which they returned the completed forms.

The most frequently appearing postmark on the returned envelopes of the nudists was California: the second most prevalent postmark was New York. Other postmarks noted were from the following twenty-two states: Florida, Georgia, Illinois, Kansas, Kentucky, Maryland, Massachusetts, Michigan, Minnesota, Missouri, New Hampshire, New Jersey, North Carolina, Ohio, Oklahoma, Pennsylvania, South Carolina, South Dakota, Tennessee, Texas, Vermont, and Washington. One return carried a Canadian postmark. The predominant appearing postmark in the case of the "potential" nudists was New York; California ranked second. Returns were also sent from the following thirteen states: Colorado, Illinois, Iowa, Massachusetts, Michigan, Minnesota, New Jersey, Ohio, Oregon, Pennsylvania, Vermont, Virginia, and Wisconsin. Two envelopes were sent from Canada.

Personality characteristics of subjects

As was stated earlier, the two objective measures of personality to which our subjects responded were Maslow's Social Personality Inventory for College Women, and Security-Insecurity Inventory. The distribution of scores for these personality inventories is as follows:

TABLE 1
Social Personality Inventory Scores

	Deciles	Self-Esteem
1.	+61 to +182	Very high
2.	+32 to +60	High
3.	+16 to +31	Tendency to be high
4.	+1 to +15	Average
5.	−12 to 0	Average
6.	−13 to −28	Average
7.	−29 to −40	Average
8.	−41 to −58	Tendency to be low
9.	−59 to −81	Low
10.	−82 to −145	Very low

TABLE 2

Security-Insecurity Inventory Scores

Deciles		Security-Insecurity
1.	39–69	Very insecure
2.	31–38	Insecure
3.	25–30	Tendency to be insecure
4.	21–24	Average
5.	18–20	Average
6.	15–17	Average
7.	12–14	Average
8.	9–11	Tendency to be secure
9.	6–8	Secure
10.	0–5	Very Secure

Before presenting the self-esteem and security levels of our subjects, a brief characterization of these terms seems in order. In reference to self-esteem, Maslow has stated that "Dominance-feeling (or self-esteem) is an evaluation of the self. Operationally defined, it is what the subject says about herself in an intensive interview after a good rapport has been established. High dominance-feeling [self-esteem][7] empirically involves good self-confidence, self-assurance, high evaluation of the self, feelings of general capability or superiority, and lack of shyness, timidity, self-consciousness, or embarrassment. Low dominance-feeling [self-esteem][8] is seen as a lack of self-confidence, self-assurance and self-esteem; instead there are extensive feelings of general and specific inferiority, shyness, timidity, fearfulness, self-consciousness. Such people are easily embarrassed, blush frequently, are generally silent, and tend to be incapable of normal, easy, outgoing social relationships or forward behavior."[9] In listing the qualities of secure persons, Maslow has included the following: "1. Feelings of being liked or loved, of acceptance, or being looked upon with warmth. 2. Feelings of belonging, or being at home in the world, or having a place in the group. 3. Perception of the world and life as pleasant, warm, friendly or benevolent, in which all men tend to be brothers. 4. Perception of other human beings as essentially good, pleasant, warm, friendly or benevolent. 5. Feelings of safety, rare feelings of

[7] Inserted by the writer.
[8] Inserted by the writer.
[9] Maslow, A. H., "Self-esteem (Dominance-Feeling) and Sexuality in Women." *Journal of Social Psychology*, 1942. *16*, p. 260. Reprinted by permission of the author and The Journal Press.

threat and danger; unanxious. 6. Feelings of friendliness and trust in others; little hostility; tolerance of others; easy affection for others. 7. Tendency to expect good to happen; general optimism. 8. Tendency to be happy or contented. 9. Feelings of calm, ease and relaxation. Unconflicted. Emotional stability. 10. Tendency toward outgoingness; interest in the outside world, in other people. 11. Self-acceptance, tolerance of self, acceptance of the impulses."[1] Characteristics of insecure persons would include the opposite of those just described, e.g. feelings of not being loved and isolation, feelings that the world is a jungle, perception of other people as being basically bad, frequent feelings of anxiety, feelings of shame, guilt, and suspicion, an intense striving for status, power, and money, etc.

The self-esteem levels of the nudists were as follows: 29 per cent fell into the top three categories (Very high, High, Tendency to be high), 33 per cent into the Average categories, and 25 per cent into the bottom three categories (Very low, Low, Tendency to be low). Several subjects did not return the Social Personality Inventory for Women. With respect to security-insecurity status, 29 per cent of the nudists fell into the top three secure categories (Very secure, Secure, Tendency to be secure), 43 per cent into the Average categories, and 26 per cent ino the three insecure categories (Very insecure, Insecure, Tendency to be insecure). One subject did not return the Security-Insecurity Inventory. In view of the high degree of neuroticism in our society, based on the above overall findings, as a group, the present sample of nudists may be described as being of comparatively sound psychological health.

The "potential" nudists, as a group, were of considerably higher self-esteem than the nudists. This was denoted by the fact that 53 per cent of them placed in the top three (high) categories, 32 per cent placed in the Average categories, and only 10 per cent placed in the bottom three (low) categories. A few participants did not return the Social Personality Inventory. In reference to security-insecurity feelings, however, the picture was much different.[2] For while 19 per cent of these subjects placed in the three secure categories and 39 per cent placed in the Average categories, 41 per cent placed in the three insecure categories.

[1] Maslow, A. H., "The Dynamics of Psychological Security-Insecurity," *Character and Personality*, 1942, *10*, pp. 334-35. Reprinted by permission of the author and the Duke University Press.

[2] As reported by Maslow, the correlation (relationship) between the scores on the Social Personality Inventory for Women and Security-Insecurity Inventory is very low ($r = .08$).

Statistical computations

In addition to computing percentages for the many sexual experiences reported by the subjects, a number of phi correlations were calculated between various sexual acts, attitudes, etc., and feelings of self-esteem and security, as well as between different sexual behavior patterns. In correlating sexual acts with feelings of high and low self-esteem and high and low security, the three high and three low categories, both in regard to self-esteem and security, were dealt with as a unit. (See Tables 1 and 2.) That is, in computing correlations the three self-esteem categories (Very high, High, and Tendency to be high) were combined and treated as one, as were the three low categories (Very low, Low, Tendency to be low). Thus, comparisons were made between the sexual experiences, desires, etc., manifested by those nudists whose scores fell into the three high categories of self-esteem (who were designated as being of high self-esteem) with those whose scores fell into the three low self-esteem categories (who were classified as being of low self-esteem). The same conditions applied in connection with behavior comparisons relating to high and low security feelings.

Because of the marked imbalance of the "potential" nudists' self-esteem scores (53 per cent fell in the three high categories and only 10 per cent in the three low categories) no correlations were computed between their sexual practices and levels of self-esteem.[3]

Although the present study was based on female social nudists and "potential" nudists, and while it is felt that the various percentages noted herein with respect to the particular sexual practices and activities are generally higher than would be found in regard to many other samples of females (i.e. nonnudists or non-"potential" nudists), it is believed strongly that the findings reported in this book which pertain to the relationships between levels of self-esteem and security feelings and sexual behavior *would be* supported to a very considerable extent by random studies of females. As will be seen, this contention is substantiated by previously published research by Dr. A. H. Maslow, this writer, and others. (The writer's present on-going research with a variety of females also lends strength in this behalf).

[3] The writer would like to express his gratitude to James Diamond, who presently holds the position of Assistant Professor of Psychology at the University of Pennsylvania, for having computed all of the correlations referred to in this book.

Changing sexual attitudes

In evaluating the overall results presented in the following chapters, it is essential to keep in mind that the attitudes of females concerning sexuality have been changing significantly over the years (and especially since the Kinsey *et al.* investigations). Moreover, compared with previous decades, females now feel much freer in terms of discussing and disclosing their sexual desires, practices, experiences, etc. These observations are confirmed not only by this writer's overall continuing research with several different samples of females, but also by the studies and experiences of many other researchers as well.[4]

[4] See especially: Reiss, I.L., Issue ed., "The Sexual Renaissance in America." *The Journal of Social Issues,* 1966. 22, No. 2, pp. 1–140.

3

ATTITUDES TOWARD SEX AND STRENGTH OF SEXUAL DRIVE

ATTITUDES TOWARD SEX

Since one's attitudes have a direct bearing on the behavior one displays, it was felt to be of major importance that the attiudes of our subjects concerning sexuality be discerned. The following question, therefore, was the first one asked of the participants: How would you describe, qualitatively, your general attitude toward sex? That is, do you feel it is desirable, good, bad, something unpleasant, etc.?

An analysis of the responses revealed that almost all of the nudists described their attitudes in positive terms. Many in doing so used very glowing and exhilarating phrases. In only a few instances were any comments of a negative nature reported. This finding was in line with our expectations, since it is difficult to imagine how any female could endure the sight of completely nude bodies (of both sexes) for any length of time if she did not have an essentially positive attitude toward sex. Because of the extreme one-sidedness of our findings, it was not possible to compute any meaningful correlations between sexual attitudes and personality characteristics or specific sexual acts. In this regard, it is very significant to note that in his study of female sexuality Maslow found the highest correlations to be between sexual attitude and sexual behavior.[1]

Like those of the nudists, practically all of the responses of the "potential" nudists to the above question were positive. Interestingly enough, several of the lesbians stated that while sex with another female was desirable, sex with a male was another matter, e.g. bad, unpleasant, indifferent.

[1] Maslow, A. H., "Self-esteem (Dominance-Feeling) and Sexuality in Women." *Journal of Social Psychology*, 1942, *16*, 259–94.

Some of the attitudes expressed by the respondents relating to sex were as follows:

Nudists

"Sex is as necessary to an 'all-around' good and happy life as is breathing." "Sex is wonderful and can be beautiful when used properly." "It is desirable, good, very pleasurable—a physiological reaction. It is not sacred, mysterious, precious." "Sex is the greatest thing there is, provided it is based on a real interpersonal relationship of love. 'If God had made anything better he kept it for himself,' someone said. A true communion of mind and body. It colors my whole life and work. I enter into it wholeheartedly and with real delight. I am completely involved with one man, my husband, and he fulfills me completely." "Desirable, pleasurable, rewarding, exciting." "Sex is life and I enjoy life." "Love is the most important object in this world. It is based on kindness and a willingness to put another being first—with regard to sex and every other phase of human relationships. Sex in this regard is not dirty but a pleasure in making another happy." "Desirable; meant to be enjoyed, not merely reproductive; I prefer not to see the sexual drive exploited in advertising, movies, etc., in a way that is unrealistic." "Whoopee!" "With the right person, sex to me, is the most beautiful experience, very desirable. Without it I feel like a dead person—but satisfied I feel wonderfully young." "It is fun, desirable, a necessity. A way of sharing and giving. A means of physical and psychological pleasure. At its best, a fulfillment and recreation." "Sometimes I feel it is a duty, but other times I get a great deal of enjoyment from it." "Unfeeling most of the time." "It is usually desirable, but sometimes it is unpleasant because my husband likes to have intercourse more often than I do." "Sex is a very necessary (for everyone, married or single) and enjoyable thing. There is nothing shameful about it." "Great!" "Most desirable and most necessary." "Sex is enjoyable, a good way to show your love—helps give a person a feeling of well-being and a feeling of being loved. It is bad if used exploitatively or selfishly." "I think sex is natural and the sex act is one of the most wonderful experiences a human can enjoy. It is desirable and good when practiced by two consenting adults." "I think it is absolutely essential to a well-adjusted adult. It's great!" "Desirable when both are in the 'mood' or when a woman teases or aggresses." "A satisfying sexual relationship is very desirable. After a very satisfactory relationship the world seems more beautiful, people are nicer, a sense of well-being and a zest for living, and loving everyone." "A pleasurable necessity. I think of sex as a most pleasurable, natural activity. There has been a lot of claptrap written about sex which implies either that sex is 'holy' and only to be performed with one person or something 'dirty' if performed with someone other than the one person. We feel quite differently—that demanding a monopoly of sex is both unrealistic and damaging to the relationship we have while living together. Our extramarital sex has only enhanced our capabilities for living together." "I believe it is the most important thing in a marriage, and if you don't have a good sex relationship you really don't have a good marriage." "I feel sex is good. Sex is always going to be a part of our lives and should not be thought of as bad or evil. It is necessary but should be confined to the marriage." "I consider sex a very desirable part of a good, well-balanced life—a natural function and a projection of the male and female into the fusion of two separate identities into one being. I feel that a good, well-balanced sex life is a must and the ultimate climax of complete compatibility, respect and understanding of two people who are in love. I believe that for complete compatibility in sex, there must be a give and take attitude on the part of both participants, that there must be an awareness of the desires and likes of both partners. I feel that in marital happiness, anything that makes either party happy is complete, natural and morally right." "Sex is desirable and good. Sex in marriage is a wonderful thing. Outside of marriage it is good but must have its limits. There must be some knowledge of sex (education) before it can be fully appreciated and applied." "Sexual relations in general are a necessary, biological function, necessary for the individual and survival of the species. My own sex life is pleasant, delightful, exciting, satisfying, fulfilling, desirable and good in anticipation, reality and in memory." "I find sex good, desirable, necessary and beautiful . . . I cannot separate sex from emotion. It is a learning experience, and more than that it is a building block in an interpersonal relationship. It may be the first block or it may not come until later, but it is a necessary part. To separate love and sex is ridiculous." "I feel that sex is wholesome and necessary, as much a desirable part of life as exercise or the arts." "Sex is extremely desirable and enjoyable with a partner who is genuinely affectionate and unselfish and who truly desires to please his partner. Once in a while I enjoy sex for sheer lust, where there is no special affection involved." "Desirable, necessary and enjoyable. I am bi-sexual, but favor sexual experience with women." "[Lesbian] It is a good and desirable part of a relationship between two people in love, but not all of that relationship." "It is good when I need it and my husband gives it to me. I don't like it too much of the time as I get tired too easily after I have had it." "Sex is a very real necessity, a thing which should be nurtured and kept beautiful—not abused." "I think sex is a wonderful gift from God for the most perfect relationship between a man and a woman." "Desirable, good and necessary for a happy marriage and true love. Anything that two persons who love each other do sexually to bring pleasure to each other is good and right." "Sex has been a completely foreign element of life to me. Presently, I'm trying to develop constructive attitudes about and toward it." "I think sex is very desirable and good. It's too bad sex is regarded as evil or dirty in our society. Our sexual attitudes are making generation after generation sick and ashamed." "I feel sex is 'wonderful.'"

"Potential" nudists

"I enjoy sex and would like to have it everyday. I think sexual satisfaction is essential for a person." "Sex is desirable. This is a feeling which is brought about naturally and I don't think it should be suppressed." "Sex is a natural function of the body just as eating and sleeping—but sex can be overdone. Although quite desirable, sex should not become the all or end of one's existence." "Very desirable and enjoyable." "Very desirable and fun. It provides an excellent release from many kinds of tension." "I think it is very good, but my religious upbringing sometimes forces me to pretend I don't know it exists or I'm not interested in it—underneath I have a good attitude." "I call it healthy. I *like* it—find it very pleasant." "I feel it is natural and usually good. I don't believe in waiting until after marriage, but I don't believe in having relations with just anybody." "Sex is a very pleasant experience, an important part of my physical existence. Also a very good way to learn of another person (from the inside out so to speak)." "It is a desirable and healthy activity. I would very much like to see it take its place alongside the socially accepted bodily needs such as eating, sleeping, etc." "I think it is one of the most wonderful things there is in life. It is very desirable." "I believe that sex is a natural (morally) human pleasure. However, I have many emotional guilt feelings about it and some very difficult to understand complications involving sex as punishment, sin and shameful." "Sex is healthy, desirable and good. Sex should not be thought of as dirty and be hidden." "Desirable. It is a way of becoming closer to and more aware of another person." "Desirable, highly pleasurable if it is someone I'm attached to and I don't feel I am being taken advantage of." "Gradually beginning to accept it as something pleasant—with as few governing rules as friendship . . . had feared it as evil." "I feel that sex can be a very enriching and fulfilling aspect of life. I feel I differ with many of my close friends to whom sex is a questionable or negative word." "I'm all for it. It may not be the only thing that makes the world go round but I'd hate to have to do without it." "I think sex is great! I find it a wonderful avenue of expression. Anything which gives pleasure (methods new approaches) makes sexual experiences even more interesting and stimulating as time goes on. This area is a tremendous release for me in that I can 'be myself,' let myself go— just have a good time. Generally speaking, sex is just as desirable— I feel badly for young married couples we meet who are all bound up with guilt feelings over sex. I often wonder how they can possibly enjoy one of the most enjoyable parts of life. I doubt that they do— thus your study is a beginning for enlightening." "I find sex under desirable conditions (i.e. right mate) good, pleasant, satisfying, exciting and morally right. I find sex with my husband unpleasant and in a sense morally wrong. [Subject dislikes her husband.]" "Sex is desirable, preferably between two people really in love. It is the height of feelings with the utmost relaxation as an aftermath along with a psychological feeling of well-being." "I feel that sex is desirable and certainly good. I think it is healthy and something that women as well as men can and should enjoy. It is one of the most important and pleasant parts of life and I'm greatly looking forward to that part of marriage." "Basically, I think sex is good and desirable, yet I think many conflicts—i.e. guilt—are yet to come to the surface." "I *love* many types of sexual activities; I regard them as good and highly desirable." "Delightful." "Speaking honestly, it can be a combination of all four [desirable, good, bad, something unpleasant]. I don't at this time assume a general attitude toward it. I've had some really disgusting experiences due to punk men." "Intellectually, I feel it to be most desirable—beneficial in every way, an important factor in maintaining real good health. Emotionally, I have guilt and anxiety feelings as a small child who has been thoroughly taught that sexual pleasure is wicked." "I feel I have a healthy attitude toward sex which is not along the so-called 'right' or 'moral' or 'standard' lines. I think it is a marvelous attitude and wish more thought so." "It is the greatest thing there is, practically." "I feel it is desirable in the right situation. But it can be very dirty and bad. I want it to be beautiful."

"Potential" nudists (lesbians)

"Desirable with same sex. Bad with men." "Sex with another female is desirable—with males completely indifferent—no sexual reaction on my part." "Homosexual sex is good. Heterosexual sex—? ?" "Sex with men is completely unpleasant; with women it can be marvelous." "In combination with love, desirable—necessary, good." "I like it. It is beautiful, something shining. A thing of joy to share with another you care for. To give pleasure and receive pleasure." "Sex is one of the finest things in life. This is especially so when it's with one you love dearly." "It is desirable only with someone I love *and* who loves me in return." "I feel that sex is a necessary, natural, beautiful, and fulfilling thing. No aspect of it shames me."

STRENGTH OF SEXUAL DRIVE

With respect to the relationship between the factors—strength of sexual drive and practice of social nudism—one could hypothesize that, in general, social nudists tend to have either strong (a direct relationship) or weak (an inverse relationship—based on the defense mechanism, reaction formation) sexual drives. As will be seen from the results presented below, the former of these suppositions appears to be the more correct one (at least in reference to the present sample of social nudists). For in response to the question: How would you describe the strength of your sexual drive or desire? That is, would you say it is average, above average, strong, very strong, weak? Actually, there is no way of measuring this objectively: 26 per cent of the nudists reported their drives to be average, 58 per cent to be above average, strong, or very strong, and 8 per cent to be below average or weak. Several responded in such a vague manner that their comments were unscorable. The following summarizes the responses of the "potential" nudists in regard to the strength of their sexual drives: average 23 per cent, above average, strong, or very strong 68 per cent, and weak or below average 5 per cent. A few comments were not scorable. In my study of the sexual attitudes, desires, practices, etc., of Mensa females (females of very high intelligence) very similar findings to those of the nudists were disclosed.[2]

While no significant relationship was found between the strength of the sexual drives of the nudists and self-esteem, somewhat surprisingly a significant correlation was noted in connection with security status

[2] The female Mensa study is based on over 300 females, most of whom have I.Q.'s well above 130. While the great majority of these subjects were residents of many different parts of the United States, a number of them lived in such places as Australia, British Columbia, Canada, England, Hong Kong, Italy, New Guinea, the Netherlands, and Switzerland. Throughout this book, whenever feasible, reference will be made to the Mensa study in the hope of enhancing further, the reader's frame of reference in evaluating the overall results presented herein.

$(r = .35 \ P < .05).$[3] No similar relationship, however, was revealed in the case of the "potential" nudists. In Maslow's study the correlations between sex drive and self-esteem for his two groups of females were reported to be very low $(r = .10$ and $.20).$[4] This writer, in a previous study, stated that "there appeared to be a *slight* tendency for the sex drives of high-dominance women to be *somewhat* stronger than those of low-dominance women."[5]

The following are some of the comments which were reported by the subjects:

Nudists

"Strong." "Slightly above average in so far as I am not inhibited in expressing my sex desires." "Very strong. I need to feel close to a man." "Under the influence of alcohol, above average, otherwise, probably below average." "I occasionally have quite strong sex desires—and often am astounded because they are weaker than expected." "Average." "Above average." "At times it is very strong. The most important factor in this drive is the mood of a woman, when sex is suggested or how a man approaches her. One wrong word can kill the drive." "Weak unless provoked correctly—that is, mentally not physically." "Varies from very weak to very strong." "Very strong with some few select people—absolutely nil with others." "Very strong." "My sexual drive is rather weak and easily sublimated." "I would say my sexual drive was very strong at times of desire. If I think I'm not in the mood and don't wish to participate, my husband usually changes my mind for me with sex play and then my sex drive is very strong, even though I might not have had the desire a few minutes before." "I think it may be strong. I would hate to be without sex. If I'm not in the mood, I can usually be aroused by foreplay." "Depends on my partner—but I would say that generally I would find myself in the very strong class, passionate, desirous and desirable." "In comparison, with my husband—it is very strong." "It varies. It is usually pretty weak. But there are times when I actually get 'horny' and desire sexual contact." "I am average, but once in a while, I feel I have a slightly above

---

[3] For those who have only a limited statistical background, it may be of some help to point out that this description of the statistical findings shows the existence of a relationship between the factors involved, such that there are only 5 chances in 100 that it (the relationship) could have arisen by chance.

[4] Maslow, A. H., "Self-esteem (Dominance-Feeling) and Sexuality in Women." *Journal of Social Psychology*, 1942, *16*, p. 273.

[5] DeMartino, M. F. (ed.), *Sexual Behavior and Personality Characteristics* (New York, Grove Press; 1966, p. 117). By permission of the Citadel Press, Inc.

average drive." "My sexual drive is very strong and something I look forward to daily." "Varies, strong for several days past menstruation—gradually lessening. Usually weaker during pre-menstruation." "Usually strong—sometimes very strong and sometimes I consider myself 'dead'—it is cyclic. Very often, I become very interested in having intercourse during menstruation." "Average. About every four months, I get a *very* strong sexual desire that will last for three days. It takes a lot of sex activity to satisfy me and after the third day I no longer have that driving desire and I can think of the other things without sex." "Strong. Am the aggresor with both men and women." "I would say average most of the time, although I can be aroused almost anytime. Just before, during and after my period I have very strong sexual desires." "Probably average unless I am unusually attracted to a prospective sexual partner, or for the time being re-infatuated by a former sexual partner." "Probably stronger than most 'average' women my age." "I separate sexual drive into physical and emotional. My physical drive is low, probably, and only long abstention or a new appealing man will arouse it. My emotional sex drive is high. I enjoy tremendously making love to the man I love, in some way or another everyday." "My drive depends much on externals and general well-being—currently it is strong and continuous." "I expect it is above average, though being divorced, I've had to put restraints on it. I'm easily aroused when with a man." "A bit below average, but wish I had more." "My sexual drive is abnormally strong. It is not to the point of a nymphomaniac, although it might have been when I was younger, but not now. However, there is little up and down to the desire range." "I consider it average (or normal), but others would probably consider it above average or strong. For instance, the past month I have had sex almost every day—sometimes two-three times a day." "Extremely weak." "My sexual drive is very strong at times and weak at other times. It depends on the way I feel, how tired I am, whether I'm upset or not." "At times I feel my desire is very strong and at other times I have the desire but less strong."

"Potential" nudists

"Depending on my menstrual cycle, I would say it ranges from strong to very strong." "Strong, especially for someone who is intelligent, sensitive, and whose personal philosophy corresponds to mine." "Strong, I was willing to go against my religion because of it." "Very strong, I enjoy sex very much." "Very strong—easily triggered specific drive, fairly constant general desire." "About average or a little above." "Very strong." "Strong". "Normal, I guess. I like it—I want it—but am afraid to indulge!" "Very strong—I like and want more affection (degree of sex depends upon boy or man involved) than I think is usual." "Average or slightly below. There is, however, a marked heightening of desire during the warmer months of the year." "Very strong, very much in my control. I can usually turn it on and off at decision, until launched into love-play." "About average or somewhat above. Depends *very much* on such factors as business, weariness, exposure to erotic sensual stimuli—time of month, etc." "My sexual drive is far above average. I've been told, I think more like a man in regard to sex than most women ever thought of." "I have conscious desires to be kissed and petted, usually with a specific boy in mind. It seems pretty strong." "According to my husband, it is strong. I enjoy sex often." "Very strong, since I have sexual thoughts at the back of my mind most of the time." "My sex drive is fairly strong—I sometimes feel stimulated by minimal contact." "I believe that my sexual desire is strong, very strong, but not satisfied. But I don't think it will diminish any because of non-satisfaction." "Sexual drive is probably average but I don't often fight it which I suppose, at least among single women, is not average." "My sexual drive varies depending on the everyday interpersonal relationships with my husband. In earlier years above average, now average." "My guess is that it is average, or possibly stronger than many women my age permit themselves to feel." "*Very strong* unless my mind is against the one I am having sex with—if my thoughts fight it, my desire is practically nonexistent."

"Based on my limited knowledge of other women (from some confidences, men's remarks, etc.) I have a very strong sexual desire." "I think my sexual drive is at least average—possibly above average—for a girl my age. I am judging by my fantasies, masturbation and slight heterosexual experience I have had." "Very strong, sometimes practically nymphomania; other times very weak. Seems to vary with good and bad moods respectively. Possibly menstrual cycle?" "I would think 'very strong'—but very directed. Many men just don't interest me at all—but if I am involved, then 'very strong' " "Weak." "With the right male very strong—it is not a strong desire for sex alone." "Average. However, it depends on the partner and my desire for him."

"Potential" nudists (lesbians)

"Average." "Strong." "Weak." "It is above average—extremely strong." "It isn't necessary for me to have sex every night—but it's nice.

Very strong—as once a day—or maybe two or three times per day is what I really enjoy." "Strong to average—depends upon female love object and extenuating circumstances." "Sex is necessary for me. It provides, for me, a healthy mind and a clearer, more active and full life."

4

**MASTURBATION: AGES PRACTICED, HOW LEARNED,
METHODS, ORGASM, FANTASY, SINCE MARRIAGE,
ATTITUDES, EFFECT ON MARITAL SEX LIFE**

As a result of the studies by Kinsey and his associates, as well as those
which preceded and have come after them, it has been firmly established that masturbation on the part of both males and females is a
very common practice. Research has also disclosed that this is an
activity which is experienced by infants, young children, adolescents
of all ages, the middle-aged (both single and married), and the aged.
In short, it may be stated unequivocally that masturbation is a universal behavior, and one which occurs at all ages. In an effort to add
to the research concerning female masturbatory activity, which at
present is not as abundant as that in connection with males, the following series of questions were asked of our subjects: Has masturbation ever been a part of your life experience? —— If so, at about what
age or ages did it occur? —— How did you learn about it? ——
What methods were used? —— Was it to the point of orgasm? ——
Was fantasy ever used? —— If so, describes same. —— Have you
engaged in masturbation since marriage? —— If so, describe circumstances. —— How do you feel about the practice of masturbation; is
it acceptable to you, good, bad, etc.? —— Do you feel it has had an
effect on your marital sex life in any way? (e.g. has it helped, hindered,
etc.?)

Prevalence

That masturbatory activity on the part of both the nudists and
"potential" nudists was very widespread, was made apparent by the
fact that 84 per cent and 80 per cent of them respectively indicated
having masturbated at some time during their lives. The female Mensa

group, interestingly enough, yielded quite similar results to those of both the nudists as well as the "potential" nudists with respect to the practice of masturbation. Kinsey *et al.* reported that "About 62 per cent of all the females in the sample had masturbated at some time in the course of their lives."[1] They also pointed out that "The number of females who had ever masturbated to the point of orgasm differed somewhat in educational levels . . . the accumulative incidences at age forty ranged from 34 per cent among females who had never gone beyond grade school, and 59 per cent for the females of the high school level, to 63 per cent among the females who had gone beyond college into graduate work."[2] In a previous study this writer noted that 53 per cent of the female participants had masturbated during some interval of their life span.[3] Recently McCary stated that "From 50 per cent to 80 per cent of all women masturbate at one time or another, the variance in figures resulting from differences in results of several investigations on the subject."[4]

Noteworthy is the fact that the practice of masturbation in the case of the nudists, was found to be significantly related to high self-esteem ($r = .44$ P$< .05$). No significant relationship, however, was revealed in regard to the security feelings of our subjects.[5] Maslow reported a correlation of .41 between dominance test score and masturbation.[6]

Ages of occurrence

The earliest age recorded by the nudists at which masturbation first

[1] Kinsey, A. C., Pomeroy, W. B., Martin, C. E., and Gebhard, P. H., *Sexual Behavior in the Human Female.* (Philadelphia; Saunders Co., 1953, p 142). By permission of Dr. Paul H. Gebhard and the Institute for Sex Research, Inc.— Although the Kinsey *et al.* findings are still very important and useful, they no longer can be viewed as representing *present-day norms* with respect to female sexuality. This is because of the fact that many significant changes in sexual attitudes and behavior have occurred on the part of females since the Kinsey studies. Actually, no universal norms exist for contemporary female sexuality in our American society.

[2] Ibid, p. 148. By permission of Dr. Paul H. Gebhard and the Institute for Sex Research, Inc.

[3] DeMartino, M. F. (ed.), *Sexual Behavior and Personality Characteristics.* (New York: Grove Press, 1966), Chap. 5.

[4] Reproduced from *Human Sexuality,* by James L. McCary, Van Nostrand-Reinhold Company, Princeton, 1967, p. 213.

[5] Since a little over half of the female Mensa subjects were of high self-esteem and only a very small number were of low self-esteem, no attempt was made to compute any correlations between their sexual experiences and levels of self-esteem. Correlations between their levels of security feelings and sexual activities have not been computed as yet, and so it is not possible to refer to them in the present book.

[6] Maslow, A. H., "Self-esteem (Dominance-Feeling) and Sexuality in Women." *Journal of Social Psychology,* 1942, *16*, p. 269.

occurred was two years and the oldest age was forty years. The median age at which masturbation was first practiced was thirteen. In the great majority of the cases masturbatory activity was indulged in over a span of years, including the adult years.

Three years was the earliest age indicated by the "potential" nudists at which masturbation was first experiecned, and the oldest age was twenty-three years. The median age was twelve years and like the nudists, the large majority of these subjects continued masturbating for a number of years, including during adulthood.

In relation to the factor of age, the Kinsey group stated "In our sample, masturbation had occurred among females of every group, from infancy to old age. . . . We have records of 67 infants and small girls three years of age or younger who were observed in masturbation, or who as adults recalled that they had masturbated at that age. We have one record of a seven-month-old infant and records of 5 infants under one year of age who were observed in masturbation."[7] Kinsey and his associates in discussing the duration of masturbatory behavior disclosed that "Among the females who were between thirty-one and thirty-five years of age at the time they contributed histories to the present study, 9 per cent of those who had ever masturbated had done so for only a single year or less than one year. About one-sixth (16 per cent) had extended their activities over a period of two to five years. For 16 per cent the activity had been continuous between six and ten years and more than half (59 per cent) had masturbated for more than ten years. The average (median) female in this group had masturbated for something near fourteen years. Among the females who had ever masturbated and who were over fifty years of age at the time they contributed their histories, 73 per cent had masturbated for more than ten years, and the median female in the group had masturbated for twenty-four years."[8]

How masturbation was learned

The predominant manner in which masturbation was learned by the nudists was through self-discovery (experimentation, personal exploration, accidentally). Other major sources of learning included the following categories: husband or male friends, reading, and girl friends.

---

[7] Kinsey, A. C., et al., Sexual Behavior in the Human Female. (Philadelphia: Saunders Co., 1953), p. 141. By permission of Dr. P. Gebhard and the Institute for Sex Research.

[8] Ibid., pp. 147–48. By permission of Dr. P. Gebhard and the Institute for Sex Research.

The "potential" nudists learned to masturbate in essentially the same ways.

Kinsey and his co-workers reported that "Most of the females . . . had discovered how to masturbate as a result of their exploration of their own genitalia."[9] They also indicated that about 43 per cent of the females who had ever masturbated had learned to do so from verbal and/or printed sources of information. Heterosexual petting or pre-coital activities accounted for the occurrence of masturbation in about 12 per cent of the instances. About 11 per cent of their female subjects learned to masturbate from observing others doing so, and homosexual activity resulted in masturbatory behavior in about 3 per cent of the cases.

Responses related by the subjects concerning the age or ages that masturbation occurred and how it was learned, included the following:

Nudists

"A.[1] First at 6 years, as a teenager, and until marriage . . . and [since marriage]. L.[2] From a boy my own age." "A. 32 [and since marriage]. L. From a friend (a male lover)" "A. 30–34 [and since marriage]. L. General knowledge." "A. Began at about 6 years. [and since marriage]. L. Accidentally—by climbing a pole at the park." "A. 6 yrs. [and at present]. L.?" "A. 11 [and since marriage]. L. Through a sister." "A. 15 years old [and since marriage]. L. Books, word of mouth, jokes." "A. Only in recent years—age 25 [and since marriage]. L. From my husband." "A. 16–20–30–40 [Not since marriage]. L.?" "A. Generally unconscious. L. I was not aware of what masturbation was in women until after I had had considerable heterosexual relations. Recently [since marriage] I have used masturbation in conjunction with intercourse." "A. Started about 10 years of age and also during marriage. L. From my brother." "A. 6–7 [and at present]. L.—." "A. Late teens, early 20's [and at present]. L. Literature regarding sexual behavior, etc." "A. About 11, and as an adult. L. By experimenting, perhaps reading; from husband and others, more reading and experimenting." "A. From 8 years old at least [and later]. L. Experimentation." "A. Mostly during college—18–21. L. I think I just discovered it on my own." "A. At 14 [and later]. L. Felt a need for some satisfac-

---

[9] Kinsey, A. C., Pomeroy, W. B., Martin, C. E., and Gebhard, P. H., *Sexual Behavior in the Human Female.* (Philadelphia: Saunders Co., 1953), p. 137. By permission of Dr. P. H. Gebhard and the Institute for Sex Research, Inc.

[1] A. stands for an abbreviation of the word Ages.

[2] L. stands for an abbreviation of the word Learned.

tion." "A. About 20 [and later]. L. Through experimenting and following the good sensation." "A. 10–13, also after mariage in 20's [and later]. L. Reading, girl friends, and sex play with boys and men." "A. 14 [and later] L. Accidentally in the tub." "A. Teenage, 34, L. A girl friend (aunt, younger than me)." "A. 10–on. L. I was reading a marriage manual at age 10 and stumbled across the subject." "A. 24 and up. L. From my husband." "A. 3 or 4 [and at present]. L. I didn't 'learn.' It just felt good to touch my clitoris." "A. The only time I ever masturbated was just before marriage because I thought it would be wise to see what excited me. L.—." "A. As long as I can remember. L. Observation." "A. 7 [and later]. L. When the outpouring water [in the tub] hit my vagina—I think." "A. 38. L. Reading, talking." "A. 7 to 10 [and later]. L. From cousins." "A. 40 (I think). L. Read about it." "A. Approximately 24. L. A male friend gave me a vibrator." "A. 35–40—during divorce period. L. Through reading." "A. 12 or 13. L. Girls at school." "A. 16 years old [and later]. L. From a girl friend." "A. About 17 [and later]. L. Discovered it myself through curiosity." "A. I don't know, I think I've always liked to arouse myself." "A. 30 to present. L. Reading." "A. 23 [and later]. L. On my own after sexual desire had been aroused by a man with whom I could not have relations for various reasons." "A. Started between 2 and 3 years of age and continued regularly till marriage—after that only occasionally. L. By touch." "A. From age 6 to present. L. Seems to have been an instinctive source of comfort in childhood." "A. 16 to 20 [and later]. L. From other girls in our high school group." "A. Started at 11 [and later]. L. From a girl friend who was two years younger." "A. From 4 years to present. L. I don't know." "A. From puberty on. L. Was masturbating before I was aware of what it was." "A. About 8 [and later]. L. The boy and girl next door." "A. 19 years [and later]. L. My husband showed me." "A. I learned to masturbate at the age of 4 [practiced through adult years]. L. Taught by a neighbor boy of the same age. Our relationship was perfectly normal and happy because we examined each other to our heart's content and mutually masturbated." "A. Early, 6–7–8? [and at present]. L. Playing in the bath tub." "A. 18 to present. L. From fiancé (ex-husband)." "A. 11, 12 frequently, 23 rarely [and later]. L. Self-experimentation, no knowledge of it as masturbation." "A. 12 [and later]. L. Accidentally—through exploration." "A. Started when I was 9 or 10 [and at present]. L. Self-discovery when washing myself, I suppose." "A. 18 through 23 [present]. L. Accidentally. I didn't know I was doing it until it started to feel good."

"Potential" nudists

"A. Early teens on. L. Personally—individually." "A. 11 or 12 [and later.]. L. From a girl friend." "Ages 4 or 5. L. I don't remember." "A. 12, 14, [and later]. L. Self-experimentation." "A. Since 18. L. From sister." "A. 8 or 9 on. L. From accidental contact." "A. 18 (I have no memory of infantile masturbation). L. Extensive petting and sex play with a boy friend." "A. 17 and 18 also at present. L. Partially from reading, also experimentation." "[Lesbian]. A. 13 [and at present]. L. Discovered it quite naturally when reading Peyton Place." "A. 13, 14, 15, 16. L. Cousin —books." "A. 9 to 15. L. Through play with other children." "A. 15 on. L. I think there was a gradual progression starting when I was in my early childhood—at which time I would occasionally play with myself." "A. Started at age 9— until present. L. At a Girl Scout Camp." "A. 21 to present. L. Had heard of it many times—exploring myself one night at age 21 and inserting objects into urethra, vagina and rectum; and rubbing clitoral area, I accidentally had an orgasm." "A. 8 [and later]. L. A little boy played with me and it felt good, so I did it when I was alone." "A. 18 and at present. L. Seemed a natural thing to do to relieve frustration." "A. About 13 [and later]. L. From a sex manual." "A. I consider earliest masturbation was an invention of sexy day dreams from about 6 or 7. I never used physical means or hands until . . . 15. I then used picture stories (I told myself) and hands to duplicate the experience. First at 15—sporadically to now. L. Made a sexy mind picture and experienced full climax." "A. 22–25 [to present]. L. From the opposite sex using it to stimulate me." "A. 20, right after divorce [and later]. L. My first husband told me women could do it." "A. Approximately 8 years [and later]. L. From another 8-year-old girl." "A. 3–6, 18 on [to present]. L. Re-introduced by homosexual episode." "A. Around 12 years old [and at present.] L. Through discussions with older girl cousins." "A. I believe it started at 18. L. From a boy I was dating at the time." "A. 4–9 [and as an adult]. L. Playing doctor with others of same age." "A. 13–18. L. Self-discovery." "A. 23. L. Reading." "A. Between ages 10 and 19. L. I don't recall exactly though I think it was from the sensation I got from lying on blankets which produced friction with the clitoris." "A. About 8 years of age [and at present]. L. I just happened to be rubbing myself and decided it felt good." "A. Beyond age 18–19 or so and at present. L. Accidental stimulation in bed from thoughts, bed clothes, etc." "A. 21 [and at present]. L. I suppose I 'stumbled' on it accidentally." "A. Approximately 16 and on. L. Accidental clitoral stimulation from leaning on something." "A. 12 [and at present]. L.

Didn't know what I was doing; it just happened." "A. 10 through 17, mostly [and later]. L. Accidentally while clamping legs together to delay going to the bathroom." "A. About 16 or 17 [and at present]. L. By accident." "A. 8 or 9 and at maturity. L. Reading (oddly enough) about it's dangers!"

"Potential" nudists (lesbians)

"A. Since I was 8 or 9 years old. L. Sisters and neighborhood children." "A. 12 years—continuing. L. Experimentation." "A. Early teens [and later]. L. In recent times I participated in an open discussion of masturbation. I discovered many others masturbated and have since tried masturbation. However, not too successful but sometimes enjoyable." "A. 10 to present [age 23]. L. Stumbled upon it in course of exploring my own body." "A. 5 years to present. L. Came naturally; was never told." "A. 12 years and since. L. Don't remember." "A. 12. L. Instinct." "A. Began at 10–12 [and later]. L. Accidentally discovered from swinging on and climbing hand over hand on gym rope."

Methods

By far the most frequently described method of masturbating by both the nudists and "potential" nudists involved in some way use of either the finger (or fingers) or hand (manual) and clitoral stimulation (manipulation). Other masturbatory techniques described by the nudists included: hand manipulation of the vagina; some form of clitoral manipulation through crossing of the legs and rubbing thighs together; water from bathtub faucet or shower running on the clitoris; use of a pillow (placed between thighs—genital area) and rubbing against it; rubbing against objects such as a chair, bicycle seat; pressing the vulva; insertion of finger into vagina as well as such objects as pencils, toothbrush handles, bananas, a carrot, a bottle, and a piece of paper; use of a vibrator or massager;[3] and anal (rectal) stimulation. Noteworthy is the finding that no nudist made any specific mention of either breast or nipple stimulation as part of her masturbatory activity. Three "potential" nudists, however, did make reference to hand contact with nipples and/or breasts. Except for the use of hand-nipple (breast) contact, in general the masturbatory techniques recorded by the "potential" nudists were very similar to those of the nudists.

[3] There are indications that vibrators are being used more and more by females to enhance their masturbatory activity.

Kinsey *et al.* found that "Masturbation among the females . . . had most frequently involved some manipulation of the clitoris and/or the labia minora."[4] Stimulation of the breasts and nipples had been involved in the masturbatory activity of about 11 per cent of the females, and almost 10 per cent of those who masturbated did so at times "by crossing their legs and appressing them to exert steady or more rhythmic pressure on the whole genital area."[5] The use, at times, of vaginal insertions during masturbation was noted by approximately 20 per cent of the females. These investigators also reported that "There were still other masturbatory techniques which were regularly or occasionally employed by some 11 per cent of the females . . . Some had rubbed their genitalia against pillows, clothing, chairs, beds, or other objects. Douches, streams of running water, vibrator, urethral insertions, enemas, other anal insertions, sado-masochistic activity, and still other methods were occasionally employed, but none of them in any appreciable number of cases."[6]

Based on their direct observations of the masturbatory techniques employed by females, Masters and Johnson have stated that "No two women have been observed to masturbate in identical fashion. However, there is one facet of general agreement. Women rarely report or have been noted to employ direct manipulation of the clitoral glans. In those isolated instances when the technique is used it is limited to the excitement phase only and frequently a lubricant is applied to this normally quite sensitive tissue. Additionally, the clitoral glans often becomes extremely sensitive to touch or pressure immediately after an orgasmic experience, and particular care is taken to avoid direct glans contact when restimulation is desired.

Those women who manipulate the clitoris directly concentrate on the clitoral shaft. Usually they manipulate the right side of the shaft if right-handed, and the left side if left-handed. Occasionally, women have been observed to switch sides of the shaft during stimulative episodes. A relative degree of local anesthesia may develop if manipulation is concentrated in just one area for extended periods of time or if too much manipulative pressure is applied to any one area.

Women usually stimulate the entire mons area rather than concentrating on the clitoral body. Regardless of whether the clitoris is

[4] Kinsey, A. C., Pomeroy, W. B., Martin, C. E., and Gebhard, P. H., *Sexual Behavior in the Human Female.* (Philadelphia: Saunders Co., 1953), p. 158. By permission of Dr. P. H. Gebhard and the Institute for Sex Research, Inc.

[5] Ibid., p. 159. By permission of Dr. P. H. Gebhard and the Institute for Sex Research, Inc.

[6] Ibid., p. 163. By permission of Dr. P. H. Gebhard and the Institute for Sex Research, Inc.

stimulated by direct means or indirectly through mons area manipulation, the physiologic responses of the clitoris to elevated sexual tensions are identical. Most women prefer to avoid the overwhelming intensity of sensual focus that may develop from direct clitoral contact. Instead, mons area manipulation produces a sensual experience that although somewhat slower to develop is, at orgasmic maturity, fully as satiating an experience as that resulting from direct clitoral shaft massage."[7]

Orgasm attainment

Of those nudists and "potential" nudists who masturabted at one time or another, 90 per cent and 84 per cent respectively reported having experienced an orgasm from this activity. Kinsey *et al.*, in this connection revealed that "About 62 per cent of all the females in the sample had masturbated at some time in the course of their lives. About 58 per cent had masturbated at some time to the point of orgasm. The 4 to 6 per cent which had masturbated without reaching orgasm was chiefly a group of females who had made only single or desultory and infrequent trials of their capacities, for nearly all of those who had seriously experimented soon learned to reach orgasm."[8]

Use of fantasy

The use of some form of fantasy during masturbatory activity at some time during their lives was noted by 53 per cent of the nudists and 72 per cent of the "potential" nudists. Kinsey and his collaborators, in this regard, found that "For more than a third (36 per cent) of the masturbating females in the sample, nothing more than physical stimulation seemed to have been involved. For the remaining two-thirds (64 per cent), psychologic stimulation through fantasy concerning specifically sexual situations had sometimes accompanied the physical stimualtion. For just about half (50 per cent) of the females, fantasies had occurred in connection with most of their masturbation, at least during certain periods of their lives. For a fair number, fantasies had not begun until some years after the masturbation had begun. In

[7] Masters, W. H., and Johnson, V. E., *Humn Sexual Response*. (Boston: Little, Brown & Co., 1966), pp. 63-64. By permission of Little, Brown & Company.

[8] Kinsey, A. C., Pomeroy, W. B., Martin, C. E., and Gebhard, P. H., *Sexual Behavior in the Human Female*. (Philadelphia: Saunders Co., 1953), p. 142. By permission of Dr. P. H. Gebhard and the Institute for Sex Research, Inc.

consequence, fantasies were more common among the older females and less common among the younger females."[9]

With respect to the nudists, the use of fantasy during masturbation was found to be significantly related to high self-esteem ($r = .32$ $P<$ $.05$). No significant relationship was observed in regard to the secuirty feelings of the subjects. In referring to his high dominance females, Maslow has commented as follows, "masturbation is often (not always) found to be a highly sensual affair, protracted and making use of all sorts of titillating and stimulating thoughts, objects and acts. In both masturbation and sexual intercourse the whole body, rather than just the restricted genital area, is apt to be involved. Every spot or area that is erotically stimulable is apt to be enlisted in the game that the act has become, and in building up to a tremendous orgiastic climax."[1]

Although a variety of fantasies were experienced by the participants, the one recorded most predominantly by both the nudists and "potential" nudists involved the subject making love (having sexual intercourse) with a desired male. Other fantasies reported by the nudists included the following: being raped or forcefully taken; having sex with a Negro (and a Mexican); sexual thoughts about animals; being the "belle of the ball"; how other people masturbated or had sexual intercourse; group sexual activity (and with numerous men); looking at other men and women performing the sexual act; visualizing females and males in the nude; thoughts of a penis substitute for intercourse; imagining conversations with a man; recalling previously experienced events and those seen in the movies and burlesque shows; and rubbing against trees and "father's leg." Among the fantasies indicated by the "potential" nudists which were different from those described by the nudists, were the following: being kissed in the gential region; thoughts of men or the subject urinating or deficating in inappropriate places; thoughts of engaging in fellatio and cunnilingus simultaneously; sadomasochistic scenes; watching someone being beaten; being a male aggressor; being in a nudist camp with many men with huge penises; having intercourse with a man with an unbelievably huge penis; being a prostitute or an older woman seducing a young, naïve boy; dancing suggestively in the presence of males; getting virtuous women to yield to men unwillingly; Roman baths, cannabalism, and dreams of conquering the world.

[9] Kinsey, A. C., Pomeroy, W. B., Martin, C. E., and Gebhard, P. H., *Sexual Behavior in the Human Female.* (Philadelphia: Saunders Co., 1953), p. 164. By permission of Dr. P. H. Gebhard and the Institute for Sex Research, Inc.

[1] Maslow, A. H., "Self-esteem (Dominance-Feeling) and Sexuality in Women." *Journal of Social Psychology,* 1942, *16,* pp. 286–87. By permission of Dr. A. H. Maslow and The Journal Press.

Comments recorded by the participants concerning the methods used during masturbation, orgasm attainment, and fantasies experienced, included the following:

Nudists

"Pressing the vulva against the clitoris. As a teenager and until marriage [in the twenties] masturbation was engaged in frequently. O.[2] Yes. F.[3] I don't remember." "Finger manipulation, and rubbing the clitoris against some narrow surface. O. Only after teens. F. Occasionally. Simply of intercourse." "Manual. O. Yes. F. Occasionally, but only after knowing the real thing. Masturbation lost some of its charm, and fantasy is sometimes necessary. I fantasy before—not during—I prefer to concentrate on one thing at a time—of making love with a current lover (when they are unavailable). If there is no current lover I enjoy a rape fantasy with a number of men—preferably a Negro." "A pillow. [Pressed against genital area.] O. Yes. F. Dreams of having a lover and from reading sexy books." "Hand. O. Yes. F. Thoughts of what it would be like to make love with a man." "A massager. O. Yes. F. No." "Finger manipulation. O. Yes. F. Various—more recently in life, fantasy has been less fantastic." "Finger. O. Yes. F. Usually I think of some man, especially in the act of intercourse." "Recently, [since marriage,] I have used masturbation in conjunction with intercourse. O. Yes. F. No." "Sometimes with fingers—often with object to simulate penis. O. Yes. F. "Rubbing with hands. O. Occasionally. F. If being stimulated by reading is considered fantasy." "Squeezing legs together in a curled-up position and tightening them rhythmically; clitoral, with fingers. O. Yes. F. "Yes—seldom as a child, I imagined being captured and tied by a forbidden (or threatening) and attractive Prince, etc., and forced to do as he said. Enjoyable, but only with use of fingers to climax." "Running water on clitoris in bath tub or shower. O. Yes. F. In later years (high school and college), fantasies of being 'raped' or forcefully taken by some appealing male of the moment." "Clitoral stimulation mostly, followed by insertion of finger into vagina at orgasm. O. Yes. F. I sometimes became aroused from something I was reading (e.g. descriptions of sexual practices in a primitive tribe, in an anthropology book), but I didn't engage in fantasy during masturbation. I concentrated on physical sensations." "I used my finger, at the same time clenching my legs together and reached satisfaction. O. Yes. F. No." "I squirted water in my cunt from the faucet [while in

[2] O. is an abbreviation of the word Orgasm.
[3] F. is an abbreviation of the word Fantasy.

the bathtub], by doubling up my legs and getting close. *O.* Yes. *F.* No. The physical sensation was enough—the force of the water at about half-force directly on the cunt." "As a child—fingers, rubbing against things, pressing things against vulva, bicycle seat. *O.* Yes. *F.* Sometimes. Usually think of a particular man and imagine us in the sex act." "Hand, rubbing, shower. *O.* Yes. *F.* Copulation like animals." "Hand—and flowing water from nozzle in bathtub. *O.* Yes. *F.* I would think about my boyfriend." "My whole hand pressure and friction, 2) My finger found an orifice with no known function, 3) Rough, scratch, bulky blanket between my legs. *O.* Yes. *F.* No." "Hand and pencil, carrot and hand. *O.* Yes. *F.* No." "Touchng and gently rubbing my clitoris. *O.* Yes. *F.* When I was little, I'd be the Princess in fairy tales. When I was older I'd be the 'belle of the ball.' It was such a nice way to become sleepy." "Hands and various objects. *O.* Yes. *F.* Visualized 'male' angels, etc." "Sliding down poles, massaging with the hands. *O.* Yes. *F.* I used to pretend it was whatever boy I liked at the time." "With a vibrator. *O.* At first I didn't have an orgasm. Gradually, I was able to relax and have them. *F.* Having intercourse, rubbing against trees, father's leg; animals (deer, horse, dogs); sinking into warm water, etc." "Finger manipulation—also pressing two legs together in a sideways position. *O.* Yes. *F.* No." "Rectal stimulation and at age [in the twenties] clitoral as well as rectal. *O.* Yes [In the twenties]. *F.* No." "Playing with myself. *O.* Yes. *F.* No." "Clitoral stimulation with finger—also pillow at one time—self-manipulation, touching all parts of my body. *O.* Yes. *F.* Sometimes. Thinking about men and situations in which love-making took place—settings, descriptions of actions, imagining of conversation." "I have rubbed myself. *O.* No. *F.* No. Occasionally during periods of sexual abstinence, I have awakened from sleep with a sexual throbbing—at these times I have rubbed myself to ease the throbbing. Very frustrating and I have never been able to achieve orgasm this way." "Gentle manipulation of clitoris by crossing legs and rubbing thighs together. My masturbation is very anal oriented and even alone I am apt to masturbate with an object or finger in my anus. *O.* Yes. *F.* Not when masturbating alone." "Exploring my vagina with my finger . . . with my finger, sometimes from behind to give an effect of someone else doing it. *O.* Yes. *F.* I used to fantasize to a great extent, but I don't believe that it was anymore than just my 'dream' man in variety of ordinary situation." "In nearly every instance in the last [several] years, an Oster vibrator was used. I still use the vibrator on a regular basis if a man is not available. *O.* Yes. *F.* Fantasies generally take the form of having several or numerous men raping me (nonviolent) in succession, or of having two men at the same time, having normal intercourse with one and anal intercourse with the other (I have actually engaged in this several times). Most often the men in the fantasies are Negroes with whom I've had actual experience." "Some manual stimulation of genitals until very excited; final stage, contraction of thigh muscles to massage clitoris. *O.* Yes. *F.* Yes, sometimes all that was needed. Clear visualization of situation (never faces) in which victim (me) is tickled while helpless or forced to assume humiliating postures. Often so vivid that manual stage can be eliminated. (Final stage always used.)" "Hand. *O.* Yes. *F.* Yes. How other people masturbated or had sexual intercourse." "[Lesbian]. Manual manipulation. *O.* Yes. *F.* Sometimes I imagined a male partner sometimes a female. Most frequently, I imagined myself as a male making love to a woman." "Hand—and water pressure. *O.* Yes. *F.* A female who is experiencing something exciting—a variety of things— looking at other women and men in the sexual act, etc. Always seen through the eyes of someone unknown to me. For some reason I choose *personally* (physically) to stay out of the fantasy." "Lie on my stomach and stroke my clitoris with my right hand. *O.* Yes. *F.* Sometimes. Usually in connection with a dark man; sometimes of Mexican descent. He undresses me and we both become greatly aroused as he is very much taken with the beauty of my body. The variance of our skin colors is very stimulating to me also." "Straddling and rubbing against objects such as chairs, and when possible manual stimulation of clitoris. *O.* No. *F.* Yes—later on. Fantasy occurred after I learned of what the sex act consisted, and usually was just an imaginary sexual relation with whichever man seemed most desirable at the time." "Fingers at first, then devices, bananas, etc. *O.* Always. *F.* Usually mental visualization of other girls and sometimes boys in the nude." "I had a secret invention [when a young girl]—I rolled up a piece of paper and inserted it; then felt it as I walked. [When an adult]—clitoral manipulation and a bottle (clitoral is never enough). *O.* Yes. *F.* [When an adult] I would dream men up." "I have used every kind of long object such as pencils, fingers, toothbrush handles, etc. *O.* Always had orgasm. *F.* I just remembered things seen in movies, burlesque shows, my own experiences with boys and men." "Insertion of fingers into the vagina with the heel of the hand stimulating the clitoris. *O.* Yes. *F.* Thoughts about having intercourse." "Running water full force over my genitals—later by hand manipulation—lately with an electric hand massager. *O.* Yes. *F.* During the last [number of] years I have imagined making love with some very dear lover or husband at that time." "Finger manipulation while lying on back prone. *O.* Yes. *F.* Yes at age 23—the idea of a penis substitute for intercourse." "Pillow between thighs and rubbing against a pillow. *O*. Yes. *F*. Imagine myself having intercourse (or trying to—as I had not experienced same) or more often projected myself into a beautiful girl having foreplay and intercourse."

"Potential" nudists

"Hand. *O*. Yes. *F*. Occasionally. As I grew older and learned more about the male sex, I imagined having relations with a man." "Outer vaginal are stimulated by fingers. *O*. Yes. *F*. Yes—mostly boys I know, a few times—girl friend; few times—grandfather and father (in early teens), celebrities." "Just digital stimulation. *O*. Yes. *F*. I would think of the sex act or else heavy 'making out' with my boyfriend." "Manual manipulation, insertion of small objects. *O*. Yes. *F*. Being kissed in genital region." "Rubbing upper part of genitals, finger stimulation of clitoris, rubbing cylindrical objects in vagina, massaging nipples with fingers. *O*. Yes. *F*. Men or myself urinating or defecating in inappropriate places, having marital sex relations in bedroom or premarital or extramarital relations in bedroom or elsewhere." "I at first thought I had a slight itch in the vaginal area—then every night the itch got bigger. By itching it I got much satisfaction. Then I started using fingers—pretending I was being raped. *O*. No. *F*. I dreamt of boys being with me—them doing it, not me." "Hand stimulation, electric vibrator, artificial penis stimulation. *O*. Yes. *F*. Fantasy of beautiful surroundings, handsome people, or some historical time period." "My finger or a pencil inserated as far as possible. I gave very little attention to the clitoris. *O*. Yes. *F*. My fantasies were usually sadomasochistic, involving overpowerings, being tied down and stripped, etc." "Picture stories, (I told to myself) hands on breasts and thighs and vaginal region, kiss the wall and 'pretend.' *O*. Yes. *F*. Fantasies of superability; able to change form at will, be a man or a woman. Stealing bodies, getting virtuous women to yield to men unwillingly, staging sexual plays, breeding people like cattle, beautiful places and things and people, ownership, secret domination, people taking care of my own and other's bodies, borderline to homosexual fantasies, Roman baths, group orgies and cannabalism, dreams of conquering the world." "Voluntary muscle-spasmatic motions in genital area, pressure from cloth, against mattress, etc. *O*. Usually. *F*. Often. Generally either recalling satisfactory sexual contact (current lover, usually), or imagining such relations with individuals of my acquaintance in whom I was developing a sexual interest. Masturbatory activity was usually initiated in order to allow me to get to sleep." "Sometimes lying on my stomach with my hands underneath me. *O.* Yes. *F.* Thinking of engaging in fellatio and cunnilingus simultaneously." "Manipulation with fingers and against a blanket or other soft object between my legs. *O.* Sometimes. *F.* These involve punishment either as part of a routine or because rules are too strict to be met by any person. Sometimes intercourse of a highly punitive and often regulated type is part of these." "Hand. *O.* Not at first. *F.* During masturbation the fantasy will be of the person with whom I wish to have intercourse. Or of a situation of which I have read or seen in a movie, etc." "Fingers on clitoris and anus. *O.* Yes. *F.* Always. First it was someone who loved me very much and I'd go over in my head all the things he'd do to arouse me. Now I fantasize about people watching me and I am not copulating with anyone in particular which is sort of sickening." "Stimulation of clitoris, later used small objects, clothespins, etc. *O.* Yes. *F.* To some extent. I think it was the thought of someone I was attracted to sexually that stimulated the desire." "Tight crossing of legs to cause pressure on the clitoris. *O.* Yes. *F.* No." "Rubbing of genital area. *O.* Yes. *F.* Sadistic—of watching someone being beaten. (Life for me at that time was a feeling of being beaten.)" "Finger on clitoris. *O.* No. *F.* Of handsome sexy type boys." "Running water through shower hose. Manual is too painful and lengthy to be worthwhile. *O.* Sometimes. *F.* Sometimes I'm female, but more often I'm a male aggressor in fantasies. Involve rape occasionally." "Hand— water from tub spigot—pressing against the bed. *O.* At times. *F.* Making love to an attractive man that I knew or a former lover, or one I was having an affair with." "Manual clitoral stimulation. *O.* Yes. *F.* Imagining myself with different sex partners. Thoughts of seduction— sometimes forceful. Animal coitus. Group sex activity. Recalling erotic literature." "Using the water running out of a bath tub faucet (clean method). *O.* Yes. *F.* No." "I almost always used my fingers in clitoral manipulation. Sometimes I would crumple up tissue paper in a penis-like structure and use this. However, it didn't hold up too well, so I would often resort to the finger again. Another method used was squeezing my legs together applying pressure to the clitoris. This was not as effective as direct manipulation though. *O.* Always. *F.* Almost always. My fantasies always involved boys or men that I knew. Usually older men whom I found sexually attractive. I often fantasized about fellows I was dating and would masturbate after they left me off from a date." "At first I rubbed against a piece of furniture, later manipulation by hand. *O.* Yes. *F.* Occasionally. Imagined being with a group of men or boys and dancing sexy or suggestively. Occasionally imagined act of love." "Folded towels between my legs, later and particularly, between the vulva and slightly into the vagina, and later a frankfurter inserted. O. Yes. F. Being in a nudist camp with many men with huge penises. Having intercourse with a man with an unbelievably huge penis. Intercourse as a baby which made my breasts grow very large and the boy's penis increases greatly in size." "Finger on clitoris, or anywhere in that area. O. Always. F. Usually a face of someone I thought to be attractive, would be part of getting sensation. Fantasy of animals is nice, if you can keep from feeling guilty about it. Water and wind are things that I use in fantasy because not only are they helpful in getting the orgasm but I dig nature." "Manipulation of clitoris and/or general region. O. Yes. F. About half the time. Usually an elaboration of some incident with a man (e.g. suggestive conversation continued and intercourse imagined) or imagined intercourse with men that I considered 'out of bounds.'" "Manual clitoral stimulation. I masturbate about five times a week. O. Yes. F. Always. I cannot become sexually stimulated unless I accompany masturbation with fantasies. They are always of a heterosexual nature. I usually visualize myself and my first lover engaged in a variety of positions. Often my fantasies take the form of memories. I like to masturbate to African drum music." "First, only the clitoris and opening of vagina stimulated by hand; later on, there were two fingers inserted in the vagina. O. Yes. F. Always. Generally a scene where I am relieved of responsibility—some kind of seduction. Or where I am completely 'shameless,' either as a paid prostitute or as an older woman seducing some young naïve boy. Have occasionally imagined myself the female in a group of men, all taking turns." "Massaging to point of orgasm. O. Yes. F. No." "Douche bag and manual manipulation of clitoris and breasts (nipples). O. Occasionally. F. No." "External manipulation (manual). Also in shower. O. Yes. F. Would imagine having intercourse with my latest crush." "[As a child]. Using tongue depressors on one's self in a group [later another method]. O. Yes. F. Yes. First playing medic—later pretending romantic involvements with movie stars."

"Potential nudists (lesbians)

"Very, very rarely used inanimate object. Generally used my own hands. O. Yes. F. Only occasionally. That the girl I was going with at the time was doing it." "Digital manipulation. O. Yes. F. I imagine I am indulging in sex acts (not intercourse) with a man or sometimes with a woman." "Digital manipulation and penetration. *O*. Yes. *F*. Often fantasize the person I love. Sometimes fantasize being pregnant and having sex with a woman." "Inserting finger into vagina after stimulating clitoris. *O*. Sometimes. *F*. No." "My own finger manipulation only. *O*. Yes. *F*. Consistently of having sex with a man. Rarely of viewing a male gang-bang." "Stimulation of clitoris with finger. *O*. Yes. *F*. Always would think of a setting more where a girl would be mistreating me—or I would make myself out to be noble—a hero." "Fingers—manipulation of the clitoris. Not entering the vagina at all. *O*. Yes. *F*. I picture someone I've enjoyed having relations with (or would like to have relations with) and imagine them performing cunnilingus on me." "Clitoral manipulation—rarely vaginal insertion. *O*. Yes. *F*. Fantasizing about female (unknown) performing act to myself."

Circumstances in which masturbation occurred since (after) marriage

Of those nudists and "potential" nudists who were married (or were married at one time), and indicated that masturbation had been part of their life experience, 93 per cent and 87 per cent respectively signified that they had masturbated since being married.[4] While the circumstances reported in which masturbation occurred were quite varied, the situation mentioned most frequently by the nudists was one in which the husband was away for some reason. Among the other more prevalent circumstances described were the following: when not satisfied by husband, when unable to achieve an orgasm from intercourse, to relieve feelings of tension—sexual release, when separated (away) from husband, when alone and sexually excited due to reading or thinking, when inspired and encouraged by husband to do so, when husband was ill, when unable to have intercourse with husband due to his feeling tired, at time of poor relationships with husband, as part of sexual foreplay or intercourse, due to a feeling of boredom or frustration, when unable to fall asleep, and when no suitable male was available. One nudist stated that she masturbated "for the edification of friends."

The circumstances related by the "potential" nudists in which masturbation had occurred since marriage were basically the same as those stated by the nudists.

Responses noted by the subjects included the following:

[4] The "potential" nudists (lesbians) were not asked any questions relating to masturbation after marriage. (Almost all of the lesbians were single.)

Nudists

"First marriage: After intercourse which was never long enough to satisfy me. Second marriage: When my husband had [illness]. Also occasionally as initial stimulus. It excites him to watch and I can have many more orgasms as the love-making proceeds." "Unsatisfactory sexual adjustment in marriage." "Very rarely. Only when my husband is away from home on trips or the . . . period of the month when my feelings seem to reach the highest peak." "It is a necessary part of my life." "When very alone and frustrated. At times when obsessed with adulterous thoughts when husband was cold." "My husband bought a massager for me to use as I have a long build-up." "Mostly to see if I could do it. I wanted to break my inhibitions." "Occasionally to relieve tension when away from home. Rarely for same reason at home." "When my husband was unavailable—while he was ill and since he died." "Usually as foreplay to intercourse (either by myself or husband). Often as an adjunct to intercourse." "Occasionally when unable to reach an orgasm with my husband. Also when my husband is away for a long period of time." "Occasionally—during absence or separation from husband." "Occasionally. Primarily when my husband was out of town. Only when intercourse was unavailable for any reason and there was no other sexual contact initiated." "Perhaps once. Visiting at home, wanted to try again." "First year of marriage. I couldn't reach a climax, so I used a finger method which brought relief." "Only when very tired and cannot sleep." "When I get sexually aroused and my husband is not around." "It is engaged in more often when having a full and satisfying sex life and less when sex life is not as good." "1) Husband is finished too soon and will not [do it again]; 2) No lover available for days or months." "I feel sometimes that it is a necessary thing. It is better than having fights with your husband." "Occasionally when orgasm was not reached after intercourse . . . to relieve desire built up when no sexual activities take place for a month or so." "I did a lot of reading and attended some meetings regarding the subject and at times I needed sexual release when my husband was not available." "When my husband has been tired for long periods I have indulged." "For sexual foreplay." "On occasions when I desired intercourse and my husband did not. I couldn't 'unwind' to fall asleep; I'd pretend we were having intercourse." "Needed one or more orgasms after sex with partner." "In the early years of our marriage, I seldom had satisfaction and it [masturbation] would happen when the build-up was too great." "Solitude, boredom." "Always unconsciously. I feel 'itchy' and find myself rubbing—not after intercourse." "My husband was away for several months." "In the last several years, I have read so-called, off-color books. These will almost always excite me. If alone, I will masturbate." "Suitable males were unavailable." "To relieve tension, when mate is absent." "With vibrator. With approval of husband, too. When extremely tense, nervous, etc." "Lack of relation with mate." "With husband and in his absence." "Sometimes alone or with my husband as a spectator or jointly." "After intercourse—when my husband [left] and I was still 'horny.'" "In later years, it was preferable to intercourse." "Reading a sexy novel." "Reading, thinking when husband ignores me." "When excited through reading and husband wasn't home." "During prolonged separation from husband. Sometimes feel disinclined to sex yet want release." "Husband likes me to masturbate during intercourse. I don't do it very much—it doesn't give me any satisfaction." "For edification of friends." "If I do, it is usually right after my period when I feel sexually excited throughout the whole day." "Usually when I am alone in the afternoon reading or taking a nap, etc. Generally, it consists largely of imagination, i.e. fantasy masturbation." "Usually happened earlier in marriage—in the afternoon; usually out of boredom." "Under nervous situations. I find it will relax me—during the middle of the day, etc." "When nervous, works like a potent tranquilizer. Occasionally use masturbatory technique in heterosexual relations . . . I started having wet dreams in which I was masturbating to orgasm. I didn't know women could have wet dreams and I would wake up in a panic because I was sure I had been masturbating in my sleep." "I couldn't sleep at times, without it." "When unable to have intercourse with my husband." "When not satisfied by husband, or when husband was away." "Twice after failure to climax. Four times during intercourse, currently." "When I am alone and desire sexual release." "Not too often—on several occasions a thought or item read would arouse me—but it was not enjoyable."

"Potential" nudists

"During first years of first marriage I was frigid and sought release from tensions in this way." "Wake up after sexy dream about 'dream man' type—and masturbate." "When my husband was away for a time. I also found a few times when I had no desire toward sex and I felt quite frigid that masturbating once returned my sexual urge." "I seldom achieve orgasm with my husband. Leads to frustration. I could not live with him otherwise." "When I wanted relaxation." "Since divorce. On rare occasions when sexual tension keeps me awake and

I do not have a lover or boy friend." "Usually when I'm separated from my husband for any great length of time." "When husband didn't satisfy me or when I desired someone I couldn't have." "To help achieve orgasm during coitus.—When alone if I have not had intercourse for several days." "If I haven't been satisfied or when I'm lonely." "When my sexual contact with my husband has been too frequent." "When I have a feeling of extreme tension, excitement or am extremely bored." "Alone, as an outlet for tension or when desiring female lover [subject is bi-sexual]; with my husband to show him how I do it, and with him in intercourse with his consent to heighten sensation." "My husband would cuddle and inadvertently arouse me, then decide he was 'too tired' and rapidly fall asleep, leaving me too aroused to fall asleep." "When I felt sexually stimulated and no man was available." "When I have felt tense and crotchety and feelings of being deprived of sex because of society, etc." "After an intercourse when I did not have an orgasm and bad feeling between my husband and me prevented him doing it for me. Or during a time when bad relations precluded sexual activity altogether." "When my husband and I could not have intercourse for physical reasons, or when he was away." "When husband was in the military service for [few] months." "When my husband is gone for long periods of time I will masturbate if I feel stimulated. There are times too, when he may not be immediately aroused when I will masturbate should I feel the desire."

Acceptance and nonacceptance of masturbatory behavior and its effect on subject's marital sex life

In terms of the responses of the nudists as well as the "potential" nudists to the question: How do you feel about the practice of masturbation; is it acceptable to you, good, bad, etc.? it may be stated that a considerable majority of both groups of subjects viewed masturbation as an essentially acceptable form of behavior. For although 13 per cent of the nudists and 6 per cent of the "potential" nudists indicated that masturbation was not acceptable to them, 76 per cent of the nudists and 76 per cent of the "potential" nudists reported the practice to be acceptable. A number of the comments by both the nudists and "potential" nudists were not scorable.

Consistent with the correlation reported at the beginning of this chapter in regard to the indulgence of masturbation and self-esteem, in the case of the nudists a significant relationship was also found between an accepting attitude toward the practice of masturbatory activity and high self-esteem (r = .41 P< .05). No meaningful correlation, however, was revealed in relation to the security-insecurity feelings of our participants.

The important question of whether or not masturbation has an effect on a female's marital sexual behavior is one which has received attention from several previous investigators. For instance, Katherine B. Davis in 1929 stated that "There is at this point apparently no relation between masturbation and reaction to sex experiences in married life."[5] Some years later Kinsey et al. commented as follows: "It has been claimed that premarital masturbatory experience may so condition an individual that she may want to continue solitary activities in preference to having coital relations after marriage; but we have seen very few histories of this sort. There are more cases of marital relations which were disturbed by some guilt which the wives had acquired during their premarital masturbatory experience. Much more important is the evidence that premarital experience in masturbation may actually contribute to the female's capacity to respond in her coital relations in marriage."[6] The results of the present study suggest that, if anything, masturbatory activity on the part of a female tends to have a positive effect on her marital sexual life. For while 34 per cent of the nudists and 29 per cent of the "potential" nudists who reported having masturbated and were married (or had been married) disclosed that this practice had an essentially positive effect (helped) in some way, on their marital sex lives, only 4 per cent of the nudists and 9 per cent of the "potential" nudists indicated that masturbation had a negative effect. The majority of both the nudists (53 per cent) and "potential" nudists (51 per cent) stated that masturbatory activity did not have any effect on their marriages. Several of the responses in both groups of subjects were not scorable.

Among the responses noted by the subjects in reference to the acceptance and nonacceptance of masturbatory activity, and its effect on their sex life, were the following:

Nudists

"Only acceptable out of necessity. E.[7] It kept me from stepping out." "It is a solitary thing and therefore not as enjoyable to me as real

[5] Davis, K. B., *Factors in the Sex Life of Twenty-two Hundred Women*, (Harper and Bros.: N.Y., 1929), p. 171. By permission of the publisher.

[6] Kinsey, A. C., *et al.*, *Sexual Behavior in the Human Female*, (Saunders Co., 1953), pp. 171–72. By permission of Dr. P. H. Gebhard and The Institute for Sex Research, Inc.

[7] E. stands for an abbreviation of the word Effect—in reference to the subject's marital life.

sexual activity. However, it certainly is better than nothing and I am glad I can get pleasure from it. E.—." "Good, very enjoyable. E. Helped in second marriage. Helped me—but not good for marriage the first time around due to my lack of understanding of masturbation." "Neither good nor bad, not satisfying. E. No." "I regard it as part of being human and therefore perfectly normal behavior, but no substitute for fucking or an end in itself. E. It has been beneficial. It helped me to establish my own identity." "Good; no guilt. But not a substitute for sex play with a man, preferably on love basis. E. No." "I'm not sure, it seems rather artificial, but it does the job. E. Haven't been at it long enough to tell." "Certainly acceptable. E. I was unhappily married before, for [over 10 years]. Yes, it has certainly helped me." "O.k. E. Certainly has not hurt me." "I kept it under control—o.k. But I'd dislike to see young folks taught it as I was. It can get out of control. E. No great effect." "Good and healthy. E. I do it so seldom, I feel it has no effect." "Acceptable. E. If anything, it has helped." "It is stimulating, pleasant, on rare occasions preferable to intercourse. E. Helped, enriched the potential sexual feelings." "An acceptable outlet. E. No." "It is a very good form of sexual outlet, especially when no babies are wanted and contraceptive information is not available. E. It has helped definitely, as I am aware of how I achieve orgasm, and how to do it." "It's acceptable but far less satisfying to me than intercourse. E. No." "I say it is good because to me it acted as a safety valve. I always indulged before going out on dates to prevent myself from getting too aroused. E. No effect, but it worked fine until I began to actually experience a climax from intercourse—then masturbation did not work for me." "In moderation it is satisfying (good). Over-indulgence would tend to rob normal husband and wife intercourse in which orgasm is much more *soothing* and not so intense as in masturbation. E. No." "It is sometimes necessary—but a very poor second. E. No." "It is acceptable and good when needed. E. It has helped my general sex life and therefore my marital sex life." "Acceptable, no guilt feelings at all. E. Helped." "I feel sometimes that it is a necessary thing. It is better than having fights with your husband. E. It has helped by keeping me from being mean from lack of sexual intercourse. [Subject's husband is away often and is not very demonstrative.]" "It is acceptable but a very poor release. E. Perhaps it has been a help." "Completely acceptable. E. Helped—kept tensions down." "Acceptable, but I much prefer my husband's loving. E. Helped break the 'taboo' and I found my husband approved of it." "It does not really appeal to me but it seems to stimulate my husband. E. No effect from my viewpoint." "I feel it is good, *in addition* to sexual relations with another person.

E. Absolutely not detrimental. Actually a help when partner is involved." "It has always been a part of my life. I think it is natural. E. Yes. I suppose it is the reason I cannot reach an orgasm by intercourse alone. My clitoris must be fondled in some way, but my husband has always done this and I didn't have to ask him to. So, I can't say it has hindered us." "All right for me but disgusting to think of someone else. E. No effect." "Acceptable to me when no suitable males are available. E. When one has a regular sex life it is unsatisfactory to do without sex for any extended period." "Acceptable. I do not feel that moderate masturbation is bad. I have always felt that all children go through a certain phase of this, personal and two party and I have never thought that moderate masturbation should be made an issue of. E. None." "Acceptable as a normal release of tensions when heterosexual intercourse is temporarily suspended. E. Helped materially in avoiding extramarital relationships." "I suppose it is acceptable but I don't like to think of my children doing it. E. No." "Not good—ashamed. E. No." "It is good—enjoyable. But enjoy [engaging in cunnilingus] and having intercourse more. E. It has helped in times of great emotional stress and strain—when close physical feelings for husband are hard to come by." "It is not acceptable to me unless my husband does it to me. E. No." "It is good and has been used as stimulation. E. Good effect, has been used as part of foreplay."" Acceptable. E. I expect it has hindered—satisfaction obtained this way, I have no desire for marital sex." "I usually feel a little guilty because it is an injustice to my husband. I have never turned him away after I have masturbated. E. No." "I feel it is most desirable when one is consciously aroused and a suitable man is unavailable. E. No." "Acceptable. Able to follow own peak better than man. E. Helped some." "I have no feelings one way or the other. E. Probably not. If it has had any result it would be merely that of spurring me to obtain sexual gratification a little more energetically." "I see nothing wrong with it in moderation. At times I believe it is a necessary practice. E. If any I think it has probably helped—reducing my tension." "Acceptable and good. Useful function in my life. E. Another method of fucking." "Acceptable, but would usually prefer partner in sexual act. E. Don't think the actual act had much effect. Although letting my husband know I sometimes masturbated probably helped." "It is a necessary release. I worry sometimes about injuring myself. E.—." "Acceptable in order to release tensions and frustrations. E. No effect." "It's perfectly acceptable to me—and anyone who feels like it. I don't tell my husband when I do. He connects it with lack of satisfaction. E. I'm no different now sexually than I was before I was married." "Much prefer a man to be involved in any sexual activity. No guilt feelings." "Acceptable, necessary at certain moments. E. Helped. Releases sexual tensions." "Created guilt feelings in the teens, presently acceptable. E. Influenced totally clitoral orientation to intercourse. Husband feels ineffective." "It's perfectly acceptable to me although not as good as two people enjoying sex. E. It has probably helped, since it relieved tensions and made me happier." "If keyed up, it is better than chewing one's finger nails. E. My husband is happy to have me reach the climax, even if he is unable to help me."

"Potential" nudists

"Acceptable, but would much prefer a male partner if I was attracted to him and I achieved an orgasm. E. I am afraid I might have been unable to stay married to the same man otherwise. Whether this is good or bad." "Acceptable—not necessary when there's a man around. E. No." "It is definitely a substitute when my husband is not available—it can never replace the real thing. E. Perhaps it tended to center sexual stimulation around the clitoris and make it more difficult at first for me to achieve sexual satisfaction except by direct clitoral manipulation." "Good in that it seems to relieve frustration—but I would rather have my satisfaction come directly from someone. E. Helped. I felt less antagonistic toward my husband if he didn't satisfy me, or if he refused me because of my wanting to use some kind of contraception." "Acceptable and necessary. E. Yes—helped." "I don't like it but I can't seem to stop. E.—." "It relieves my tensions and leaves me with no guilt. E. No." "It is acceptable. E. It has helped in the respect I am not so demanding of my mate. On the other hand it makes me feel as if perhaps I should expect these demands answered." "If one is not completely satisfied, it is sometimes the only source of relief. E. I don't think its had any effect at all." "I feel it is not as good as intercourse but is an acceptable substitute when intercourse is not possible. E. Has made intercourse more desirable." "It's a poor substitute for the real thing; not emotionally satisfying. E. No." "I feel that it is not really desirable; I certainly wouldn't like to get caught at it and wouldn't admit it to most people; but I don't think it is harmful. E. Not unless I would have been more demanding otherwise, which I doubt." "I believe it to be a good outlet and source of relief of sexual tension. The fantasies I use make it clear that I feel it as bad. E. I generally feel I am less able to give myself to my husband, the next contact after I have masturbated." "I know it is natural, but I am kind of ashamed of it. I would not mind if anyone else did it. E. Helped by developing sex drive, although the center of stimulation was the clitoris at first." "Acceptable. Don't know if I'd like to have my children masturbating—no definite ideas. E.—." "Mixed reactions; feels good, but somewhere there lurks the idea that it is 'bad.' E. No." "Not acceptable. E. I feel it's probably had much to do with lack of achieving orgasm."

Potential nudists (lesbians)[8]

"You might say I consider it a necessary function when no other relief is available." "I feel that it is good and acceptable." "I do not object to the practice." "I would like not to have to do it—i.e. to have my sex needs fulfilled by love-making." "I have never experienced strong guilt feelings but wish I could curb the frequency because I feel it is a bit immature." "Indifferent." "It is acceptable in the absence of other ways of satisfaction. The church, of course, considers it a sin. This causes me to feel guilty in some ways." "It is acceptable and a pleasant relief from tension." "It's natural, therefore acceptable." "Occasionally necessary to relieve strong need—not wholly satisfactory—preferable to no release at all."

[8] The lesbian questionnaire did not ask if the practice of masturbation had any effect on the subject's marital life.

5

VIRGINITY AND NONVIRGINITY, AND EFFECT
ON MARRIAGE

Although there have been conflicting reports regarding the frequency with which premarital intercourse is being experienced by females at present, as compared with previous years, it is this writer's belief that the trend definitely is in the direction of increased premarital sexual behavior and thus an increase (percentage wise) in the number of single nonvirgins.[1] This tendency toward increased premarital sexuality, it appears, has been due to a number of factors, including a change in the sexual attitudes held by females; a heightened emphasis on sexuality by our society as witnessed in such mass media as the movies, TV, plays, advertisements, magazines, and many literary works; a change in attitude on the part of males (especially those who are educated) concerning the importance of virginity in a wife; as well as the realization that simply because a female is a virgin at the time of marriage it is no guarantee that she will automatically make a "good" wife or mother, and that just because a female is a nonvirgin at the time of marriage she will *ipso facto* make a "bad" wife and mother.

With the aim of contributing additional information relating to virginity and nonvirginity, the following questions were asked of the subjects: Were you a virgin at the time of marriage? —— If not, with how many men did you have sexual relations? —— If unmarried, are you a virgin? —— If not, with how many men have you had sexual relations? ——.

Our results revealed that 72 per cent of the nudists and 73 per cent of the "potential" nudists had been nonvirgins at the time of marriage

---

[1] For a preview of what may eventually occur in America see the interesting article on the sexual behavior patterns of Swedes: Moskin, J.R., "The New Contraceptive Society," *Look Magazine*, February 4, 1969, 50–53.

(or were nonvirgins and single). The results obtained from a study of the Mensa females in this regard were almost identical to those of both the nudists and "potential" nudists. By comparison with percentages reported in previous studies concerning the prevalency of female nonvirginity, the above figures are somewhat high. In an earlier study, this writer noted that 50 per cent of the female subjects were nonvirgins at marriage.[2] Kinsey and his collaborators indicated that "Very nearly 50 per cent of the females who were married by age twenty had had pre-marital coitus. Similarly those who were married between ages twenty-one and twenty-five had had pre-marital coitus in nearly 50 per cent of the cases. Those who were married between the ages of twenty-six and thirty had had pre-marital coitus in something between 40 and 66 per cent of the cases."[3] These investigators also discovered that "Ultimately only 30 per cent of the grade school group had had pre-marital coitus, in contrast to 47 per cent of the high school group and more than 60 per cent of the girls who had gone on into college."[4]

Interesting, too, was our finding that nonvirginity and high self-esteem, and virginity and low self-esteem were significantly related ($r = .28$ P< .05). Maslow, in line with this disclosure, reported a negative correlation ($-.66$) between dominance test score and virginity.[5] Virginity and nonvirginity, however, were not observed to be correlated significantly with the security feelings of the subjects.

Masturbation and nonvirginity

With respect to both the nudists ($r = .22$ P< .05) and "potential" nudists ($r = .26$ P< .05), masturbation was found to be related more to nonvirginity than it was to virginity. Similar observations were noted in previous studies by this writer,[6] and by Maslow.[7] In reference to this finding, Maslow has remarked, "This indicates that masturba-

[2] DeMartino, M. F. (ed.), *Sexual Behavior and Personality Characteristics*. (New York: Grove Press, 1966), Chap. 5.

[3] Kinsey, A. C., *et al.*, *Sexual Behavior in the Human Female*. (Philadelphia: Saunders Co., 1963), p. 287. By permission of Dr. P. H. Gebhard and The Institute for Sex Research, Inc.

[4] *Ibid.*, By permission of Dr. P. H. Gebhard and the Institute for Sex Research, Inc.

[5] Maslow, A. H., "Self-esteem (Dominance-Feeling) and Sexuality in Women." *Journal of Social Psychology*, 1942, *16*, p. 269.

[6] DeMartino, M. F. (ed.), *Sexual Behavior and Personality Characteristics*. (New York: Grove Press, 1966), Chapter 5.

[7] Maslow, A. H., "Self-esteem (Dominance-Feeling) and Sexuality in Women." *Journal of Social Psychology*, 1942, *16*, pp. 259–94.

tion in normal people need not be thought of only as a method of compensating for lack of love or heterosexual experience, nor as solely a product of fear of heterosexuality."[8]

Effect of nonvirginity on marriage

Whether it is desirable or undesirable, from a psychological viewpoint, for a female to experience premarital intercourse is a question that has received much attention over the years, but it is one that as yet has not been resolved. In our society, nevertheless, the prevailing attitude (especially among the older generation) is that a female should maintain her virginity until marriage, and whenever this topic is discussed, one of the main points of consideration is the effect of nonvirginity on marriage. It was with the hope of shedding additional light on this important problem that the following question was asked of our subjects: Do you feel that having been a nonvirgin at the time of marriage has had any effect on your marriage? If so, explain in what way.

In response to this question 38 per cent of the nudists and 40 per cent of the "potential" nudists (who were nonvirgins at the time of marriage) indicated that having been a nonvirgin had a positive effect on their marriage, while only 14 per cent of the nudists and 16 per cent of the "potential" nudists stated that having been such had a negative influence.[9] A number of the nudists (35 per cent) and "potential" nudists (36 per cent) reported that having been a nonvirgin did not have any effect on their marriage. In both groups of subjects there were some responses which were not scorable.

In light of these results it may be concluded that in the case of both of our samples of nudists and "potential" nudists, the experiencing of premarital sexual intercourse tended to have a beneficial effect on their marriages.[1]

As to whether or not females in general should engage in premarital coital relations, the writer feels that this is a matter which each female needs to decide for herself. In making such a decision the following considerations should be borne in mind: possible guilt feelings, religious training and feelings, possibility of pregnancy, personality factors (especially level of self-esteem), reaction of future husband, and possibility of venereal disease.

[8] Ibid., p. 273. By permission of Dr. Maslow and The Journal Press.

[9] The above question was not asked of the "potential" nudists (lesbians).

[1] In reference to the practice of premarital coitus and its effect on the relationship of fiancees, see: Burgess, E. W. and Wallin, P., Engagement and Marriage. (Philadelphia: J. B. Lippincott Co., 1953), pp. 371–72.

The following are some of the responses noted by the subjects who disclosed that having been a nonvirgin at marriage did have an effect in some way on their marriage:

Nudists

"It gave me a basis for comparison and I made a better choice later." "I was more experienced than my husband and he was unwilling to grow and learn." "First marriage—I did not let my husband know and therefore could not share my knowledge with him. Second marriage— He knew everything and we have felt free and relaxed together." "We got emotionally involved and guilt feelings developed. Married due to our affair. *Obligation* on both sides." "It prepared me for sex itself by being gradual. My marriage night was a blissful one—and every night thereafter." "No and yes. I think at first I may have felt a little guilt due to my background . . . It was helpful in that a wedding and all the excitement and first-night trauma didn't occur." "My husband often stated he would never have married me otherwise; he wanted to know what he was getting." "I think the previous experiences were important to my knowing about my own reactions to learning some modes of sexual expression and some techniques. I was both more tolerant of his approach and preferences as well as appreciative of different sensations which he elicited in me—as a result of knowing other men." "It helped in putting sex in its proper perspective." "I don't know. I think the more *good* sex experience one has, the better one's marital sex life will be. But my premarital experiences were too full of anxiety. I never had an orgasm until my relationship with my husband." "Yes. Gave me a mental block." "A good one [effect] be- cause I had *some* knowledge of my own sexuality. I had a free attitude toward sex. I had a basis of comparison and didn't marry just so I could have sex." "The first year of marriage was easier because we had adjusted to each other sexually before marriage and I trusted him completely." "It made me a better bed partner." "My husband stated he was fortunate to know he was marrying a woman who would not reject his advances, or ever say she was 'too tired' to have sex." "I believe that we were sexually adjusted by the time that we married." "I think *not* having to become sexually adjusted to each other after marriage has helped us to such a happy marriage for the past [many] years." "Felt more 'free' with men—'stepping out' came easy and I don't think this is good at all. However, I had no inhibitions and this my spouses liked." "My former spouse was very puritanical and claimed to think less of me because of our premarital sexual experience together." "I wouldn't be able to be as free and un-fucked up now if I had never experienced sex before marriage." "Yes. Do you try on shoes before you buy?" "I think it is foolish to enter marriage as a virgin. You wouldn't know what to expect and might never be able to adjust to the situation." "My second husband wouldn't have married a virgin." "Superficially. When my husband decided he wanted a divorce, he threw it up to me—but he was using it as an excuse." "I felt terribly guilty at first, my husband was jealous. This was only the first year or two of our marriage." "I probably would have felt I had missed something which could have left me restless and wishing for different experiences." "Our relationship would never have gotten off the ground if I had been a virgin. It was a sexual attraction that made us think twice about each other—we gained the rest later." "If I had been as inhibited when I married my present husband as I was when I was a virgin we would have probably had a more dull and routine sex life." "I am certain that it helped me to adjust sexually to marriage and also to be more certain of my choice of men. I have found my husband by far the most satisfying." "Probably. Experience made for more open attitude." "Helped me choose a sexually satisfying husband." "Helped to do away with earlier preconceived sexual ideas." "It was beneficial because it gave me some experience." "Wasn't frightened of sex." "Yes. I was pregnant."

"Potential" nudists

"I felt closer to partner." "For the better. Experience sure helps with sex and the more you know about it the better you can satisfy your partner." "Made sexual adjustment easier." "Yes. I haven't been able to reach a climax." "Yes. Only that I wish I were pure for my husband—otherwise, no." "I believe it had an effect; both good and bad." "I need never have sorry qualms about 'what I may have missed' in other men. Also, the experience of premarital affairs made me a more capable lover for my husband." "I feel it was desirable as it enabled me to discern if a man would be a potentially good marital partner and saved me, in one instance, from marrying a man with a rather undesirable sexual fetish." "No. Although I'm beginning to wonder if my husband feels special enough to me." "I knew too much of the wrong kind of sex—without love." "No for first marriage. Yes, for second. It is far, far preferable to be experienced. It was the one thing that was 'right' from the start, so we had no difficulty in that area to compound the growing pains in other aspects of our relationship." "Can't imagine how impossible sexual pleasure in intercourse would have been for me, had I maintained virginity til marriage." "Allowed for better sexual adjustment." "I had already overcome any natural hesitancy to enjoy sex play and intercourse. Also, familiar with birth control methods—avoided fear of pregnancy. If you try on shoes before buying a pair, you *must* 'try on' a prospective husband." "Husband occasionally used it as a weapon—which wouldn't have been successful, if I hadn't already felt guilty about it." "[Virgin—single] I do not believe in premarital sex . . . I would rather have my husband be my first man—not he being inexperienced though—then it really would be difficult!" "[Single] I regret not being a virgin and in a sense 'preserved' for my future husband. However, I also feel having had sexual relations with men before marriage may be an asset in my sexual relations with my husband—in terms of experience, procedure, reaction, and mental state of confidence."

✴✴✴✴✴✴ 6 ✴✴✴

SEXUAL EXPERIENCES (MARITAL, PREMARITAL, EXTRAMARITAL, POSTMARITAL): POSITIONS USED AND MOST PREFERRED POSITION[1]

With the purpose of obtaining information concerning the variety of positions employed during acts of sexual intercourse, the following question was asked of the subjects: Describe in as much detail as possible your marital sex experiences, e.g. positions used by you in intercourse (on bottom, top, sitting, standing, in shower, etc.)[2]

While, as expected, the position mentioned most by the nudists was the bottom, many others were also described by a substantial proportion of the respondents.[3] Such positions included the following: on top, sitting and its variations (e.g. sitting on top in a chair, sitting on him while he is lying down, both of us sitting, etc.), standing, rear entry ("dog fashion," woman kneeling on her hands and knees—man enters vagina from rear), lying on side (facing partner), in the shower, in the bathtub, and lying on side (subject's back toward her mate's stomach). Specific reference to anal intercourse was indicated only by eight nudists.[4]

Among the more unusual locations reported in which coitus occurred were: on the kitchen floor, garage floor, in swimming pools, lying on

[1] The findings presented here pertain to marital, premarital, extramarital, and postmarital sexual relations.

[2] A similar question relating to premarital sex experiences was also included in our questionnaire.

[3] Since a fairly large number of the subjects did not state specifically the positions used, but made such comments as all positions, various, all positions we could think of, etc., it was not possible to derive meaningful percentages for the positions utilized.

[4] For an interesting discussion on the use of various coital positions, see: Goldberg, M., Brill, N. Q., Chez, R. A., Gallant, D. M., Laidlaw, R. W., "What Do You Tell Patients Who Ask About Coital Positions?" *Medical Aspects of Human Sexuality*, 1968, 2, 43–48.

a table (kitchen, picnic), on the toilet ("john"), in a lake, in the ocean, on a beach, on a patio, in a jeep, cramped in the front seat of a car, leaning over the tub.

In general, the responses of the "potential" nudists were the same as those of the nudists.

Responses noted by the participants included the following:

Nudists

"I have experienced just about every possible mode of loving except rear entry or anal stimulation, which would repel me. My husband feels the same and has never attempted it either." "On bottom, top, sitting, standing in shower." "All positions." "In bathroom (shower, tub—on the john), in ocean (salt water burns), on kitchen floor after waxing into corner, tried various positions—legs over man's shoulders, sitting, rocking back and forth, woman kneeling—man from rear." "On bottom, top, sideways, from rear (kneeling), from rear (sideways) laying on table, in chair (sitting), on top with my head toward his feet." "I have a wonderful, patient husband, always trying new and different ways to keep our sex life exciting." "We are well-adjusted people sexually. We enjoy sex to the utmost in every position." "On bottom, top, sitting. Such variety takes away the monotony of one position." "Usually in bed—on bed, on floor (water is too astringent for comfort). Many positions; on bottom, on top; lying parallel both facing and with back to husband. Lying in crossed position with legs at different angles. Kneeling or lying on stomach and rear approach. Sitting on husband's lap in a chair or the edge of bed. Lying down with husband sitting on top. Both of us sitting." "Have not found standing practical. Prefer bottom, slightly on side when tired or I want relaxing relations. When especially excited I prefer top position. Generally our relations are in bed at night because of day separation, children are around, etc. I like to occasionally get variety by being outdoors or 'swept off my feet' during the day." "Mainly on top position (very few orgasms experienced in any other position—except in the beginning—due to a need for petting of breasts). We have experimented with many other positions (above mentioned ones included)." "Sitting on top in a chair, lying on a table in bottom position, sitting on top in bed, in the tub while bathing, cramped in the front seat of the car." "On the bottom, on top—both most satisfying. Husband is much taller—standing doesn't work too well. Sitting, and rear entry occasionally. We experiment." "I have tried every position except hanging from a chandelier, but I prefer getting on top of my mate or lover." "On bottom, top, sitting, in shower, in tub. When I'm on the bottom my husband likes me to put my legs over his shoulders or with my legs together. I like to sit on him while he is laying down and I do all of the movement. Standing is not so good. The legs get to weak. My husband likes to catch me leaning over the tub." "On bottom, sitting on partner, standing, rear insertion, sideways, sitting forward or backward, clinging around partner's neck ('the tree'), etc." "On bottom, top, sitting, standing, in shower, on floor, on our sides, bottom's up (knee chest position). One leg on floor the other over mate while on top, backwards on top. Oil over all our bodies and varied positions to climax, etc." "On bottom, on top, bottom-up [buttock up] and face on pillow, standing on shoulders with legs up and husband standing on his own feet—penis inserted, standing in shower." "All of above. In bathtub, in a jeep, in a car, on the side, rear (dog fashion), many other positions. On a coach train using the hands through the rectum—which I find distasteful because it is extremely painful, but once in a while, I submit to please my husband." "Bottom, top, standing, in bath, shower, swimming pool, sitting, fellatio, cunnilingus, masturbation, backwards, on sides, etc." "On bottom, top, sitting, from the back (woman on her hands and knees, the man squatting behind her); woman on her back lying on the edge of a low bed—(legs up around the man) with the man squatting on the floor in front of her." "Most often man on top position, with my legs bent, or sometimes bent and parallel with my body. In shower and tub many times—very satisfying for me. Also rear entry. We have enjoyed all positions." "Mostly male superior. Sometimes female superior or side by side. Occasionally front [male's] to back [female's] especially if my husband feels stimulated while I am sleeping." "Positions mentioned [in questionnaire]. Tried it in bathtub, but not practical, '69' [mutual mouth—genital contacts], dog fashion, side by side with penis between my buttock from underneath. Left arm under me, left hand pinching left nipple. Kissing right breast, right hand rubbing my clitoris." "Usually me on bottom. Sometimes me on top. In swimming pool in a hotel. On couch in living room while guest and son watched TV. Husband approaching from behind. Both on side." "On bottom, top, sitting, standing, in shower, edge of bed, top, bottom, sideways, on knees (female) with husband behind me. Sitting with back to husband, while sailing. Husband standing with my legs round his waist, etc." ". . . Sometimes sitting on the couch with my husband on his knees . . ." ". . . Me lying at edge of bed with husband kneeling on floor." "Prefer me lying on back with husband on top. Except when engaging in fellatio and cunnilingus, that is done lying on our sides."

"On bottom, top, sitting, standing in shower, in bathtub, on floor, while swimming, on beach, dog fashion, '69,' side position, on kitchen table." ". . . Husband standing beside the bed while I lie below him." "Above positions [on bottom, top, sitting, standing, in shower] plus in bathtub, anally, husband enters from rear." "We have tried about every position we could think of. In bed, on floor, in bathtub, outside on the grass, garage floor, picnic table. About always we end up in usual man-above position. One most enjoyable to me is a side position. Being approached from behind is very stimulating also." "In shower, sometimes. Otherwise, on my back, legs spread and raised high and drawn against upper body so exposure is complete. At other times lying face down while male enters in normal fashion, but from rear. Also sitting on edge of bed and lying back on elbows so I can see entry and movement of penis—while male performs in a kneeling position at bedside." "We mostly do it with me on the bottom. Sometimes I get on top but he hurts me because I get too much of his penis that way. We twist and push a lot and usually do it for about forty-five minutes each time." "I guess everything within what might be considered 'normal'—lakes, outdoors, bottom, top, sitting, standing, bathtub, shower, car, on hands and knees." "Position used most is man flat on back and me straddling him; either facing his head so that I can kiss his mouth, or facing his feet so that he can finger my anus. One position used less often, but exciting is what is considered 'dog fashion'—with me on my hands and knees with my head down and my partner either standing by the edge of the bed behind me, or on his knees on the bed behind me. Lying on my side on the bed with him lying behind me. He sits in an armless chair and I straddle him, facing him. Me sitting on the edge of a table with legs spread, he standing by table facing me. Occasionally, I lie flat on my back and he stretches on top of me. In this position, I frequently wrap my legs around the trunk of his body. Any of these positions can be varied a little by moving a leg or twisting the body. Any of these positions can be used for anal intercourse but more caution must be taken not to hurt me. Although my anus is considerably tighter than my vagina, (especially if I am tense) it is somewhat more exciting to my husband so it is best to attempt this when he is either already tired or fucked out." "Female on bottom . . . Experimented with sitting, female on top, standing, 'dog fashion,' anus intromission (painful—not too successful). Do not have a shower or would try that too." "Include the above [bottom, top, sitting, standing, in shower], kneeling, swiming pool, lying on beach, lying on table, bent over table. In patio in sunshine, lying on side, insertion from both front and back (not rectal). Anyway we are physically able to have intercourse." "All in bed—on bottom, side, or top (If I entered the bathroom when he was in the tub, he laid the wash cloth over his penis!!!) We enjoyed intercourse, fellatio and cunnilingus—all often. (I usually came three times when we had a 'good one.')" "We use different positions frequently—me on top most, because my husband likes it—I prefer bottom though! Also used standing—lying on sides, husband sitting with me on top, in shower, my kneeling him from back, me lying on back—him sitting up and vice versa." "We have tried every position; had sex in cars, swimming pools, bathtubs, on tables, in chairs, on the floor, on the grass. We have tried and enjoyed many things." "*Post Marital*—Bottom, top, sitting, kneeling, standing. We have also experimented with rectal sex. Also, I enjoy a *small* amount of sadism—slapping, spanking, etc.—a little bit of this is enjoyable." "*Post Marital*. Since many of the men I have been with were of foreign backgrounds, I was taught many things not known to the average American male." "*Post Marital*— sitting, standing, dog fashion, bottom, top—on top with my back turned—I can lean over and kiss his feet while he caresses my bottom as it moves up and down on his penis—in the shower, lying in tub, in front of mirror, '69,' etc."

"Potential" nudists

"Bottom, top, sitting, standing, shower, bathtub, top sitting, in swimming pool, perpendicularly, dog position, sideways." "We have engaged in foreplay in bathtub. Usually use female on bottom. Husband likes female on top for a change." "We have tried just about all, I think. I'm partial to being on the bottom and I like doing it in the woods in a sitting position." "On bottom, on bottom face down, on top, in the bathtub, standing, sitting, spoon fashion, kneeling." "On bottom, top, standing in the shower, sideways, rear entry. It's been mostly supine, usually bed, mostly before bedtime or upon waking. Nothing unusual." "On the toilet with me sitting on his lap. My husband has held me against the wall with my legs around his waist. My husband lying on the bed with me sitting upright on top." "On top to achieve orgasm in union with husband. On bottom to complete the act since he likes orgasm that way. Sitting is no fun, standing is no fun—not enough play—sitting once." "All of the above [mentioned in questionnaire] plus intercourse while lying face to face; on the side with the man's penis entering the vagina from the rear, lying on the side with the man's penis entering the anus from the rear, same from the front." "Bottom, top, sitting, standing, in bathtub, on floor, on sides, on edge of bed with husband standing." "Marital sex relations involve cunnilingus and regular male-female intercourse with male on top. Occasionally I will take top position. The pitch of my excitement is dependent on my husband's virility." "We have used as many positions as we are aware of. (If you have any new ones, we sure would appreciate trying them out!) We find this a lot of fun, and sometimes will be just the kind of thing to kindle extra special sexual feelings (titillations). We have tried male on bottom, which is probably the preferred way for both of us. I get more clitoral stimulation this way and am able to move my body freely, thus applying greater pressure to the penis, which is most pleasurable to my husband. Also, we are able to hold and kiss one another in this position. The position I enjoy best of all is from the rear position. I have never actually had a climax without manual manipulation of the clitoris. (Even in the woman-above position, though certainly giving the most stimulation, I do not feel enough pressure against the clitoris.) The from-the-rear position (either on our sides or back to front on top [subject's back to husband's front, while lying on top of him] is particularly pleasurable because I am able to enjoy the feeling of penetration of the penis and clitoral manipulation—at the same time. (There is no greater feeling.) Usually I am able to reach a climax in a matter of seconds—this being what I consider the best orgasm—that which includes and encompasses both the clitoral area and vagina as well. This type of orgasm takes over the entire body and is the most gratifying type to me. We have also tried the sitting position, which is fun for a change . . ." "We mainly had intercourse in the 'standard' position, man on top. During the first year of marriage we experimented a good deal with the other positions; standing, man on bottom, entering from the rear. We sometimes had intercourse in the shower or in a different room of the house (on living-room carpet) and we had more frequent intercourse on camping trips, in motels, etc. My husband used to like to tie my hands, sometimes; I enjoyed it too. He liked the idea of me resisting or lying passive. I usually felt like being more active and sometimes wished I could take the initiative. He rarely would cooperate unless he initiated the incident." "Short of charging admission to an audience or having my children watch—you name it!" "Lying face to face female under; male lying on back, female astride; slumped female in stuffed chair, male kneeling on floor in front; in shower; male sitting in chair, female with legs around waist; female lying face down, male kneeling between legs or lying on top; male standing, female with legs wrapped around waist; begin with coitus posterious (both lying on side) female turning over on back with penis in place.

Female puts one leg over husband's body, other leg between his legs."

"Potential" nudists (lesbians)

"Under the male." "All positions." "Under the male, on top of the male, foetal position, sitting, on hands and knees." "Under male, on top of male, sitting on male." "Every which way—probably majority of time under the male."

PREFERRED POSITION DURING SEXUAL INTERCOURSE

In response to the questions: Which position with respect to sexual intercourse do you prefer most? Why?—the dominant one mentioned by both the nudists (56 per cent) as well as the "potential" nudists (58 per cent) was the bottom. The second most predominant position indicated by both the nudists (29 per cent) and "potential" nudists (16 per cent) was the top.[5] Among the primary reasons given by the nudists for their preference for the bottom position were that: a) They like the man to be the aggressor and to feel dominated by him. b) It is easier to achieve an orgasm in this position. c) It is comfortable and enjoyable. d) It affords close bodily contact as well as contact between the penis and clitoris. e) It is natural. And f) It is least strenuous. Essentially similar comments were made by the "potential" nudists in regard to their preferences for the bottom position. The major reasons stated by the nudists for preferring the top position included the following: a) It permits greater freedom of movement. b) It facilitates the attainment of an orgasm. c) It empowers better control of the situation. The "potential" nudists reported basically like reasons for their preference of the top position. Some of the other preferred positions noted by the nudists were the following: rear entry-subject on her hands and knees ("dog fashion"); sideways (on sides, facing); on sides—subject's back to mate's front (rear entry); sitting on top of male; standing. Additional preferred positions designated by the "potential" nudists included the following: standing, sitting (facing one another), sideways—legs alternating, on our sides—my back to his stomach, on hands and knees. Masters and Johnson, in their highly unique study, have reported the following in reference to the degree of contact between the penis and clitoris: "Although anatomic placement

[5] These percentages are based on the comments of subjects who had experienced sexual intercourse.

and physiologic reaction preclude any consistency of direct clitoral glans stimulation during coition, the significant influence of secondary stimulation should not be overlooked. The fact that the clitoral glans rarely is contacted directly by the penis in intravaginal thrusting does not preclude the coital development of indirect clitoral involvement. Clitoral stimulation during coitus in the female supine position develops indirectly from penile-shaft distention of the minor labia at the vaginal vestibule . . . . Only the female superior and lateral coital positions allow direct or primary stimulation of the clitoris to be achieved with ease. In these positions the clitoris can be stimulated directly if apposition between male and female symphyses is maintained. There also remains the constant factor of secondary clitoral stimulation provided by traction on the minor-labial hood during active coition in these positions. The influences of both direct and indirect stimulation are essentially inseparable in these coital positions. Clitoral response may develop more rapidly and with greater intensity in female superior coition than in any other female coital position. In the knee-chest coital position no direct stimulation of the clitoris is possible. Yet glans tumescence, when it occurs, and clitoral-body retraction, which is a constant factor, occur in the response patterns established for the supine or superior coital positions. The intensity of physiologic reaction usually is less pronounced than in either supine or superior coital positioning."[6]

In regard to the nudists, a preference for the "top" position (in some manner—including sitting on top) either solely or as one of several mentioned, as compared with a preference for the "bottom" position, solely or as one of several indicated, was found to be significantly related to high self-esteem ($r = .29$ P$<$ .05). In discussing the significance of various positions used during intercourse, Maslow has pointed out that "Many of the women very high in dominance-feeling get a tremendous thrill out of occasionally assuming the 'above' position in the sexual act; . . . In those couples in which the wife has dominance status over the husband, these women to some extent, regardless of level of dominance-feeling, are impelled to assume this position as the only or the best means of obtaining erotic pleasure."[7] He has also stated that "The above position often has a deep connection with dominance, both feeling and status, and the below position seems

[6] Masters, W. H., and Johnson, V. E., *Human Sexual Response.* (Boston: Little, Brown & Co., 1966), pp. 58–60. Reprinted by permission of Little, Brown & Company.

[7] Maslow, A. H., "Self-esteem (Dominance-Feeling) and Sexuality in Women." *Journal of Social Psychology*, 1942, *16*, p. 276. By permission of the author and The Journal Press.

often to be connected with subordinate status and feeling, although this latter connection is more influenced by other variables than is the former. For instance, we are forced to the conclusion that, in certain women whose high self-esteem is of the 'ego-secure' type, the below position seems to carry with it no implication of submissiveness nor the above position any implication of dominance (the sexual act is not for them a 'dominance act'). Also, religious dogma has standardized the below position as 'normal' for women."[8]

Responses related by the participants included the following:

Nudists

"On the bottom with my legs in the air feeling the full thrust, then as orgasm approaches, I lower my legs and move actively like a dance. W?[9] I like the top position, the side position too, but they are not as deeply satisfying. My husband has a large penis. I am penis oriented and experience orgasm with clitoral stimulation alone, as only a prelude to deep penetration." "I like to be on top. W? I achieve orgasm more quickly." "Depends on the man. Usually, I prefer to be on top. W? I can control the depth of penetration." "Conventional—man on top. W? I like to feel ravished and find this the best way." "Woman on bottom for climax—like to have man dominate. But I like to be side by side or on top for play—greater contact, hand movement, kissing and playing." "Me on the bottom. W? It's the only way I can have an orgasm." "Backward or sideways. W? Because my husband can masturbate me at the same time." "On top. W? Sharper reaction." "On top. W? Because then both breasts can be fondled at once while approaching orgasm." "Being on top or bottom. W? Greater freedom of movement for me. The penis seems to touch the most sensitive areas—more internal sensation than from some other positions." "The bottom position with my lover first and then the side [on our sides with husband entering my vagina from the rear] position for reaching a climax with my husband. W? In this side to side position, I can take hold of his testicles which helps in my orgasms. (Entering me from the rear.)" "Woman on bottom. W? The movement of the penis gives me more satisfaction and a closer feeling to my husband during intercourse and after." "On top of my mate or lover. W? Because I am small; my lovers weight more and I can create the movements to orgasm easier." "A variety. The best is vaginal penetration from the rear with simultaneous stimulation of the clitoris. W? Orgasm is more likely to take place in

[8] *Ibid.*, p. 277. By permission of Dr. Maslow and The Journal Press.
[9] The abbreviation W? stands for the word Why?.

this position." "When I sit on him while he is lying down. W? It feels better that way and sometimes I can 'come' that way." "Lying on bottom, partner on top. W? Least strenuous, also deepest insertion." "Bottom's up (knee chest position)—man on his knees. W? The penis is touching the most sensitive area of the vagina in this position." "Kneeling—from the rear. W? Feels the best." "I prefer to be either on the bottom or top depending on whether I'm the aggressor (on top) or he is the aggressor (on top) because if I am the aggressor, it is more mobile to be on the top." "Bottom. W? More body control." "Male dominant position in all its variations is the one we use most frequently. My preference for this is ever so slim compared to any of the others. W? Each position has a certain advantage over the other, but all the main body areas of stimulation are in contact and I like the feeling of my husband's weight on me." "On bottom. W? I like to feel dominated by my husband—and submissive." "Woman on her hands and knees, man squatting behind her; woman on her back on the edge of a low bed, legs a limbo, the man squatting on the floor in front of her. W? Both partners have greater freedom of movement, the penetration is deeper, the rhythmic pounding is more stimulating and the orgasms of both partners are much more vigorous." "I, on the right side, my husband on his left side. W? Not as tiring, much easier to reach a climax." "Rear entry. W? I enjoy deep penetration; the head of the penis swells as orgasm approaches, thus triggering mine. My vagina is more sensitive in this position." "The man above—also from behind. W? I can have a climax easier—from behind because the penis penetrates deeper." "Most often I lie on the bottom. W? It is the most comfortable position. Although sitting on the couch, with my husband on his knees is nice. The penis can go in quite deeply in that position." "Him on top of me. W? I love this feeling of male domineering or possessiveness on his part." "Side position. W? Best stimulation of clitoris." "On top and stretched. W? Because I always have an intense clitoral orgasm in this position." "Back to front, that is, receiving penis from the rear. W? I find that I can always reach a climax that way." "The first position I like best (me straddling husband) is just an all around handy position where I have a great deal of control over the situation. I can control the tempo and the amount of insertion. The second position I like best (dog fashion) I have less control, but it is sexually more exciting." "I get the most pleasure from being on top. The deep penetration and the chance to move at the waist to change the areas of pressure. Also, I have enough internal muscles now to squeeze and 'nibble' with." "Me on bottom. W? Gives the man more freedom of movement. Also, I want to feel dominated or 'taken' at that time." "On the bottom. W? I feel more comfortable and I like my partner to be the aggressor which to me means man on top." "The male on top of the female. W? I love to feel his body pressure on me and I enjoy wrapping by legs around him." "I like a variety of positions. The man I've loved the most gets me to do everything with him—with marvelous pleasure to us both—and absolutely unself-consciously; sitting, standing, dog-fashion, bottom, on top, on top with my back turned—I can lean over and kiss his feet while he carresses my bottom as it moves up and down on his penis (this is especially exciting)—lying in the tub, in front of a mirror, '69,' etc." "I prefer to be on the bottom. W? Psychologically, I get a stronger feeling of love, or affection and warmth." "Top. W? It's quicker and I don't get tired as quickly as when I'm on the bottom." "Sitting on edge of bed and lying back on elbows so I can see entry and movement of penis—while male performs in a kneeling position at bedside." "Bottom, top and standing—in that order. W? Bottom actually feels best, top—can see mate better and have better control, standing—feels good because of position inside." "Generally prefer being on top. W? More freedom of movement and self-expression." "My huband lies on left side while I lie on my back with my left leg between his and my right leg over his hip. W? His penis seems to penetrate about the farthest in this position. It is also a very relaxing position." "Probably the face-to-face —husband on top—although the crouching position runs a close second. W? I especially like the feeling of body closeness in a face-to-face position; seeing the pleasure shown in husband's facial expression." "On my back with him all the way inside of me. W? I like the feel of his penis when it is hard and inside of me when I need it." "I prefer to be under him on my back, but sometimes I enjoy a side-by-side position. W? I am more comfortable on my back and intercourse requires less energy. Also there is more penetration. The 'side' method seems more natural and spontaneous, however." "The position with me on top. W? Can always reach orgasm." "Lying on my back, husband on top. W? I achieve my best orgasm—probably because I am comfortable and I seem to have more feeling in the clitoris." "Man on top. W? More driving power." "The woman on top of man. W? I prefer the deep penetration of the penis and the orgasm is strongest that way. I can also move myself more freely to agitate the clitoris."

"Potential" nudists

"Standing. W? Both partners can move quite freely." "On the bottom with my legs up in the air. W? Then he can get it all the way in and you can feel every bit of it." "On bottom. W? Requires least exertion. When on top penetration is sometimes too deep." "Being on the bottom with my legs up and around him. W? I can get more feeling that way." "Although I've only been on the bottom—I'm sure that's what I would always prefer. W? I would rather feel weaker than the man." "Face down on the bottom. W? I find I receive the greatest pleasure due to the depth the penis can reach." "Either sitting (facing one another) or man on top. W? Sitting position is more stimulating, an on top position is more comfortable." "For myself to be on top. W? To be free to move about more." "Sideways—legs alternating." "Usually on the bottom. W? I feel engulfed, protected, loved and secure." "On bottom. W? I can manipulate better to reach a climax. I can always reach an orgasm when I am on the bottom because I know how to hold my husband back when he might reach his too soon." "1) On bottom facing partner, 2) or standing. W? 1) Fullest appreciation by each lover of the other, 2) Most voluptuous sensation." "My favorite is when my partner and I are on our sides, my back to his stomach. W? It seems to arouse me more." "Bottom. W? I feel most loved and protected." "It depends—If I feel especially agressive, I like to be on top. (When I'm pregnant and it's more comfortable, too). Generally prefer a position where I can see and embrace my husband during the sex act." "My being on top. However, this only comes about when my desire is intense. W? Find it very enjoyable, thrill is greater as though I am flying." "Man on top (with this particular man). W? I enjoy my arms around him and the way he feels on me." "From the rear position and woman on top. W? Rear position—I am able to enjoy the feeling of the penetration of the penis and clitoral manipulation at the same time. On top—I get more clitoral stimualtion this way and am able to move my body freely, thus applying greater pressure to the penis, which is most pleasurable to my husband. Also, we are able to hold and kiss one another in this position." "On bottom with my legs high; from back. W? More depth—more clitoral contact." "Depends on the intensity of passion. The first time on the bottom, then all other methods are enjoyable and satisfying with the right partner." "The man on top. W? I prefer to be the more passive." "Conventional female on bottom, male on top W? Most comfortable, best contact, most romantic (face close to face), conducive to feeling 'possessed by' rather than 'possessing.'" "Man on top. W? Probably because I am most used to it. I like the feeling and warmth of having someone over me and contact of the penis seems most comfortable in that position." "Prefer to be underneath the man. W? I am comfortable that way and have had the best orgasm feeling. I like the feeling when I'm on top, but have never had an orgasm that way." "Female puts one leg over husband's body, other leg between his legs. W? It does not strain either of us, we can easily change from one position to the other; stimulating angle of penetration." "1) On top—facing, 2) on bottom, pillow under pelvis. W? 1) More active position, control selfish relationship. 2) Depth of penetration stimulation." "On bottom. W? My clitoris is very small and my uterus is tipped; maximum stimulation without discomfort."

"Potential" nudists (lesbians)

"Under the male. W? Not so tiring." "Under. W? Less effort." "On hands and knees. W? I could pretend (fantasize) it [he] was a female." "None."

7

FELLATIO, CUNNILINGUS, AND HAND-GENITAL
CONTACT (MASTURBATION) WITH PARTNER

Of the various forms of sexual expression possible between males
and females, the one which, in our conservative society, tends to
be viewed as the most "abnormal" by the average unsophisticated
person is that which involves mouth-genital contact; i.e. fellatio
(female mouth on penis) and cunnilingus (male mouth on female
genitalia). Consequently, one rather strong measure of an individual's
limited or liberal acceptance of sexuality is in terms of the practice or
nonpractice of such techniques. In view of the findings noted in
Chapter 3 concerning the sexual attitudes and drives of our subjects, it
would be imagined that a very significant number of them would
participate in some form of oral-genital contact. This was borne
out by the results in that in response to the questions: Did you ever
engage in fellatio (female mouth on male genital), cunnilingus (male
mouth on female genitals), masturbation of partner? Specify. Were
these practices acceptable to you? (These questions were asked in
connection with both premarital and marital sexual experiences)—
84 per cent of the nudists reported having experienced fellatio and
92 per cent cunnilingus at one time or another. Moreover, 83 per cent
of the nudists disclosed that they had participated in *both* fellatio and
cunnilingus. Of those nudists who ever performed fellatio, 93 per cent
indicated an acceptance or liking of the practice, while 94 per cent of
those who had experienced cunnilingus related an acceptance of this
activity.

In the case of the "potential" nudists, 72 per cent noted having
participated in fellatio, and 73 per cent in cunnilingus, while 68 per
cent stated that they had engaged in *both* fellatio and cunnilingus.
An acceptance of fellatio was revealed by 90 per cent of these subjects
and an acceptance of cunnilingus was indicated by all except one of

74

those "potential" nudists who had ever experienced the act. The overall percentages of the female Mensa subjects with respect to the practices of fellatio and cunnilingus, or both, were appreciably lower than those disclosed in connection with the nudists, but similar, for the most part, to those of the "potential" nudists.

The present writer, in a previous publication, reported that 53 per cent of the females studied had indulged in fellatio, or cunnilingus, or both.[1] The Kinsey group, in describing the precoital techniques experienced during marriage by their sample of females, pointed out that fellatio occurred in 49 per cent of the cases and cunnilingus in 54 per cent of the instances.[2] McCary informs us that "Many marriage counselors believe that considerably more than 60 per cent of the higher-educational-level group indulge in oral-genital sexual expression, but that they are reluctant to admit it because they fear the disapproval of others."[3]

In view of the various percentages presented above, relating to the prevalency of fellatio and cunnilingus among females, it is clear that these acts on the part of our sample of nudists were particularly widespread.

The practice (by the nudists) of *both* fellatio and cunnilingus was found to be significantly related to high self-esteem (r = .40 P< .05). No significant relationship however, was noted in regard to the security feelings of our subjects. Maslow, in his very important study of female sexual behavior stated that "cunnilingus is liked very much and indulged in as frequently as possible by a large proportion of the subjects who rate in sex attitude from seven up, and by practically none who rate five and below. (Because of the very high correlation [r = .85] between dominance rating and sex attitude, these remarks hold true for either dominance or sex attitude.) To a somewhat lesser extent the same is true for fellatio. Generally the higher the dominance (with ego-security held constant), the greater attractiveness the penis has for handling, looking at, and thinking about."[4]

Presently in the psychological and psychiatric literature, manipulation of the penis by a female (or another male) is characterized as an act of masturbation. Since, however, masturbation by definition

[1] DeMartino, M. F. (ed.), *Sexual Behavior and Personality Characteristics.* (New York: Grove Press, 1966) Chapter 5.

[2] Kinsey, A. C., *et al., Sexual Behavior in the Human Female.* (Philadelphia: Saunders Co., 1953.)

[3] Reproduced from *Human Sexuality,* by James L. McCary, Van Nostrand-Reinhold Company, Princeton, 1967, p. 157.

[4] Maslow, A. H., "Self-esteem (Dominance-Feeling) and Sexuality in Women." *Journal of Social Psychology,* 1942, *16,* p. 286. By permission of the author and The Journal Press.

involves *self-stimulation* (autoeroticism), it is suggested that in the future any behavior involving manual manipulation of the penis by a female be referred to as "hand-genital contact." In the present study, hand-genital contact with a male partner was reported by 69 per cent of the nudists and 65 per cent of the "potential" nudists.[5] Of those nudists and "potential" nudists who had ever engaged in this act, 95 per cent and 89 per cent respectively described it as being acceptable.

The following comments were related by the subjects in regard to the practices of fellatio, cunnilingus, and hand-genital contact (masturbation) with partner, during premarital and marital experiences:

Nudists

"*Premar.*[6] Fellatio and mutual masturbation. *A.*[7] Very much so. *Mar.*[8] All three, fairly often. A. Yes." "*Premar.* Both [fellatio and cunnilingus] A. Not at first. *Mar.* Both. A. Yes." "*Premar.* No. A. Not acceptable. *Mar.* Yes, all three. This has been a recent development in our sexual activities after about more than five years of sexual relations. A. Very much so; they add variety and further enjoyment to what is considered normal sexual relations." "*Premar.* Yes. Taught all methods by my husband. A.—*Mar.* Yes. A. Yes." "*Premar.* Fellatio and cunnilingus, but not masturbation of partner. A. They seem part of loving. I love to touch, to feel the whole person. *Mar.* Fellatio and cunnilingus, but not masturbation. A. Yes, they delight me." "*Premar.* Both [fellatio and cunnilingus]. A. Cunnilingus, yes, fellatio, no. *Mar.* Yes. A. Fellatio, no." "*Premar.* All three. A. Yes. *Mar.* All three. A. Yes." "*Premar.* All three; mutual masturbation and manipulation by hand, mouth, foot etc. A. Yes—greatly attractive. *Mar.* Yes A. Good way to arouse a man, especially if he's not interested or is unable to get aroused." "*Premar.* Mutual masturbation. No oral play. A. I can't remember being approached (or invited) to oral practices. I think I would have been slightly horrified at first, then interested. *Mar.* Yes. All. Sometimes mutual or 'taking turns.' At times as foreplay, and at times to climax for either or both. A. Yes." "*Premar.* All three. A. Very much so, although prefer practices which arouse self to petting partner. *Mar.* Yes. All three whenever husband wants to. A. Yes." "*Premar.* Yes. Masturbation of penis, oral genital—both as part of foreplay. A.

---

[5] It seems quite possible (in terms of the responses) that a much greater percentage of both groups of subjects may have actually experienced hand-genital contacts, but for some reason they simply omitted making reference to them.

[6] *Premar.* is an abbreviation of the word Premarital.

[7] *A.* is an abbreviation of the word Acceptable.

[8] *Mar.* is an abbreviation of the word Marital.

Yes. If I cared about the person. *Mar.* Yes. We both enjoy all kinds of body contact either as foreplay or instead of intercourse during the part of my period when I bleed heavily—after childbirth, etc. Masturbation, mouth contact anywhere, including testes, anus as well as penis. A. Yes." *"Premar.* Yes, all. A. Yes, they were; they helped a great deal when sexual intercourse was performed in reaching an orgasm. *Mar.* Not too often. Once in a while when he asks me to. When first married, we used to do so more often until boredom with the same old sex methods set in as the years passed. A. At times." *"Premar.—Mar.* Yes. I have been unable to learn fellatio but my husband is an expert with cunnilingus. Masturbation of husband is used whenever we're in a hurry or I'm menstruating. A. Yes, all but fellatio." *"Premar.—Mar.* Fellatio. I use my tongue on the 'balls' and push the cock pretty deep in my mouth—once in a while I take the orgasm in my mouth and spit it out—mostly I save it for regular intercourse.—Cunnilingus.—I jerk him off till he comes. A. My husband wanted me to for a long time before I did—and I didn't like it. Gradually I came to like it and now I love it." *"Premar.* Sometimes fellatio, manual stimulation of genitals but not usually to orgasm for myself or partner. A. Yes. Athough I had to get used to fellatio. *Mar.* All. Cunnilingus was at my initiative and because of my encouragement, at first. A. Yes." *"Premar.* Fellatio, cunnilingus and masturbation of partner. A. Yes. Cunnilingus was the only way I could reach an orgasm. Masturbation of partner satisfied him and kept me from becoming pregnant. *Mar.* Yes. Fellatio and cunnilingus at the same time because that is the only way I can reach an orgasm. Masturbation of husband sometimes. A. Yes." *"Premar.—Mar.* Yes. It is my current stimulus of love play; fellatio as well as cunnilingus from husband and friends. A. Yes, very—adds variety to playing." *"Premar.* All—including '69.' A. Yes. *Mar.* Yes. A. Yes." *"Premar.* Fellatio, masturbation of partner. I've done just about anything you can do when making love. A. Yes. *Mar.* I suck on him, he sucks on me (which I don't care much about). He plays with me and I play with him. Before he 'comes' he puts his penis in me. A. Yes." *"Premar.* Fellatio —cunnilingus. A. Yes. *Mar.* Yes. Husband taught me to masturbate him. Husband more and more demanded fellatio. I desired his mouth on my genitals but he never made the attempt. I was too shy to suggest. A. Certainly.—They are extremely delightful, sensitive, loving means of giving and receiving pleasure. *Post-mar.*[9] Several lovers since do this frequently. Three or four men I've known seem to prefer cunnilingus to any other form of love-making. One in particular likes me to 'come' in his mouth, likes me to sit on his mouth—likes to go to sleep

[9] This stands for an abbreviation of Postmarital.

with his mouth sucking on my vagina—either lying below me with his head between my legs or in *soixante neuf* position." *"Premar.* Fellatio, masturbation of partner. A. Yes. *Mar.* Fellatio to climax and not to climax. Often as part of love act, not as often with cunnilingus as it isn't too desired by me; it seems more to hurt than to excite. A. Yes." *"Premar.* Yes. '69.' I learned to swallow (and enjoy) the semen as an older man convinced me it was a 'life force that was energizing.' I like cunnilingus from either a male or female (to point of orgasm). A. Yes. *Mar.* Yes. In a car, bed, beach, anywhere. A. Yes." *"Premar.* Mutual masturbation but not fellatio or cunnilingus. We didn't know about it then. A. Yes. *Mar.* We engage in fellatio, cunnilingus and mutual masturbation. A. Yes. Very enjoyable especially cunnilingus. I don't want him to have an orgasm in fellatio—fellatio is part of the foreplay." *"Premar.* All three. A. Yes. Any method used between two persons in love is acceptable and good. I can find nothing morally wrong with anything or any circumstances pertaining to sex as long as both people are in agreement and desirous for the furthering of sexual intercourse between themselves. *Mar.* All three. A. Yes." *"Premar.* No. Unknown to us at the time. *Mar.* In foreplay, we often masturbate each other, using hands. Sometimes we use our mouths one at a time, then simultaneously. A. Yes, very much so." *"Premar.—Mar.* Yes. [fellatio and cunnilingus] One time after a particularly beautiful LSD [drug] experience. I [engaged in fellatio] and actually swallowed his semen. It really surprised me and the fantasy that went along with it was very pleasurable. Extreme closeness and acceptance of all parts of him. A. Yes." *"Premar.* No. A. No. *Mar.* Fellatio, cunnilingus—masturbation of husband and myself at same time. A. Yes." *"Premar.—Mar.* Fellatio, no; however, kissing of the velvet-like foreskin of the beautiful penis is practiced with great satisfaction and enjoyment to both my husband and me. Cunnilingus, yes, with great satisfaction and enjoyment to both, as our mental and physical attitude accepts this sexual activity as normal—concluding with intromission of the penis for full and complete orgasms by both my husband and I. Yes, very definitely." *"Premar.—Mar.* Yes. I find fellatio difficult. It is painful to open (and keep my mouth that wide open) for such a long period. Cunnilingus I enjoy; in fact it's great fun. I have masturbated by husband with my hand. A. I don't enjoy fellatio for the reason mentioned above—although I think the male organ is beautiful and I love to touch the genitals, etc. But the practices are acceptable to me—and if it were not for the pain associated with keeping my mouth open so wide, I would enjoy fellatio. I do enjoy cunnilingus." *"Premar.* I've engaged in fellatio, cunnilingus and masturbation of partner and self-manipulation. A. Yes. Cunnilingus especially gives me great pleasure and arouses me more deeply than perhaps any other kind of foreplay. I enjoy fellatio, but at first felt uneasy about doing it. Masturbation of partner is also good—like to touch my partner. [Single]."[1] "*Premar*. Yes. All A. I consider fellatio and cunnilingus an integral and desirable part of the foreplay between a man and woman. I do not care for masturbation of partner except as part of foreplay, nor do I care for cunnilingus to orgasm. *Mar*. Fellatio and cunnilingus were used in nearly every instance, masturbation only in sense of fondling and caressing. A. Very desirable." "*Premar*. Both. Derive much pleasure from tonguing a man and having him reciprocate in kind. No masturbation of partner. A. Yes. *Mar*. Both [not masturbation]. A. Yes, usually." "*Premar*.—*Mar*. My husband uses cunnilingus quite a bit and once in a while, if I am badly in need of my husband and see him, I kiss his penis. A. Yes, because we are in love and are married to each other." "*Premar*. I have used fellatio, cunnilingus, masturbation of partner. The only things I have not used are artificial devices. A. When he is tired or we don't feel like actually having intercourse, I use fellatio or, more frequently, masturbation. Naturally, I have nothing against any of these practices. Quite often he brings me to a climax orally. [Single.]" "*Premar*. Cunnilingus, also fellatio. A. Yes. *Mar*. Yes. Either separately or together; frequently to ejaculation. He usually lies on his back with me on my hands and knees over him. A. Yes. I would say that my mouth and sucking is my main source of gratification as well as of sexual pleasure and excitement. I think I get more overall pleasure out of sucking cocks than any other one thing I do with another person. My husband and I occasionally fall asleep with my head on his stomach and his cock in my mouth. Other times we use this purposely for a relaxing technique, especially if I am nervous and fidgety." "*Premar*. (With future husband at time) Cunnilingus and masturbation. A. Cunnilingus was hard to accept at first. *Mar*. All three at various times. A. Yes." "*Premar*. Can't remember the first time I engaged in fellatio but it was something I wanted to do. Same with cunnilingus. Someone did it and I loved it. Mutual masturbation with a man is better than alone. A. Sexual activities are between two people for their mutual joy and help. So, sometimes, when I am asked to do something I do not care about I do it because it gives pleasure to the man of my life. [Single.]" "*Premar*. Engaged in all three during sexual intercourse with my husband before marriage. A. Not at first, but are now and are enjoyable. *Mar*. Yes. Done to increase sexual desire prior to intercourse. Occasionally done to have a different sexual experience.

[1] Subject is not married and has never been married.

A. Yes." "Premar.—No *A.*—*Mar.* He [husband] has tried cunnilingus but I don't like to be breathed on down there—too chilly. *A.* I like to be kissed *while* other things are happening to me, or while I am otherwise active." *"Premar.*—*Mar.* My husband taught me after marriage—fellatio and cunnilingus together—the results were like fireworks. It was always in conjunction with coitus the same night, to calm down. *A.* Yes. I enjoyed them very much. *Post-mar.* Met a man and found a special magnetism at once and we were 'all over each other' the first night. Must be an unusual attraction to desire fellatio though. *A.* Yes.—natural." *"Premar.* No. *Mar.* Engage fairly often in fellatio; seldom in cunnilingus, as female partner derives hardly any pleasure therefrom. Hardly ever in masturbation of husband. *A.* Yes." *"Premar.* No. *A.* No. I thought they were filthy, dirty, and degrading. *Mar.* Yes. We do any of these things whenever one of us wants it done or wants to do it. We stop when the act is no longer comfortable or pleasing. *A.* Yes." *"Premar.* Mutual masturbation. *A.* No. I did not like it at all. *Mar.* Yes. I have engaged in all. *A.* All but fellatio." *"Premar.* I did 'hand' masturbate my mate on several occasions prior to our having sex experience. *Mar.* Many times my husband has engaged in cunnilingus with me and me in fellatio on him. I have 'hand' masturbated him and he has used his fingers on me. *A.* Yes." *"Premar.*— *Mar.* All three. Use fellatio and cunnilingus to achieve excitement prior to intercourse. Masturbation of husband when I am menstruating. *A.* Yes."

"Potential" nudists

"Premar. All (fellatio, cunnilingus). *A.* Not before I was married. *Mar.* Yes. *A.* Yes, you have to learn to like it." *"Premar.* I've engaged in both [fellatio and cunnilingus]. At times I've been the active partner, the passive partner—and I've also participated in both at the same time. *A.* Yes. [Single.]" *"Premar.*—*Mar.* Yes. My husband enjoys this sort of thing. *A.* No. Any of these practices tends to cool my ardor rather than enhance it. I have tried to reconcile myself to this but find it impossible to achieve orgasm or even remain interested." *"Premar.*— *Mar.* Yes. All of them at different times in my marriage. *A.* Yes. But not at all times. I enjoy them when I have a feeling of deep sexual satisfaction and closeness with my husband. I have to be in a passionate and sexy mood." *"Premar.* Both [fellatio and cunnilingus]—also mouth on anus. *A.* All but mouth on anus were acceptable—but not favorite practice. [Single.]" *"Premar.* Yes. Fellatio.—hard work and no satisfaction for me. *A.* No—guilt feelings. *Mar.* Concurrent fellatio and

cunnilingus as foreplay—to orgasm for [a period of time when subject was unable physically to engage in intercourse]; mutual masturbation as foreplay to arouse interest. A. Yes." "*Premar*. Have done all at some time or other, but only when I've known the man for sometime or if he appeals to me very much. A. Usually acceptable. *Mar*. Sure, all. A. Yes." "*Premar*. Fellatio, cunnilingus, and masturbation of partner. A. Yes. Oral intercourse has been somewhat gratifying, more so than was masturbation. [Single.]" "*Premar*. No. *Mar*. Yes. Have only practiced this with my husband. For the sake of variety and when coitus is prohibited; e.g. before and after childbirth. A. Of course." "*Premar*. Cunnilingus often with future husband, who enjoyed it more than I did. A. Sexually exciting to the point of orgasm, but accompanied by guilt and psychic distress. *Post-mar*. (with lovers) [Subject is divorced.] Cunnilingus often if they desire it. Fellatio with two men. Masturbation when necessary to excite a man (if he requests it). A. Yes. Cunnilingus is very enjoyable. Fellatio only enjoyed with one man who was extremely attractive to me." "*Premar*. Yes. All of those mentioned. A. The first two definitely desirable. The third is acceptable as stimulation prior to actual intercourse. *Mar*. Yes, all. A. Yes." "*Premar*. All of them. A. Yes. *Mar*. Rarely. I'd like to but he doesn't seem at ease and I'd hate to be a leader and teacher. A. Yes." "*Premar*. Yes. A. Yes, very much so. *Mar*. Yes. Sometimes before and after our love-making we engage in all three. A. Yes, very much so." "*Premar*. Both [fellatio and cunnilingus]. I have kissed and caressed his penis with my mouth although I have never taken it into my mouth. He has also kissed and caressed and used his tongue to penetrate. A. They do not bother me. However, I did not enjoy extensive oral caresses, etc., very much either way. Light kissing and caresses with the lips was quite acceptable both ways [Single.]" "*Premar*. All three in a variety of situations; masturbation of partner to orgasm was rare; all three were employed basically as precoital techniques and only rarely as substitutes. A. Yes. My occasional objection to fellatio has been in cases where genital secretions tasted unpleasant. *Mar*. Fellatio and cunnilingus invariably as precoital techniques only; masturbation of husband—to arouse him sometimes. All three somewhat uncommonly, but not rarely. Usually when we have much leisure. A. Quite." "*Premar*. I have engaged in both, [fellatio and cunnilingus] often at the same time. A. Acceptable, but not extremely pleasurable. I much prefer regular intercourse. [Single.]" "*Premar*. Yes. All mentioned. A. Yes. *Mar*. Fellatio and cunnilingus. My husband told me to do it. At first I was quite shocked but now I enjoy it. He also does it to me. A. Yes." "*Premar*. Both [fellatio and cunnilingus] A. At first I thought it was pretty awful, but now I rather enjoy it. But of course it again depends on the boy. [Single.]" *"Premar.* No. *Mar.* Yes, all. *A.* Yes." *"Premar.* Fellatio, cunnilingus and masturbation of partner. *A.* Yes, especially cunnilingus. Prolonged fellatio gags me. I prefer fellatio and cunnilingus to occur simultaneously. *Mar.* Yes, all three. *A.* Yes." *"Premar.—Mar.* Fellatio and cunnilingus. I'm always playing with his penis. *A.* Yes. Find it very stimulating." *"Premar.* I have mostly engaged in fellatio over masturbation—for intercourse took the place of masturbation. My partner has participated in cunnilingus to get me sexually aroused. *A.* Yes, they are acceptable to me now, for I feel that sex in all forms is beautiful and right. [Single.]" *"Premar.* Yes. With one partner in particular, I frequently gave him a climax with my mouth on his penis. I once 'escaped' sex with an undesired partner by doing this as an alternative. *A.* I do not find it objectionable, but have some feeling of repulsion at the point of his ejaculation and have worried in case the penis would touch my vulva. *Mar.* Have given my husband climax with my mouth on a few occasions. He has occasionally put his mouth on my genitals as part of foreplay. *A.* Yes." *"Premar.* Cunnilingus as often as possible, masturbation of partner once and fellatio infrequently; only for partners who meant a great deal to me spiritually. *A.* Yes, except for masturbation of partner which was tiresome to me and completely unexciting. *Mar.* Fellatio very infrequently, masturbation never, and cunnilingus always. *A.* Yes." *"Premar.* Fellatio, cunnilingus and masturbation of partner. *A.* Yes. Oral intercourse has been somewhat gratifying, more so than was masturbation. [Single.]" *"Premar.* Seldom fellatio, never cunnilingus before marriage, masturbation of partner whenever intercourse was not possible due to periods of limited time. *A.* Yes, I would have liked to experiment more. *Mar.* We went through a period of fairly intense experimenting along these lines during the [early] months of marriage. He did not like fellatio very much or cunnilingus either for that matter; he enjoyed it but seemed inhibited. We eventually came to a pattern of mutual masturbation, sometimes of ourselves and sometimes of each other, when intercourse was impossible. He would never engage in intercourse during a period [menstrual] or in later stages of pregnancy.— I wanted it more than he did. *A.* Yes." *"Premar.* With the man I had intercourse, I practiced both fellatio and cunnilingus. With the other man, we practiced mutual masturbation everytime we had relations. *A.* Yes, they were acceptable to me. [Single.]" *"Premar.* Yes, all three. *A.—*Cunnilingus reminded me of dogs, fellatio with one was nice because I wanted to do that for him, but for another it was foul because it was forced on me rather fiendishly. *A.* Yes, I feel it is acceptable to me if I want to do it. [Single.]" *"Premar.—Post-Mar.* Yes. Female mouth on male genital to the point of his orgasm. A. Not always— depending on me as an individual and my sex drive at that time." *"Premar.* Yes. Very satisfying experience (although I have found several men who initiate the idea are repulsed as a climax is approached on the part of either party.) A. Very. *Mar.* Yes. A. Yes." *"Premar.* Yes—All, plus a few recipes from the Kama Sutra, etc. A. Very rewarding [Single.]" *"Premar.* Fellatio, cunnilingus, manual stimualtion of each other. A. Yes. *Mar.* Yes, all three. A. Yes." *"Premar.* Masturbation of the partner, fellatio and cunnilingus. A. Masturbation of the partner is acceptable, however, the other two cause me to be ashamed. Actually, I believe disgusted is a better word [Single.]"

"Potential" nudists (lesbians)

"All.[2] A. Acceptable but not pleasing." "Yes. A. Fellatio is repulsive. Cunnilingus is delicious." "Yes. I've jacked them off on dates after petting and kissing.—Ick! ! A. No. These questions are making me ill." "Male mouth on female genitals. A. All right—no trauma." "Yes— not more than once with any male who wanted it. I didn't like this type of activity. A. No." "Yes, cunnilingus. A. Yes." "Yes. Both at the same time . . . A. Absolutely not." "Yes. Once we practiced fellatio and cunnilingus. A. I didn't mind too much when his mouth was on my genitals, but having his penis in my mouth made me sick."

[2] The lesbian questionnaire did not make any mention of premarital or marital status in reference to fellatio, cunnilingus, or masturbation (hand-genital contact).

****** 8 ***

FREQUENCY OF ORGASM ACHIEVEMENT

There seems to be a fairly widespread belief that female nudists, for the most part, are basically frigid and thus are unable to experience an orgasm. In terms of the findings of our sample of nudists, however, this notion appears very much to be incorrect. For in response to the question: How often do you achieve an orgasm from your sexual activities? (i.e. always, almost always, sometimes, never, etc.)—27 per cent of the nudists said "always," 47 per cent "almost always," and 14 per cent stated "sometimes." (Six nudists made it know that they experienced multiple orgasms).[1] One subject in responding used the phrase, "almost never," two others employed the word "seldom," and a third said "rarely." Some of the responses were not scorable. Although no respondent utilized the word "never," three reported that orgasms occur only from certain sexual practices (other than intercourse); such as contact between clitoris and penis or hand, cunnilingus, masturbation, and finger-genital contact.[2] Then, too, while one nudist revealed that she was able always to achieve an orgasm from masturbation, and a second disclosed that it was possible for her to obtain an orgasm "always manually or during cunnilingus," these females, respectively, attained an orgasm from intercourse "almost never" and "hardly ever." With respect to the "potential" nudists, 16 per cent reported having "always" experienced an orgasm from their sexual activities, while 45 per cent said "almost always" and 16 per cent "sometimes." Two of these females indicated having had an orgasm "seldom" and three responded with the word "never." Several of the responses were not scorable.

[1] In reference to marital coitus, Kinsey *et al.* found that 14 per cent of their female subjects regularly experienced multiple orgasms. (p. 375).

[2] There is no longer any doubt that from a biological viewpoint, there is no difference between a so-called vaginal and a so-called clitoral orgasm. See: Masters, W. H. and Johnson, V. E., *Human Sexual Response.* (Boston: Little, Brown & Co., 1966). See also: Ellis, A. "Is the Vaginal Orgasm a Myth?" In *Sexual Behavior and Personality Characteristics.* (M. F. DeMartino, ed.) (New York: Grove Press, 1966).

In view of the percentages presented above relating to the frequency of orgasm attainment by our subjects, the following comment by the Kinsey group is especially interesting, ". . . a goodly number of the married females never or rarely reach orgasm in their marital coitus."[3]

No significant relationship was observed between the frequency of orgasm attainment by the nudists and levels of self-esteem. When, however, the security ratings of those nudists who had responded with the words "always" or "almost always" were compared with those who stated "sometimes," "seldom," "rarely," or "almost never," although no statistically significant relationship was found, a definite trend was noted ($r = .27$ N.S.). Such a trend was not revealed in the case of the "potential" nudists.

Maslow, in analyzing the meaning of the orgasm has remarked as follows; "It would seem, then, that the orgasm has psychological values in the woman. With it she may 'give in,' make herself vulnerable, and to a certain extent put herself into subordinate status. For a man to induce the orgasm in a woman supports his dominance-feeling and also, for the moment at least, gives him dominance status . . ."[4] Kinsey and his associates in discussing the significance of the orgasm have stated wisely that "It cannot be emphasized too often that orgasm cannot be taken as the sole criterion for determining the degree of satisfaction which a female may derive from sexual activity. Considerable pleasure may be found in sexual arousal which does not proceed to the point of orgasm, and in the social aspects of a sexual relationship. Whether or not she herself reaches orgasm, many a female finds satisfaction in knowing that her husband or other sexual partner has enjoyed the contact, and in realizing that she has contributed to the male's pleasure."[5]

Responses reported by our subjects included the following:

Nudists

"Always." "Almost always." "Sometimes." "Always, although I would just as soon have sex more often and orgasm not every time." "Always,

[3] Kinsey, A. C., *et al.*, *Sexual Behavior in the Human Female.* (Philadelphia: Saunders, 1953), p. 373. By permission of Dr. P. H. Gebhard and the Institute for Sex Research, Inc.

[4] Maslow, A. H., "Self-esteem (Dominance-Feeling) and Sexuality in Women." *Journal of Social Psychology*, 1942, *16*, pp. 281-282. By permission of the author and The Journal Press.

[5] Kinsey, A. C., *et al.*, *Sexual Behavior in the Human Female.* (Philadelphia: Saunders, 1953), p. 371. By permission of Dr. P. H. Gebhard and the Institute for Sex Research, Inc.

except when under certain types of medical therapy that have a depressing effect." "Always—several with my lover and one tremendous one with my husband when I pass out into a deep sleep." "Always. On most occasions, two or three. They vary in intensity." "Rarely." "Always and multiple." "Seldom." "With husband almost never—from masturbation always." "Only from husband, touching clitoris with his penis or hand—not vaginal." "First orgasm was at age [in the thirties], multiple ones after that; very often now." "Always. This is not a result of penis against clitoris. I have a high clitoris, thus the penis cannot come in contact with it. With the use of his or my finger I can always have an orgasm. Half the time we reach a climax together." "Almost always from cunnilingus; never with intercourse." "If all precautions are taken in foreplay, and to help me (and I have not had the experience of anyone not desiring this), I always have at least two orgasms to the man's one ejaculation . . . I have multiple orgasms and just once have I found a man who does." "Hardly ever during intercourse. Always manually or during cunnilingus." "Almost never." "Always, often five or six times to his one." "Almost always; depends upon how relaxed I am and how much foreplay has taken place." "Almost always when I am *previously* aroused; sometimes when I am not."

"Potential" nudists

"Always." "Sometimes." "Almost always." "Never." "I usually achieve orgasm, though sometimes delayed." "Never with a man unless it is by cunnilingus. [Subject always does from masturbation.]" "Almost always in masturbation; never with a man." "Always from masturbation whether I do it or the partner. About 50-50 from intercourse." "With right partner, always; with husband never." "Almost always and twice—sometimes three times."

"Potential" nudists (lesbians)[6]

"Sometimes (always have an orgasm when masturbating)." "Seldom with females . . . Almost always with males." "Almost always." "Seldom." "Always. I find them very pleasurable and satisfying." "I've received satisfaction by producing orgasm in my love object [female]. I've experienced orgasm sometimes when being made love to and rarely when making love."

[6] Throughout this book, the verbatim responses of the "potential" nudists (lesbians) refer primarily to homosexual activity.

FANTASIES EXPERIENCED DURING SEXUAL ACTIVITY

Inasmuch as a person's inner thoughts are completely private and personal, there is no limit to the range or extent to which one may engage in fantasy or imagination, provided he or she so desires or is stimulated to do so. Much can be learned, therefore, about an individual's underlying emotions, attitudes, desires, wishes, and frustrations from a study of his or her fantasy life. While much attention has been paid to the fantasy sexual life of males, at present little is known concerning the fantasies and thoughts of females which occur during heightened states of sexuality. In an effort to discover more about this aspect of female psychosexual behavior, the following question was asked of our subjects: Do you ever engage in fantasy (i.e. thoughts of someone else, visualize scenes, animals, etc.) during sexual activity? If so, describe nature of fantasy.

An affirmative response to this question was given by 44 per cent of the nudists and 39 per cent of the "potential" nudists. Although the fantasies described by the nudists were varied, the one mentioned most prominently involved thoughts of another male (someone else). Other fantasies recorded by several of the respondents pertained to group activity (orgies), homosexuality, various scenes (including those related to nature), and animals (sexual contact between women and dogs, etc.). The fantasies of the "potential" nudists were very much like those of the nudists.

This writer noted in an earlier study that 23 per cent of the females had fantasied during the course of their sexual activity. Among the fantasies indicated were the following: "the presence of another [substitute] man [this was reported by 3 subjects]; visualizing a previously experienced sexually exciting situation involving a 'sexy' female; being in a state of complete passivity and being subjugated sexually by the male, at other times being very aggressive; visualizing other people 'doing the same thing that we are'; assuming the role of a heroine portrayed in a book read recently [reading is very stimulating sexually to this subject]; having intercourse with a movie star or someone famous."[1]

No significant relationships were found either between the self-esteem levels or security feelings of the nudists or "potential" nudists and the experiencing of fantasy during sexual behavior with another person.

Fantasies which were described by the subjects included the following:

Nudists

"Occasionally, I visualize scenes." "Sometimes I remember things I have read—or remember a good experience with a certain man I enjoyed being with." "I almost always visualize my clitoris and vagina and his penis—but they are jumbled thoughts. Thoughts about intercourse or masturbation." "Very rarely think of someone else." "At times, though rarely. My fantasies take the form of sweeping feelings—as waves washing over repeatedly and with increasing force. Occasionally—explosions—like flashes of light accompanying orgasm." "Sometimes a particularly attractive man, or one who seems attracted to me. I visualize having intercourse with him." "Sometimes visualize the penis and imagine what the intercourse looks like—contact of the genitals." "My fantasy runs from imagining someone (women or girls) having relationships with a horse or a dog. Lately, my fantasy has been with fathers and daughters, mothers and sons—starting by giving them baths and getting aroused when genital organs were caressed and washed. I used to want a woman to put her large breasts in my face—with her over me so I could fondle and suck on the nipples." "Once in a great while—might think of a fantasy before marriage." "Sometimes. Often from books I have been reading with some erotic material." "Sometimes I think of someone else or having sex with an unidentified person, special feelings, positions, etc." "Yes. Much group activity, much interrelations." "Sometimes I visualize male friends with whom I had intercourse." "I have fantasied varied orgy situations with various of our friends; I have also fantasied a homosexual affair in an orgy situation." "Sometimes a beautiful mountain or forest scene comes into my mind at the point or just before orgasm." "I sometimes pretend we're young and starting out in our sexual life, or I'll pretend he is as he is and I'm young, or he is young and I'm as I am. Sometimes, I'll pretend my husband is someone else—usually a stranger I've

[1] DeMartino, M. F. (ed.), *Sexual Behavior and Personality Characteristics,* (New York: Grove Press, 1966), p. 130. By permission of the Citadel Press, Inc.

seen on the street or in a crowd—that looks handsome and virile—but it is never anyone I know personally." "Occasionally I visualize scenes of recent sex orgies, etc." "Occasionally, when my husband fails to put in a satisfactory performance, I am apt to think of my lover." "Thoughts of other sexually stimulating occasions, either those which have happened or those which I imagine could happen. The fantasies sometimes concern the current partner and sometimes other partners—real or imagined." "Thoughts of other couples participating in an orgy—in like manner; of animals when husband enters my rectum, of husband being a girl when I'm on top of him, etc." "Think about the ocean and about swimming and floating—and about big puffy clouds—and soft silky-feeling things—velvet, fur, etc." "Scenes such as in the woods. Being with other couples, each being with their husbands and wives. Doing a strip-tease before a male audience." "Almost always. Having intercourse, rubbing against trees, father's leg, animals (deer, horses, dogs) sinking into warm water, etc." "Fantasy only when he is manipulating my clitoris—consists of imagining that he has a hundred thousand fingers moving in a blur of speed." "Not too often. If I do it's usually about dark-complexioned persons. They are very gentle and romantic with me at first—undressing and kissing each part of my body. They then become very, very passionate." "[Lesbian, during homosexual activity]—Yes. I often picture myself as a man." "Varies between thoughts of men and women together, men together, women together, and women and dogs." "Thoughts of someone else and/or visualizing scenes are the almost necessary fantasies to achieve orgasm." "Like to hear pornographic stories both before and during intercourse; photographs are equally exciting." "Thoughts of someone else. Sometimes women." "I catch myself thinking of figures—just different numbers going through my mind but no particular order that I have noticed." "Did with husband but don't now. Thoughts of someone else (because husband was sexually unacceptable)." "Thoughts of someone else or two men at once—and visualize scenes." "Occasionally while having intercourse I think of someone I'm physically attracted to. This is when I'm very low sexually. I mean I'm not highly aroused." "Yes—several times; I have visualized dogs mating. This usually happens when I have recently seen two dogs mate."

"Potential" nudists

"A few times when having sex with my husband I thought of someone else whom I desired as being my partner. And sometimes when I couldn't reach an orgasm I imagined my partner as some other person, to see if this would aid in attaining an orgasm (it didn't)." "Yes, having genitals licked." "Sometimes I have visualized a different partner—a boy I went with before marriage." "I often think of someone I would rather be with. Sometimes I visualize being out in the country by a lake or in a beautiful place." "I've thought of several men making love to me at the 'same time.'" "Fantasy of watching others in intercourse." "Generally, pornographic scenes, naked men with erections, bunch of people engaging in fellatio and cunnilingus, etc." "Once in a while I think of someone else." "Occasionally, when I'm with someone, I think of someone I like better or think I *might* like better." "Same type of fantasies used during masturbation. [Imagining myself with different sex partners. Thoughts of seduction—sometimes forceful. Animal coitus, group sex activity. Recalling erotic literature.] At times fantasies are less specific—might be abstract or geometric forms." "Fantasy pertains to someone else. Most infrequently. Reality, dealing with everyday problems seem to interfere in regard to my husband's feelings about me." "I usually am more stimulated if I imagine some sex situation. Fantasies mainly consist of 'forbidden' sex—i.e. sex with more than one person, with someone watching, being caught by my husband, intercourse with a horrible man, etc." "I often fantasize up till a point just before climax. I usually imagine a scene where I am intensely desired, in some situation where intercourse 'should' be taboo—for instance on the beach, in the back room of a night club, in a secluded corner at school." "Sometimes I fantasize about another male. I simply place someone else in my husband's place during sexual activity (as to scene). On occasion I envision a particular spot I feel would make things more exciting, such as swimming nude and having relations or lying nude in the grass, etc." "Yes, from a wishful standpoint when I am with my husband and my desire for someone else is very strong [Subject dislikes husband]." "I imagine doing it with others, imagine other people doing it, think about penis." "Mostly sexual parties in which I am an onlooker. Sometimes houses of prostitution, etc." "I only think of my husband having it into me, 'eating me,' squirting me full of 'come,' biting my breasts."

"Potential" nudists (lesbians)

"Of having sex with a man. Rarely of viewing a male gang-bang." "Where I have become a hero in the girl's eyes." "I think of the person [female] I am with. I am often preoccupied with reaching a climax and have, at times, felt remote; i.e. I was standing off somewhere watching myself be made love to. (Pardon preposition)."

10

INITIATOR OF SEX ACTIVITY AND DEGREE OF PARTICIPATION DURING ACT

In our basically conservative society, most males as well as females still seem to adhere to the belief that in love-making and sexuality, the male is the one who is "supposed" to make the initial advances, and that during the course of sexual activity the male should *always* assume the active or major role, while the female plays an essentially passive or minor role. Consequently, in the great majority of marriages or heterosexual encounters in our culture, these behavioral patterns are the predominant ones practiced. As will be observed from an analysis of the results presented below, however, the samples of female nudists and "potential" nudists included in the present study tend to exhibit somewhat different (more spontaneous, aggressive, and healthy) modes of behavior.

In response to the questions: Who usually initiates the sex activity? (You or your mate.)—How would you describe your degree of activity with respect to initiating same, and after it has started? (That is, are you generally passive, active, very active, etc.)—17 per cent of the nudists and 16 per cent of the "potential" nudists revealed that they (e.g. Me, Myself, I do) were the ones who usually initiated the activity, while 39 per cent of the nudists and 42 per cent of the "potential" nudists disclosed that no one partner was the prime instigator. This was indicated by the responses: Both, About Equal, Half and Half, Mutual, Either, and Varies. Husband or mate (he does) was reported to be the usual initiator by 43 per cent of the nudists and 34 per cent of the "potential" nudists.[1] Several of the responses of the "potential" nudists were unscorable. That the great majority of the subjects in our study participated vigorously during love-making was

---

[1] In the case of the "potential" nudists (lesbians), the term mate refers to another female.

demonstrated by the fact that 50 per cent of the nudists and 41 per cent of the "potential" nudists reported being active, while 34 per cent of the nudists and 34 per cent of the "potential" nudists were very active, after sex activity had started. Responses signifying a tendency toward passivity during sexuality (e.g. passive, generally passive, somewhat passive, I am not usually very active) were recorded by only 6 per cent of the nudists and 9 per cent of the "potential" nudists. An almost equal percentage of nudists (7 per cent) and "potential" nudists (8 per cent) stated that sometimes they are active and sometimes passive.[2] Some of the comments of the "potential" nudists were not scorable.

In reference to the nudists, the initiation of sex activity was found to be related strongly to high self-esteem (r = .57 P< .05). No significant relationship was noted, however, in regard to the security feelings of the participants. In a previous investigation this writer observed that females "who were of high dominance-feeling generally assumed a much more active role both in terms of initiating sexual behavior and during the course of it, than did those who were of low dominance."[3] Maslow, in his highly informative discussion of love in self-actualizing persons (i.e. people who are very healthy psychologically) has commented as follows: "Another characteristic I found of love in healthy people is that they made no really sharp differentiation between the roles and personalities of the two sexes. That is, they did not assume that the female was passive and the male active, whether in sex or love or anything else. These people were all so certain of their maleness or femaleness that they did not mind taking on some of the cultural aspects of the opposite sex role. It was especially noteworthy that they could be both active and passive lovers and this was the clearest in the sexual act and in physical love-making. Kissing and being kissed, being above or below in the sexual act, taking the initiative, being quiet and receiving love, teasing and being teased—these were all found in both sexes. The reports indicated that both were enjoyed at different times. It was considered to be a shortcoming to be limited to just active love-making or passive love-making. Both have their particular pleasures for self-actualizing people."[4]

Some of the responses recorded by subjects were as follows:

[2] As we stated previously, throughout this study percentages were calculated without reference to decimal places.

[3] DeMartino, M. F. (ed.), Sexual Behavior and Personality Characteristics. (New York: Grove Press, 1966), p. 127. By permission of the Citadel Press, Inc.

[4] Maslow, A. H., Motivation and Personality. (New York: Harper and Bros., 1954), p. 245. By permission of the author and the publisher.

Nudists

"Either. I am generally active—the activity builds up." "I do—active." "In marriage I did (one major factor in our incompatibility). I have a preference for an aggressive man now.—I am very active but talk very little." "In marriage, he did. Since marriage, mutual.— Very active." "My husband always. I never initiate.—After it has started, I'd say active and sometimes very active." "My husband—but I do sometimes. When I'm in the mood (which isn't too often) I really enjoy it and would say I'm quite active. On the other hand, I can be quite passive." "Me. After initiation, I am passive." "Mate. Some-times I am passive at the start, but am quickly aroused. Perhaps I sometimes initiate it with my kiss. I've been told often it packs a wal-lop even when I didn't mean anything more than a kiss." "Me—very active." "Both. Sometimes he touches me first, sometimes I touch him first. Very active. I like to move a lot during intercourse and feel no restraints in the foreplay." "My mate. I had been passive until [a few] years ago when I acquired the help of a [much] younger male who performs all the love play—and arouses me to the heights of ecstasy. Then my husband takes over when he is finished. Then I become the active one because my desire needs to be fulfilled." "About even, for we both initiate it.—Very active." "Mate—generally active or very active. Even if I feel passive I don't let my husband know." "I do more than my husband. Very active." "Usually my husband—I am not very active usually—unless I am the one initiating it." "My husband does. If I do he gets mad; he says he doesn't like being pushed into some-thing—I am very responsive and pretty active." "Both do—except with one special man—I always wait for him to make the first move—I am as active as the man. I find too, that if I give vent to a sudden excite-ment, the man becomes even more excited—and this gives us both added pleasure." "My husband prefers that he initiate the activity. With extramarital lovers its hard to say, because I am a very active participant. I immediately 'go down' if my partner hesitates at all in his preliminary play. I would describe my activity as one who follows rather than leads—except when it flatters and pleases a man to have a woman initiate action and show her needs." "Almost equal but perhaps slightly more by me—I am active and at times very active." "About half the time I do. I usually remain very active." "Half and half. I will actively initiate the activity and actively participate if he initiates it. We 'play act' a lot. Sometimes I'll play at being a whore." "Me! I do. Depends on my mood (and the partner). I've never had anyone feel that time spent in sex with me was wasted." "Usually husband. Somewhat passive." "My mate. Active and responsive. I get as much out of it as I put into it." "About half and half.—I'm very active. I try to give as much pleasure as possible. I've read books to find out about the anatomy of men—where their sensitive places are, how they think, and what stimulates their imagination. However, if I don't receive some attention in return, my passions and interest wane. I will initiate the foreplay to arouse my mate to action." "Mate. Generally passive. Sometimes (rarely) aggressive. When I am aggressive I really enjoy it—but it is terribly hard for me to break through the passivity. I am trying though." "My mate. (If I do, he may be impotent). I am very active." "Husband. Passive because husband controls initiation of sex activities." "We both do. It just depends on who wants it the most, I guess.—I am usually very active—but my husband enjoys it when I react differently at times. So at times I just lay very passively; at least as long as possible. Other times I take over the activity in the woman-above position." "Mate. I'm usually passive toward initiating, but active to very active once stimulated." "I generally indicate that I am in a mood conducive to sex, if that is 'initiating.' If I am thoroughly convinced that sex would be the best thing to have next on the agenda I am quite open and active." "My husband. I am usually passive to active. My husband does most of the work. I move only to receive orgasm." "I usually initiate most of the actual intercourse simply because I am the more physical of the two of us. I like to hold and be held, touch and be touched much more, and more often than he does. I think that's generally common, whether women like to admit it or not. . . . However, once activity has started he takes over, and though I am far from completely passive, there is no question that he is the leader." "Either. Best when its mutual.—Very active once the desire is there. I like a man to give me a chance to kiss him back and not just take over." "Sometimes one, sometimes the other.—Generally passive; sometimes slightly active." "Man usually initiates it but usually because I let it be known one way or another. Perfume helps and certain kinds of looks. Wandering fingers (I always keep my hands above the navel until invited to put them elsewhere) and of course a sort of pressure when dancing.—My degree of activity adapts itself to the situation at hand. But whatever it is, it holds my whole and undivided attention." "It is about half and half.—Active. I fell no bashfulness or shyness in trying to arouse him—but I respect his desires to skip love-making if he definitely says he is too tired or not interested at all." "My mate—I seldom initiate sex, although I am active after my husband starts it. I am becoming more and more uninhibited in starting sexual play and taking the lead in sexual activity."

"Potential" nudists

"Sometimes me, other times him.—Sometimes very active, sometimes slow, depends on position." "Me. Active—very active." "He initiates it more times—but I do it once in a while.—I guess I lack a little confidence in myself so I play a generally passive role. Its probably due to a lack of understanding of the act." "My mate always does.—I'm very active and I have no restrictions in our relationships." "Mate. Usually passive, but it depends on what the boy wants." "Depends upon mate—often mutual. I am generally not only extremely affectionate but also extremely responsive to affection, and cannot remember ever being passive, though amount of activity depends on person." "Overtly, my mate; 60 per cent of the time. I am either passive or overtly active. I, however, become quite passive if aroused by hands on my breasts or genital area—get weak knees and yielding, lose much perception of partner." "Husband. Active." "I usually do.—I become very active after it has started." "If I am strongly attracted to the man— me. If not so strongly, its a toss up. Usually very active. This is a habit which has gotten me into some very unusual predicaments. I found out that most men (especially the younger ones) take a little time to get used to a sexually aggressive female." "Both. Very active. I feel to have a good sexual relationship, the wife should take an active part and seduce her husband quite often. I enjoy it very much." "We both. Sometimes my husband, sometimes myself—active. Sometimes he enjoys going 'around the world.'" "Varies with the mate! Too active, because usually I get the man going faster and further than I really would like. I am *very* responsive to any stimulation and I enjoy initiating although I have had to learn to hold back." "Husband. Generally passive except when I've been reading [certain books]." "Probably I usually encourage it or I don't. If my husband initiates sex activity I feel he needs the attention and I take an active part even if I do not like it. He seems to enjoy it very much; says I'm terrific, etc.—too bad it's usually an act on my part. Sad also." "Sometimes my fiancé, sometimes myself. I am generally very active. After my fiancé and I have had an orgasm I frequently am desirous of continuing and if he is not, I proceed to make him so. During intercourse, I believe I'm as active as my partner." "Mate. Usually passive until sexual urge reaches peak— then active." "He does. I might try to excite him by sitting near him (or on top of him) and kissing him or stroking him—if that doesn't work I give up and wait for him to initiate. My response is usually very strong and immediate." "Usually my husband. Occasionally, I suggest desire verbally or by initiating caressing. After the act has begun, I am fairly passive—less active than I feel I would like to be." "While married, almost always my husband. Now, it varies but usually the man.— I feel that I am generally active, although in a casual affair I am rather shy of taking the initiative. This is lessening with more experience. I don't like to do everything, however, it makes me feel as if I'm being observed with too much detachment." "That depends on my partner, some men have to be the aggressor.—Again, it depends on who it is, if I really like the thing I'm active as hell. Otherwise I feel extremely passive about it because all I have to do is masturbate and I can get ten times the satisfaction." "Since I have obtained a little more experience I've started to at times. Generally passive." "Mate. To initiate I attack him when he is sitting in his chair. I stroke his genitals through his clothes, undo his fly, etc. Or else I come out wrapped up naked in a quilt. During sex I am usually passive in that I don't make the basic movement, although I make secondary movements." "Depends on who becomes aroused first. I'm very much in love with a man now—so it's very active. If I'm not too involved, I tend to be passively receptive."

"Potential" nudists (lesbians)

"My butch, but sometimes I do. I am basically passive but occasionally am inspired to become active when I have been drinking or am with someone I love and want to please." "We both do. We're both active in turn. If I initiate the activity by taking her in my arms and kissing and petting her, it doesn't mean I will gratify her first." "Both. Very active—actually I play a dominant role—prefer making love rather than being made love to." "Mate. The butch is the aggressor. I tease and make myself available. After it has been initiated by the butch I am very active—as active as the mate." "Self. I am active in initiating homosexual activity, however, my partner or whomever, makes themselves available to these advances. This is done by kissing, talking, holding, petting and touching; also by french kissing." "Me. Very active." "Self, ostensibly; actually a look or some signal of desire from either [female]. Active, assume initiative." "Both about equally initiate activity. If I initiate am very active; if mate [female] initiates am very passive. Sometimes both at same time then we both are very active."

***** 11 ***

SEXUAL APPROACH PREFERRED AND SPECIFIC PREFERENCES

SEXUAL APPROACH PREFERRED

Previous research[1] has demonstrated clearly that there is no one or ideal approach to love-making which all females always find pleasurable or desirable. Rather, females desire different techniques, depending on such factors as their emotional states or moods, personality make-ups, and the particular circumstances involved. As will be seen, the results of the present study substantiate and are substantiated by those reported earlier. For in response to the question: What kind of sexual approach do you usually prefer, i.e. slow and gentle, quick, explosive, sometimes slow, sometimes sweeping?—Describe—while a preference for the slow and gentle (slow, gentle) approach was mentioned most often by the nudists, many of them indicated a liking for a variety of overtures; depending on their mood, partner, circumstances, etc. Other desired approaches recorded prevalently were denoted by the words: explosive, sweeping, and quick. The following terms were also used by the nudists in describing their preferred sexual advances: passionate, forceful, rough, violent, vigorous, active, furious, fast, teasing, loving, tender, and romantic. In general, essentially similar responses were noted by the "potential" nudists.

With respect to the nudists a preference either solely, or as one of several described, for a sexual approach characterized by such terms as: sweeping, violent, explosive, rough, grabbed, quick, forceful, feeling of being dominated, hot and quick, wild and abandoned, and tantalizing, as compared with a preference for an approach denoted *only* by the words slow and gentle, slow, or gentle, was found to be sig-

---

[1] See: DeMartino, M. F. (ed.), *Sexual Behavior and Personality Characteristics.* (New York: Grove Press, 1966), Chapters 4, 5, and 6. Also see Ellis, A., *The Art and Science of Love.* (New York: Dell, 1965), especially Chap. 4.

nificantly related to high self-esteem (r = .33 P< .05). No significant relationship was observed in reference to the security feelings of the subjects. In his classic study of female sexuality Maslow pointed out astutely that "The average high-dominance woman in our insecure society prefers straightforward, unsentimental, rather violent, animal, pagan, passionate, even sometimes brutal, love-making. It must come quickly, rather than after a long period of wooing. She wishes to be suddenly swept off her feet, not courted. She wishes her favors to be taken rather than asked for. In other words she must be dominated, must be forced into subordinate status. For the middle-dominance woman, gentler, long-prolonged wooing is considered ideal. In love-making, sex as such must be hidden, swathed about with veils of love words, gently and carefully led up to. It must be preceded by a general atmosphere of the type supplied by soft music, flowers, and love-letters. . . . So marked are these differences that we may say, with some inaccuracy but with illumination, that the high-dominance woman unconsciously wishes to be raped; the middle-dominance woman to be seduced. As for the low-dominance woman, it is difficult to know what she wishes. Perhaps it may be fair to say that any commerce with sex will be for the purpose of reproduction or to 'satisfy her husband' (except when there is a very high sex drive)."[2]

Among the responses reported by the subjects were the following:

Nudists

"Slow and gentle." "Slow and gentle or sometimes sweeping, depending on the mood of the moment." "It varies. Usually I prefer slow beginnings leading up to violent activity when the man reaches orgasm." "Variable. Often I like slow, teasing; but enjoy a quick explosion for a change. Depends on mood." "Almost all approaches—at different times and different settings." "Slow and gentle increasing to sweeping." "If I am tired or feel very romantic, I prefer slow and gentle. If I am not tired and it is in the middle of the day when the children are not home, I like it sweeping and explosive." "I love it in slow motion but yet sweeping at times." "Varies. Sometimes I like a gradual seduction, other times I respond to almost rough handling and force. After being aroused I usually (not always) prefer that it move quickly and am temporarily put off by delay or prolonged foreplay." "I like my lover to start slow with his mouth on my genitals

[2] Maslow, A. H., "Self-esteem (Dominance-Feeling) and Sexuality in Women." *Journal of Social Psychology*, 1942, *16*, pp. 283–84. By permission of the author and The Journal Press.

until I reach a few orgasms. Then when he enters, it becomes quite explosive with him reaching 4 to 5 orgasms. I reach numerous ones and we continue for an hour or more til he is finished—then I want my husband who is waiting and who likes me full of love juices which flow out of me." "If at night when all is quiet, I prefer it slow and gentle. If it is a stolen few minutes (because our need for each other is so great) I prefer it sweeping and furious." "Slow and gentle as though we had our whole lifetime to perform the particular act in which we're engaged at the time." "It seems to take some time for me to work into the right mood, so usually I prefer a slow approach." "I like it to last a long time." "Sometimes slow, sometimes sweeping. Usually, I like a slow approach but this depends upon the mood, the circumstances, how sexy I feel at the moment." "A slow, loving, tender approach. I like to be talked to. Once in a great while I like to be grabbed and loved." "Usually prefer a long build-up—perhaps starting with lunch or even breakfast—a swim, a sail—an expedition to an art gallery—tea—dinner with cocktails, then bed with leisurely approach. Some few times an explosive sweeping approach, followed by lazy leisurely talk and petting. Love quick spontaneous intercourse on waking up lazily in morning." "I usually prefer to get 'talked out' if something is bothering me, as I want to share something and then be swept with passion rather quickly. Sometimes, I prefer slowness to make the pleasure last longer." "Sometimes slow, sometimes sweeping. That's what makes it interesting; it's never the same. Sometimes it's a touch of the hand, or a light kiss on the back of my neck—at other times he just lifts me up bodily and carries me to bed (not an easy feat— I'm heavy)." "Depends on circumstances. When I'm kept satisfied, I prefer the slow and gentle approach. If I've been 'without' too long, I like the explosive approach." "Depends on mood—usually I like the feeling of being dominated and powerless." "First hot and quick and then slow and gentle." "I always prefer the slow gentle approach. The foreplay is as important as the act. If my passions are high before we start, I need less foreplay, but then I appreciate a long foreplay even more to prolong the love act. Why should you want to hurry and get a good thing over?" "I enjoy a different approach each time. I enjoy them all." "Depends on the situation—sometimes real quick and other times I like to engage in foreplay for an hour or so." "Gentle and romantic." "Slow and gentle. I like to have my breasts kissed and my pussy played with in order to reach a climax and then I like to have my lover enter me and reach his climax. I very seldom reach a climax from the inside. It takes a large man who can go for a long time to make me reach a climax inside. Sometimes I can reach a second climax inside after having reached one on the outside." "I prefer my husband's approach—whatever it is. Sometimes he takes an hour, makes a ritual of preparing me, massaging, lightly touching all over, giving head [cunnilingus]. Sometimes he just drags me to bed and fucks me without ceremony. Variety is the spice of life." "Slow and gentle when sex play is initiated by my husband—usually explosive when initiated by myself." "Slow and gentle approach is always preferred. Love-making and love-playing to me demands gentleness and includes licking, kissing, and sucking of nipples and breasts; gently massaging each other's genitals, touching and fingering buttock. The charm of love we practice always includes the above—providing us a greater joint harmonious satisfaction preceding sexual intercourse." "Usually slow and gentle. Sometimes explosive. Although I am afraid of being hurt if the approach is too rapid." "Sometimes sweeping—if there has been sex play during the day. Quick—if I don't particularly care if I have sex or not. Explosive—if it has been a while since any activity. Slow and gentle, if I am very passionate and desirous." "[Lesbian] Quick and explosive." "Varies with the situation. Prefer quick build up and then hold it short of climax as long as we can." "Yes—all of these. Sometimes light and in a joking manner and sometimes wild and abandoned." "Slow, gentle, prolonged, and almost tantalizing." "Slow and sweeping. I enjoy a lot of foreplay—that is kissing and feeling of bodies—getting more and more passionate as we go along." "A variety is nice.—I have been 'swept off my feet' twice and really enjoyed it." "Slow and gentle. If it's too quick I feel cheated." "Slow and gentle, usually, but without doubt of intentions." "Sometimes slow—sometimes sweeping—never explosive unless it is a mock rape scene, and that's fun sometimes." "Generally I prefer a slow and gentle approach although I appreciate a variety and gain much pleasure from an explosive demonstration." "Slow, but gradually more aggressive to point of explosion." "Prefer slow, subtle approach usually, unless my prospective partner is very exciting to me (one I have entertained notions about over a period of time either consciously or unconsciously, and who is new to me)." "Quick." "I enjoy all of the approaches depending upon my mood . . ." "It takes me a long time to warm up—so I prefer the slow and gentle approach—so far." "Depends on how much desire has been building up in me. If there is time, I enjoy a lot of foreplay, examination of each other, etc. Tantalizing teasing makes it more fun and satisfaction is deeper.—If it has been a long time since I have had intercourse, I prefer a quick dry entry with no foreplay and a vigorous bodily movement on both our parts. Orgasm usually comes swiftly and very deep within." "I prefer a very slow and gentle approach in which the penis is moved completely and slowly back until we reach orgasm and then very fast and explosive."

"Potential" nudists

"Slow, gentle, tender, few words, spontaneous and not previously discussed." "Depends on the moods of both partners. On some occasions, sexual play before intercourse is desirable—at other times, little or no play is needed." "It varies, usually slow and passionate! Occasionally fast but that is rare. It isn't so much speed that matters as it is attentiveness and care." "Gentle, but passionately desirous." "All depends on my mood. If I feel very strong about sex, I like the approach to be quick. If I'm not strong at the moment, slow and easy. Also, I like impromptu sex—just all of a sudden for no reason there it is." "Quick. Two kisses and I'm ready for action. My husband likes to play for a half hour. This is mostly the cause of my inability to achieve an orgasm, I get overdone." "Prefer sex to follow an interesting discussion which has made me feel closer to and understood by my husband." "Always gentle, sometimes slow—sometimes quick, nice to fuck unexpectedly." "Depends on the man— he should use the style he's most happy about." "Anyway—slow or explosive as long as it is strong and sexy and not hesitant." "Slow and gentle—I like to be seduced." "I like a vigorous but gentle approach usually, in which my partner is concerned with my pleasure as he is with his. This includes vigorous foreplay." "It doesn't really matter. I love sex and I'll take it anyway I can get it. It depends on position and the mood." "A slow and gentle approach most of the time because it excites me more. However, a quick approach is also satisfying to me at times because to me it shows masculinity." "Depends upon my mood. I usually prefer an 'explosive' approach." "I like both [slow and gentle, quick and explosive]. Some days (especially if I've been drinking) I like to be rough and I like him to follow." "I usually prefer a slower approach as I require ten to fifteen minutes of foreplay to be significantly aroused." "An approach which is gentle and firm but not overly slow; i.e. once I am aroused I want to be taken decisively so and will try to have my partner do this." "It usually depends on what sort of mood I am in. Generally, I prefer a slow and gentle approach at the beginning. But once my partner and I are aroused, I like him and myself to be quite passionate." "I sometimes prefer a violent and rapid approach, but on the average I like a brief period of gentle foreplay, increasing in violence and tempo." "I usually need a period of gentle tenderness before entry. Occasionally my response is quite immediate and I am eager for entry within a few minutes." "Slow and gentle, gradually—when we both are ready to reach orgasm—quick and explosive." "Depends very much on mood. If I'm in a violent animal mood I want violent animal sex. If I feel all innocent, I want gentleness." "Varied approach. Whether slow or fast I enjoy some teasing in foreplay, opportunity to stimulate partner manually and orally before penetration." "Depends. I'm lucky to have a man who's enormously responsive to my moods—but who can dominate me and make me like it." "Sometimes very slow and gentle until I can't stand it—sometimes quick and hard and forceful." "Fitting my degree of passion. Generally slow and gentle, sometimes sweeping." "Sometimes slow, sometimes sweeping—depends on the mood we're in."

"Potential" nudists (lesbians)

"Slow and gentle. Lovingly." "I prefer a masterful, self-confident, 'no nonsense' approach." "I think I'd like a quick explosive approach now. My contacts have been slow up to now." "On the street (pick-up) I like action. In the act of love (or sex)—gentle, easy, slow, tender caressing and petting, and kissing. After climaxing more of the same tender treatment." "Sometimes slow and gentle, other times rough and quick—no in-between." "Slow and gentle—stroking of the back, arms, neck, face, many preliminaries." "Slow and gentle but seriously and meaningfully." "Usually slow, gentle, increasing in intensity, rarely sweeping or swift. At recognition that this is wanted by her."

SPECIFIC PREFERENCES

Although to most males sexual expression is primarily a physical act, to most females, it is basically an emotional experience which involves the display of love and affection.[3] Moreover, females as compared to males (because they are more romantic and sensitive emotionally), in love-making generally place a greater emphasis on such factors as time, atmosphere, place, and state of undress. With these considerations in mind, the following question was asked of our subjects: Do you have any specific preferences with respect to engaging in sex during the day or night, light or dark, unclothed, partially clothed, etc.?—In relation to the time element, 22 per cent of the nudists indicated a preference for the night, 13 per cent for the daytime or afternoon, and 8 per cent for the morning. Many, however, seemed to have no special

[3] See: Ehrmann, W., *Premarital Dating Behavior*. (New York: Henry Holt & Co., 1959), p. 269.

preferences and answered simply by saying: day or night, anytime. Thus, there does not appear to be any one particular time when a preponderance of the nudist subjects desire to participate in sex. As to the absence (dark) or presence of light during sexuality, it may be said that while many of the nudists in our sample do not have any feelings one way or another in regard to these factors, far more of them (34 per cent) prefer that there be some degree of light (i.e. light, little light, semi-light, candlelight), rather than complete darkness (4 per cent). (Kinsey, *et al.* found that while 40 per cent of the males in their sample "preferred their coitus or other sexual activities where there was at least some light," only 19 per cent "of the females in the sample preferred sexual relations in the light.")[4] With respect to the state of undress, as was anticipated, the great majority of the nudists (76 per cent) reported that they prefer to experience sexual relations in an unclothed state (i.e. nude, naked). Several also stated that their mates too should be nude. On the other hand, some of the respondents did not relate any preference in this connection. Other expressed desires by the nudists included the following: a liking for sex activity when rested—not tired, while partially clothed, while wearing erotic or "naughty" garments—also hose and high heels, after a shower, on a bed, and outdoors.

While, in general, the overall findings of the "potential" nudists were the same as those of the nudists, they, however, did not indicate as marked a preference either for being unclothed (63 per cent) or for some degree of light (23 per cent).

Somewhat to our surprise, a preference for the indulgence in sex with the presence of some light or in the daytime, as compared to a preference for both the dark and at night, was not found to be related significantly to feelings of either self-esteem or security.

Preferences which were described by the respondents included the following:

Nudists

"Unclothed, no preference as to time." "Night, partially clothed." "Prefer daytime, nude, my bed." "None—but prefer not to have children awake or possible interruptions (although daytime 'quickies' can be stolen!)" "Anytime, unclothed." "Day or night, light or dark but always nude. Some of the most remembered highlights of my life have

---

[4] Kinsey, A. C., *et al.*, *Sexual Behavior in the Human Female.* (Philadelphia: Saunders Co., 1953), p. 664. By permission of Dr. P. H. Gebhard and the Institute for Sex Research, Inc.

been the times when my husband and I fucked in the woods, on a mountain top, in the field, in a great hollow log in the rain, etc. I use the word 'fuck' because I feel it is a good English word with only one meaning. To me it is a perfectly good word." "No preferences as to day or night—I simply don't want to be tired. I prefer a light to be on. I like to have both parties unclothed." "At night, dark—no light, and when I'm sure of no interruptions—unclothed." "Prefer to be completely nude and light or dark depending upon the mood we are both in. Would prefer early afternoon—as the children are not home and I am relaxed—not too tired." "Light is fine. Although, when highly excited, I tend to close my eyes (even at night). Nude is the best for contact.—But some clothes can be interesting too." "Depends on mood." "I find sex in the light more stimulating as I enjoy seeing my husband's body. Always nude except for partial covering in winter." "My best time is in the afternoon; I like the semidark with a dim blue light—completely nude." "Prefer quietness of night—a candle lighted room, unclothed, after a shower." "Sometimes light and unclothed, usually no preference. Prefer times when neither of us are tired and when I have just had a shower or swim." "At night with candlelight and totally nude." "Night or before getting up in the morning. I like the light on and unclothed." "Day or night, with lights on or in dark is unimportant. But we *must* be naked and I'd rather be in bed." "Much prefer complete nudity—feel more uninhibited in partial darkness— but I have been very excited at times when making very intimate love in bright sunlight." "I like sex best in the afternoon, usually in the nude—sometimes with erotic garments—very seldom in total darkness or at night." "I usually prefer sex in the morning or day because I'm rested then. Sometimes I prefer darkness, usually it doesn't matter one way or the other. I prefer no clothes." "Warm afternoons outdoors in the open—always without clothes and I like it anywhere, anyway, anytime." "Unclothed, in the morning, when rested." "No preference as to day or night. In the daytime, I like to see what we're doing, but at night I prefer to be in the dark. I prefer to be unclothed (both) unless we are sneaking a 'fast one' in the house with the children apt to rush in—or in the car. Then I prefer to be partially clothed." "Dark, unclothed, prefer morning—I'm usually tired at night." "Completely unclothed—preferably with light. I might prefer daytime, because I am less tired. I think a warm night outdoors under the moonlight would be divine." "Always unclothed whether day or night. Usually with a soft light at night so we can enjoy visual as well as physical sex." "Night in the light and partially clothed to start and then in the nude." "Without clothes. Day or night, no matter. I prefer to be secluded. Although making love in the same room with other people who are also, would be acceptable." "Yes, night—dark—beginning partially clothed, ending completely nude is preferred and practiced." "I prefer the morning— in the light—completely naked." "I like an intimate light and to be naked." "I prefer night, but find either daylight or lamplight very exciting." "Prefer unclothed and outdoors, light or dark—prefer enough light to see and be seen, like variety of time—morning, afternoon, evening." "If I could choose a more convenient time, it would be mid-afternoon before I get too tired. Anytime, I like *some* light to make it more interesting. If the urge is sudden, clothes are a hindrance but I like a man to undress me. 'Naughty' garments are delightful." "Nights, lights on, partially clothed." "Afternoon, usually. Naked, except for hose and high heels." "No—anything and everything goes." "The only thing I have a preference about is that both of us be completely nude. In my first experience the man left his socks on and it has left a feeling of hurry up which I don't like. I also like some light in the room, usually a candle or dim light." "Naked—enough light to see what's going on." "We take advantage of physical opportunities for variety whenever we can—prolonged nudity (swimming, sunbathing), any-time, usually a light on so we can move around without bumping each other, a warm room, occasionally outdoors." "No preference in regard to day or night, just must be unclothed." "No preference for either day or night. Prefer light to dark, unclothed. I enjoy seeing him." "I insist on complete nudity for both myself and my partner and always in a lighted room. I want to see and be seen." "Main preference is in bed, nude, and with bed covers up; it can be either day or night, light or dark; in the summer the bed covers don't have to be up." "I prefer engaging in sex during the day, without clothes." "I think I prefer night slightly to day—I'm usually completely unclothed but I enjoy variances in these things. We're always striving to vary it somewhat. It adds excitement." "I prefer mornings or afternoon-nap time. At night I usually am tired and drop off to sleep quickly."

"Potential" nudists

"Prefer day—or some light at night and completely unclothed." "If in day, prefer sex in the morning right after awakening: if at night, prefer slight illumination, especially from candle or colored light bulb. Always naked." "Unclothed, midafternoon, when possible." "At night as long as it is dark. It seems more romantic to me. Unclothed, because it gives me a sense of freedom." "Definitely unclothed completely—anytime of day or night, light or dark (not total darkness, sometimes in the early morning light, firelight, etc.—very romantic)—much better on a bed than elsewhere, privacy is imperative." ". . . I do prefer to make love in the light and I would not like myself or my mate to be partially clothed." "I love it day or night. It doesn't make a bit of difference to me." "Night—nude, when you can sleep together all night." "To be naked (both of us) and in bed as opposed to a car, chair, etc." "Lately, I've enjoyed it partly clothed—it never made any difference before." "Totally unclothed—darkness—after several hours in the company of my lover." "Night, dark, unclothed; to be less bothered by other stimuli and concentrate on sex sensations." "No, I just like it—but *not* partially clothed. Beds are most enjoyable, but a good clean rug is exciting too—as long as it is warm enough." "I much prefer engaging in sex in a fairly dim room, on a bed. I like being in an unclothed state." "No, the emotional attitudes of warmth, caring, interest, and openness are most important to me." "I much prefer to leave all my clothes off—and his too. Otherwise no preference as to dark or light, day or night." "I have no preference with regard to day or night, light or dark. I do enjoy being nude and having my partner nude. Nothing nicer than the feeling of flesh! For something different, I like being partially clothed. Whatever the mood at the time. I become more easily stimulated trying out new places in the house, such as having relations on the couch, on the rug, chair." "Unclothed, day or night, prefer some light." "No particular time, but unclothed." "Always night, dark and unclothed. Once I tried it during the daytime when we were out in the country—a group of Girl Scout hitchhikers came upon us. I'll never forget that—I learned a lesson." "I usually prefer the dark because I feel it's more mysterious but I like sex in the day, night, or light, depending on my mood. I prefer to be unclothed completely. Sex in the morning upon waking is very stimulating." "Anytime of the day or night is as good as another—it's nice to have at least a small light—perhaps a candle on during the activity. One has to be nude to get maximum enjoyment—total tactile stimulation is very important." "Night, dark. Day would be all right but children are liable to pop in. Unclothed or undressed by mate." "I like sex best at night—preferably in candlelight or with a small light on. I like to be naked." "I dislike a man wearing any type of clothing; sex in pitch darkness is particularly exciting; occasionally (depending on mate) broad daylight inhibits me somewhat." "Having a great block about the body, in the past I did it mostly at night, but I have done it all ways mentioned. The one time it was really a gas was during the day in a storm tunnel." "It varies—mostly night so that we both can relax after communion with each other and less free of entanglement of clothes." "Anytime, anywhere, any way—but not just any man." "Usually at night in the dark in bed. Sometimes we do it with the light on and look at our genitals with a mirror."

"Potential" nudists (lesbians)

"Prefer dim light, unclothed." "Anyway is fine." "Anytime. Unclothed." "Indifferent." "Night—but also day if the room is dusky. Both nude completely." "Prefer unclothed, evening. After darkness so that nothing distracts the act or feeling of the act." "Not really. If we are clothed or partially clothed during petting, we always stop and completely disrobe for the sexual act." "Prefer to be unclothed—also prefer night, but have no objections to daytime sex." "I am not adverse to sex during the day. In fact, it's wonderful in the morning. The night, however, seems best. Prefer to be unclothed." "Either day or night—partially lit and most often I like myself to be totally clothed."

✳✳✳✳✳ 12 ✳✳✳

"SPECIAL" TECHNIQUES AND "SEXY" TALK DURING SEXUAL ACTIVITIES

"SPECIAL" TECHNIQUES

Any activity which is repeated in a routine manner tends to become unexciting, dull, and eventually boring. The same holds true for sexual behavior. With the aim, therefore, of discovering the extent to which females attempt to enhance their sexual activities through various innovations, the following questions were asked: Do you ever engage in any "special" techniques during your sexual foreplay activities, e.g., doing a "striptease," dancing sexually for mate in nude or seminude, etc.? Describe. Do you ever use mirrors, music, or anything else to enhance your sexual activities? If so, describe.

An analysis of the results revealed that 70 per cent of the nudists and 53 per cent of the "potential" nudists did, at one time or another, attempt to enliven in some way their sexual experiences. As will be seen, the embellishments utilized by the respondents during sexuality were quite diversified.

Contrary to expectations, no significant correlation was noted between either self-esteem or security status and the use of "special" techniques.

Among the sexual innovations reported by the subjects were the following:

Nudists

"I have had rooms where half the walls were mirrors and I never saw them, but I am deeply moved by certain kinds of music—Rachmaninoff." "Usually, I begin activity by kissing. Since we are nudists, and go nude around the house, this means genital contact—which causes the desired stimulation. We have stood before a mirror. We

108

usually have classical music on." "Striptease." "Occasionally. Dancing nude together, listening to music. Bathing. Taking a sip of liquid and transferring to partner's mouth. Back rubbing. Kissing feet. I dance in front of a mirror, I watch penis movement in mirror—very exciting. I like to see myself move and meet it—then see it reappear." "I try to please him. If mirrors and music will help him, its fine with me." "Those things [Striptease, dancing sexually for mate in nude or semi-nude] and more—I've done because my husband wished it. But I do enjoy it too, at times." "We sometimes describe a scene or tell a story on each other's body or pretend we are someone else ('call girl' and client). When mirrors have been available we used them." "Very occasionally—striptease and dancing nude." "Perfume is good—especially around breasts and genitals. Sometimes we lick and fondle each other while reading mimeographed-type pornography." "I have danced with my brief black bra and panties, caressing my breasts and my genital organs—pubic hair and vagina—also dance nude for friends at a gathering when the music arouses me.—Have tried a vibrator once on my vagina which almost drove me out of my mind.—Another time we rubbed oil on our bodies and then had intercourse, it was sensational. I reached numerous climaxes this way. (With the vibrator four people held my arms and legs while a fifth person applied the vibrator—I am told I screamed in ecstasy—later I helped apply it to another woman present.)" "Once in a while I undress slowly in front of my sex partner—but as a rule I want to get at the sex. I like soft music—mood music—the older songs by Jackie Gleason, etc. I like mirrors." "Just cleanliness and perfume." "Striptease, posturing and 'teasing.'" "Sometimes I wear a sexy bra. Mirrors are nice at times. Unusual places are stimulating such as living room floor, kitchen table, out of doors, in the water. Sex play is stimulated by music, low lights, dancing." "Sometimes we like to stand in front of a mirror and caress each other. Sometimes we put romantic records on or have the FM radio on." "Men have taught me to enjoy viewing the sex act. It took me many years to acquire such a taste. Music can add drama to coitus. But none of these embellishments are necessary to me." "I like to dance to arouse partner. I use soft music, in the evenings dark green and blue lights—also mirror to watch." "On rare occasions I have stripped only or stripped and danced for mate in nude. Mirrors are used very seldom. In bathroom, before large mirrors. Music occasionally adds to our love mood." "We sometimes pretend that I am being raped or that my husband is being raped." "Strip to the waist and shake breasts—tease by pretending to kiss my husband's penis. On occasion we have used mirrors and we take sexy pictures with our Polaroid."

"Sometimes music. A few times in front of a fire in the fireplace with music were delightful." "Sometimes I dress 'sexy.' I have a lot of sexy lounging clothes I have made with slit skirts, low bodices, black underwear, black stockings. I have some G strings and bikini outfits.—We usually have the Hi Fi turned on low. We especially like the fireplace lit or candlelight. We enjoy intercourse on the fur rug in front of the blazing fireplace—late at night. We have had intercourse in front of mirrors, we have tried different places—the woods, sand dunes, the beach, backyard, the front porch." "Not necessarily on purpose—I'm just playful, I guess. Mirrors are nice—especially for masturbation—alone or with someone. Fire feels *so* good to the naked body! Love soft background music (classic and semiclassic preferred). I have a soft pink-and-green light in my bedroom and nude artist's sketches on the ceiling." "Sometimes I like to tease my husband by dancing while removing clothes, etc. Sometimes I sing to my husband." "Could be a rhythmical dance. Music—hot jazz, big bands, Latin-American dance beats." "Occasionally nude dancing together—tit sucking.—Records which have appropriate types of rhythm, mirrors, tape recordings of previous sexual activities." "Dance nude, do striptease. Music—incense, dim red lights—whisky". "Mainly, I take pains with my appearance and wear a little pair of panties and high heels—sometimes I dance.— We listen to our stereo and just lately started using a mirror. It is very stimulating to watch each other's sexual organs while making love to each other." "My husband likes to take Polaroid nude shots—but he does at other times also. We play the stereo. Like to make love on fluffy bedroom rugs.—I almost always perfume the sheets." "I feel awkward but my husband asks me to and sometimes I do dress in garter belt, stockings, and heels for him (rarely). On very rare occasions—music. And perhaps once or twice a mirror was used when we were in a motel or hotel room. This was for my husband's benefit." "I love sexy, pretty lingerie—like to dance sexually and strip tease for him. Sometimes music is good; he uses mirrors—but I don't like to watch." "Wearing something special, using perfume—taking showers together—having a drink in bed. Standing in front of mirror watching our movements. Using a hand mirror (magnified) in bed. Play the FM radio. Open drape to let the light shine in." "Dancing together in the nude with [another female. Subject is a lesbian]. We play pop music—something like twist music, and dance in the nude to it." "Danced twice; striptease once." "We like to see each other in a mirror. I have a long wall-length mirror reflecting my bed." "Once in a while I will model in sheer black pin-up type lingerie or negligee." "Dancing sexually clothed in hose and high heels.—Usually play with male before a full-length mirror, each of us getting nude full-length front views of our bodies." "[Lesbian] *Homosexual activity*—Occasionally. A striptease and sexy dance steps are helpful in arousing another person. Romantic music makes a pleasant background." "Striptease and sing to him." "Strip poker—tickling. If we happen to be dressed and have an evening free, we play strip poker until both are nude (winner often demands loser remove pants first). Our favorite game is to see how much tickling we can take; starting gently and getting wilder.—Music always helps. Sometimes cola drinks act as an aphrodisiac.—I like to display myself in 'naughty' clothes that scantily conceal or boldly emphasize the female parts." "At times I will pose, walk, and occasionally do bumps and grinds for my husband. Usually in the nude, but sometimes in sheer nightgowns or a bikini.—Sometimes we use mirrors. At other times we enjoy reading erotic literature or looking at pictures of both males and females usually in the nude or with very few clothes. Sometimes we enjoy talking about sexy situations we might find ourselves engaged in." "The thing I appreciate most in a sexual relationship is humor, so that one slip does not destroy the mood. A stubborn zipper or button, a running nose or sudden belch can be very inconvenient if you let it be. So I occasionally clown, use exaggerated poses and movements and am sometimes even pornographic, all in a light vein, which amuses the man, and also, almost without us realizing it, heightens our expectations and also the act itself. Music is nice as a background, but we never try to adjust our rhythm to the beat of the music. I think a mirror would be fun, though I have never been in a position to use it . . . I have attempted intercourse while under the influence of LSD-25, one of the psychedelic drugs. Whether my real inhibitions were coming out or because we tried it during the most frenzied part of the experience, I wasn't much interested in it. The feeling itself was very pleasant but it couldn't hold my attention. Also, perhaps the fact we were in the house, when we prefer to be out in nature during the times we are under the influence of it, contributed to my lack of enjoyment. We will probably try it again under more favorable circumstances." "I undress him and he does me. But most usually we are too anxious to feel that bare skin all the way down, to fool around very much. We never need anything further to excite us." "We like to have a fire in the fireplace, a huge towel on the floor in front of it, and oil each other with baby oil or 'Lanlay.' Then we finish in bed. This is done occasionally.—Clean sheets. A shower together or a Japanese bath (in regular bathtub, after a shower, a hot soak for five to eight minutes) separately. Prolonged, tantalizing kissing before we undress." "Sometimes I do a striptease and do a nude dance with suggestive hip thrusts and other sexual gestures. Sometimes, use erotic records of music, stories, and sounds of sexual activities." "Stripped for ex-husband on his insistance.—Music, sometimes; drums or romantic music." "Dancing nude, very infrequently. Music, for a short time.—Found that it induced relaxation and distraction and sleep." "I do strip dances sometimes—dance nude for him. I also wear net hose and other things he likes.—We use mirrors sometimes—also I dress in garters and hose, sexy lingerie that arouses him." "We are nudists so striptease has little effect—I reverse things and *get dressed*—usually in sexy pajamas and he enjoys *slowly* undressing me.—We both like to get high on beer and then we can play for about an hour before experiencing orgasm.—Normally my husband can't go for more than 15–20 minutes before reaching orgasm." "I find that most men in my life enjoy watching me do ballet exercises—stand on hands—do the twist or 'bumps and grinds' in the nude. . . . Makes us both feel silly and gay. We also take each other's pictures in the nude with a Polaroid camera. Music is always very exciting—bathing in a large tub when available, soaping each other's genitals and fondling them—holding a man's penis when he urinates.—My favorite lover often switches on a bright light when we get in a '69' position.—Standing in back of a man while he showers and rubbing my body against his back while caressing his penis.—If drinking and kissing—drop a mouthful of drink with small ice cubes into his open mouth.—Kiss each other's feet.—Use each other's toothbrush. Anything ridiculous and intimate."

"Potential" nudists

"At times, tried mirror—I don't like using it. Music is enjoyed if the beat isn't easily distinguished—otherwise, I am distracted." "Music excites me. Also a drink helps me to relax much more and obtain greater enjoyment." "Occasionally. Slow striptease. Music—stimulation using a rubber phallus [penis substitute] sometimes inserted in his anus, sometimes in mine." "I dance and do a striptease sometimes." "I enjoy doing a striptease and getting him all excited. Then when I get down to the last bit—I go lock myself in the bathroom or something and tease him. I like playing current rock-and-roll records and I often like using mirrors." "Sometimes at the request of mate I will undress myself as he watches. Music is often in the background—it is arranged by my mate for the most part." "Striptease, dancing sexually in nude and seminude. Mirrors, music." "I sometimes go through a coquettish teasing routine." "I like to do a striptease or move about sexily, scantily dressed. We have used music." "I had a hilarious experience once. Thinking it would be very sexy to have mirrors in the bedroom, I bought enough to literally cover the bedroom walls. When it came time to use them I found they were useless. I can't see a foot in front of my face (clearly) without my glasses and I don't wear them during intercourse." "The above items [doing a striptease, dancing sexually for mate in nude, seminude]. Mirrors, music and candlelight. Sometimes we like to get lost in our own world of sex and play it up big and enjoy it thoroughly. We find wine and candlelight our favorites and use same when we are celebrating special occasions or just want to be deliciously sexy." "Once. Mate liked to play equivalent of 'strip poker'—he enjoyed looking at me in the nude. I like to have my lover undress me. Music, candlelight on occasion. Sometimes prefer having had some wine." "Liquor makes me even more interested and more apt to have multiple orgasms." "At times have used music, colored candlelight, incense and marijuana." "I sometimes walk around in the seminude as sort of gentle hint." "Occasionally soft music was on during sexual activity, but it was not important. But I like to masturbate to African drum music." "No. Verbally we sometimes play roles during foreplay. He pretends to be a seductive person who takes various roles and I the innocent, naïve female." "Music is distracting because one keeps trying to keep in rhythm." "I very often do a striptease, disrobing in as alluring fashion as I can muster and teasing with my body (seems to work wonderfully). This is usually done in a playful manner (as compared to when we are in a more serious love-making mood). I probably most enjoy parading nude in front of my husband. —It is a tease. I usually do this when in a playful mood—sort of tongue-in-cheek attitude! I may prance or twirl around the room in pants and bra, or sway seductively (I hope) to music (if music is playing) or try to imitate the bumps and grinds I've seen. I concentrate mainly on showing off the breasts and behind, or hip area. I probably use more swaying and slow rotation of hips, as I feel more sexy doing this.—I get the inclination to do a 'striptease' most often when I am in my pants and bra—as I feel free then—plus I think I look trim and attractive. . . . As to my feelings during the process, I am not actually stimulated from doing this. I am probably in a happy mood, rather confident and feel like showing off my body. The reaction from my husband is rewarding, as he becomes very excited. I enjoy this, it makes me feel attractive and sexually exciting; it makes me proud of my figure; it makes me feel like a stimulating partner. I am also fascinated by husband's reaction—his facial expression, how quickly this excites him.—This almost always ends with sexual relations either in bed, on the couch, or on the rug. Usually there is little foreplay here and intercourse moves rather swiftly due to my husband becoming extremely excited. In most instances I concentrate more on his pleasure than my own. I prefer this way (in this case)." "Sometimes walk around nude if I'm feeling good about my body." "Yes, I like to blow a taste of soul before. In the past I took a combination of reds and whites; this enhanced it for me and my partner to the maximum. Vibrating chairs are nice." "Sometimes a mirror when standing. Sometimes music, but after the beginning it distracts me." "Yes. (I would like to use a mirror but haven't had the opportunity.) Have often had music, liquor—a drink usually makes me enjoy it more, and also wearing provocative clothes." "Sometimes we do it [engage in sex] with the light on and look at our genitals with a mirror. Sometimes we stop in the middle and chase each other around the house." "Not often. Striptease, seminude." "I have. Dancing naked is a gas! Music is marvelous but can sometimes be a little distracting." "No. I'd like it, but he's too much of a puritan, probably. Also, I'm probably too heavy to carry it off." "No. Would like to but husband doesn't seem relaxed about it. Would like to have a mirror over the bed, but so far haven't." "No, but would like to." "No, because the opportunity is very rarely available. However, I'd find this very exciting if it were possible. Especially doing a striptease, and I'm certain that after marriage we will use many techniques during foreplay. It could be very stimulating. —Mirrors, music, incense, black underclothes, perfume. Mirrors around the bed so we can see each other—frequently it's very exciting to see yourselves—frequently music during foreplay, but I never hear much after we start."

"Potential" nudists (lesbians)

"Dancing. Doing a striptease—like very much the idea that my body in the nude could excite someone [female]. Sometimes suggestive rhythmic music." "Music. Sentimental love songs or some similar type music softly on a record player, if possible." "Often enjoy exposure of mate. Did use a dildoe [substitute penis] with another partner [female] and enjoyed using same. This mate desired internal stimulation.— Popcorn in bed enjoying television." "I like classical music. Tchaikovsky's Piano Concerto No. 1.—Both partners freshly showered—teeth

brushed—perfume for me—men's cologne for the butch." "Before;
I like to read (with my mate) [female] pornographic literature."

"SEXY" TALK

Based on the knowledge that certain types of words and conversations can both intensify as well as produce distinct erotic sensations on
the part of many persons (females as well as males), the following
question was asked of the subjects in an attempt to disclose the kinds
of verbalizations that *actually* occur during private and intimate sexual
behavior: Do you ever engage in any kind of "sexy" talk during sexual
activity (i.e., describe exciting situations, use of profane words, etc.)?
Describe.

An affirmative response to this question was indicated by 57 per cent
of the nudists and 53 per cent of the "potential" nudists. In the case
of the Mensa females, significantly fewer subjects, percentage-wise,
responded positively to the above question than in the cases of either
the nudists or "potential" nudists. In marked contrast to the aforementioned percentages, this writer noted in an earlier study of female
sexual behavior that only two (6 per cent) of the respondents "reported verbalizing any 'obscene' or sexually provocative terms of a
'vulgar' nature during their sexual activity . . ."[1]

Especially noteworthy is the fact that with respect to the nudists,
a significant relationship was found between high self-esteem and the
use of "sexy" talk during sexual activity (r = .32 P< .05). No significant relationship, however, was disclosed in regard to the security
feelings of our participants. In the study referred to above, this writer
observed that both of the females who had employed "obscene" or
"vulgar" language during their sexual behavior were of high dominance
(3rd decile). Moreover, this writer further pointed out that "A third
subject (a virgin) who also was of high dominance (2nd decile)
stated (looking toward the future) that at times she probably would
like to hear profane (or 'obscene') words during sexuality, because
she associated the expression of profanity with masculinity."[2] Then,
too, Maslow has stated that "Another characteristic of high sexual attitude and high dominance-feeling is the free use of words and phrases
ordinarily considered to be obscene or 'dirty,' words that are completely
tabooed by low-dominance men and women. Generally the sexual act
is to be taken not as a serious rite with fearful aspects and differing in

[1] DeMartino, M. F. (ed.), *Sexual Behavior and Personality Characteristics.*
(New York: Grove Press, 1966), p. 128. By permission of the Citadel Press, Inc.
[2] *Ibid.*, p. 128. By permission of the Citadel Press, Inc.

fundamental quality from all other acts, but as a game, as fun, as a highly pleasurable animal act. Such couples speak about it freely to each other, smacking their lips over anticipated or remembered pleasures, and becoming excited all over again in the process."[3]

Among the comments related by the subjects were the following:

Nudists

"When, after preliminary 'Frenching' [mouth-genital] contacts we are ready to fuck, we say so." "Quote poetry, words of love songs, sexy jokes—like to laugh. Seldom use profanity, although I am getting used to men who do so." "When we were first married we talked 'dirty' to one another. (Whispered in each other's ear.)" "Occasionally, describe exciting situations." "My own tend to be more euphemistic, relating to giving up control—being possessed. My husband uses 'fuck' and 'screw' and I find this exciting. We make specific requests of each other and just asking is everything." "Have described our past experiences." "Sometimes, references to each other's genitals: 'Oh, what a pussy.'" "I always tell my young lover to fuck me hard and shoot the juice to me—this excites him and helps me reach many orgasms . . ." "We generally talk about what we're doing." "I say 'Suck my cunt'; 'Fuck me.'" "Use of endearments, and some profane words, sometimes. Attestation of pleasure is important." "We tell each other how much we love each other and how good he makes me feel or how good I make him feel." "He will talk about what he is doing to me. At that time, I like to hear profane words." "Sometimes. When in the pretense of being raped, we sometimes use such words as 'I've wanted to get you for a long time' or 'You won't be sorry.' 'Please don't, I've never been touched before.'" "I use profane words and talk about what I am doing." "Something to the effect of how good it feels, or how delightful his body is, etc." "Sometimes, I'll make up stories about being young and doing it for the first time, or vary it with him being young, etc. Sometimes I'll be tough and smutty and use profane words. I prefer him to say beautiful things about me and us together—or just not talk at all." "Describe exciting situations, profane words—but not excessively." "Often—'sexy' talk and use of profane words." "I use profane words. My partner likes to hear of my past experiences." "Discussion of how good sex feels, references to the parts of the body which feel good, 'cock,' 'peter,' 'prick,' 'ass,' 'pussy.' Words which urge

[3] Maslow, A. H., Self-esteem (Dominance-Feeling) and Sexuality in Women." *Journal of Social Psychology*, 1942, *16*, p. 288. By permission of the author and The Journal Press.

the partner on, 'Let's go,' 'squeeze me,' 'Drive it in.' Talks about past or future 'fuck parties,' when other partners are present." "Ask to be fucked. Express great pleasure and thrill from activity." "We talk about sex with other people and sex in general. Experience with others." "Describe exciting situations (real) or tell stories, but not very often." "I sure would love to fuck you, or suck you." "Foreign romantic words. Profane words also." "Telling of how we feel and what we like. Recalling past experiences. Sometimes making up situations." "Use of profane words or sexy endearments." "Use of loving, sexual profanity." "How great it feels, how large he is. How good we each are at sucking, etc." "Describing to each other about thoughts and feelings concerning intercourse." "My husband talks sweet, using four-letter words." "I tell him I enjoy doing it with him." ". . . sexy sounds." "I really don't enjoy it much myself, but my husband enjoys it extremely, so I talk about situations and use words that mean sexual intercourse, mostly for his benefit." "I tell him I enjoy doing it with him." "Telling sexual stories with exciting situations." "I like the use of profanity during intercourse and also for my partner to describe situations or experiences with others. However, the latter has occurred infrequently, but I found it very exciting, to the point of orgasm." "Yes. Such as 'Lay me, you bastard,' 'Screw me, you wonderful big man,' and others." "Not much. Just enough to say what we like, want more of, want a rest from, etc." "No profanity! Titty, pussy, etc. Like word 'fuck.' Too bad it's been so 'put down.' It's a nice word to say." "Sometimes the conversation is 'sexy' in that I ask for descriptions of a man's experiences with other women and especially when he lost his virginity. We use common terminology because it is known to everyone and makes it easier for suggestions and desires to be made known." "Enjoy making up stories that parallel our activities." "Use of profane words." "No, but I have a desire to develop this facility. Previously, used repeated phrase like 'Make me.'" "This is not a full-time thing. But at times the word fuck has been used during sexual intercourse and it has always been favorable." "It seems to arouse both of us—if one of us or both—describes in words what we are going to do, or how it feels while we're doing it. One man particularly seemed to get very aroused using the words 'fuck' and 'cunt.' He always wanted me to say them."

"Potential" nudists

"Sometimes use the words 'screw' or 'fuck.'" "Yes, but I'd rather not write it down." "Sometimes the talk is purely clinical. I want to learn more about it, so we both question each other." "I tell him how big his genitals are and I'll describe his 'fanny' and chest to him. I haven't used profane words though." "Sometimes we describe exciting situations to each other, and I like him to talk 'sexy.' " "Occasionally I find the use of profanity during intercourse heightens the atmosphere. I will use slang expressions and four-letter words in describing my feelings and will make suggestions as to what to do next in the same language." "During orgasm, I find sexy talk stimulating. I don't think it's the words as much as the sound of voice tone and the awareness of my partner." "I have used profanity when my mate requested it. It neither enhanced or detracted from the situation as far as I was concerned. I use profanity occasionally without being asked to." "Description of fantasies, describing memories I get, since affair [with a girl] I tell my husband of my desires for this girl that come up in his and my intercourse." "General love and appreciation patter is frequent and especially appreciated by me." "We tease one another about being 'loose.' Often he will say, 'If you're not careful I'll rape you,' and I sometimes threaten to 'rape' him." "Use of profanity. I talk a lot up to climax. At that time, absolute silence." "My husband will sometimes refer to me as a 'hot bitch' a good deal before we get into more intensive sexual play. I find this remark rewarding as I know he is pleased when I am 'turned on.' In this way it is stimulating . . ." "Profane talk—low sex talks." "My partner frequently says, 'I'm going to lay you,' or 'fuck you,' or 'how about some 69'? 'Stick me,' 'Feel me up.' etc. It is very exciting during sex although we don't use the language normally." "I strangely enjoy saying and shouting 'fuck' and 'fuck me,' 'eat me', 'come,' 'squirt,' etc." "Sometimes describe what I feel and attempt to elicit same from partner." "Usually words which encourage a little more in the way of helping me along." "Yes. I like to but I feel it embarrasses my husband." "Sometimes. I use a good deal of profanity in daily ordinary conversation with my husband and good friends, so it's not too unusual. I compliment my husband's anatomy during intercourse or foreplay." "Yes. One lover I had liked to use some 'dirty' words and talk about intercourse. I found it distracting." "Yes. Occasional use of Anglo-Saxon words by husband and attentive expressions of encouragement by same." "Use conventional Latin words (i.e. penis, vagina) to describe organs. Discuss sensations." "No. But I have sometimes wished he would describe his desire using words such as 'pussy,' 'tit,' etc."

"Potential" nudists (lesbians)

"Poetry. Like to recite romantic, provocative poetry to a girl." "Sometimes. Vulgarity is only in the mind of the people present. Some four-letter words such as Fuck and Love seem vulgar in the way they are used." "Sometimes with—[a certain female], I would say things like 'Come on, honey, give!' or 'Relax', or 'Don't try so hard; I won't stop till you come'; etc." "Occasionally. Enjoyed talking to her as if she was a male—spoke of 'your good, long penis.'" "Endearments, compliments, using correct terms rather than slang or 'vulgar' terms."

✻✻✻✻✻ 13 ✻✻✻

GREATEST NUMBER OF ORGASMS DURING A TWENTY-FOUR HOUR PERIOD, AND CIRCUMSTANCES

That females are able, in a short span of time, to experience a far greater number of orgasms than males, all factors being equal, is a well-established fact. This female superiority is due mainly to the physiological differences in regard to the nature of female versus male orgasms. Masters and Johnson in this connection have stated that "Aside from ejaculation, there are two major areas of physiologic difference between female and male orgasmic expression. First, the female is capable of rapid return to orgasm immediately following an orgasmic experience, if restimulated before tensions have dropped below plateau-phase response levels. Second, the female is capable of maintaining an orgasmic experience for a relatively long period of time."[1] With the aim, therefore, of learning something about the prolificacy of our subjects, in terms of attaining orgasms, and the conditions which facilitate such, the following questions were asked: What is the greatest number of orgasms that you have ever achieved during the course of a 24-hour period?—Describe circumstances under which they occurred.

The number of orgasms reported by the nudists ranged from one to "forty or fifty" and the median (average) number for the group was five. In the case of the "potential" nudists, the range was from none to thirty-five with a median number of four. The circumstances described in which the orgasms were experienced, as will be seen, were varied and included sexual intercourse, masturbation, cunnilingus, and hand-genital contacts. Essentially similar circumstances were related by both groups of subjects.

Certainly the ease and quickness with which a female is able to

[1] Masters, W. H., and Johnson, V. E., *Human Sexual Response*. (Boston: Little, Brown & Co., 1966), p. 131. By permission of Little, Brown & Company.

attain an orgasm has much to do with the quantity she is able to experience in any given amount of time. The following comments, therefore, by Kinsey and his co-workers seem to be particularly significant: "Some 45 per cent of all those females in the sample who had ever masturbated reported that they usually reached orgasm in three minutes or less, and another 25 per cent in something between four or five minutes. The median for the whole group was a few seconds under four minutes. Many of those who took longer to reach orgasm did so deliberately in order to prolong the pleasure of the activity and not because they were incapable of responding more quickly. These data on the female's speed in reaching orgasm provide important information on her basic sexual capacities. There is widespread opinion that the female is slower than the male in her sexual responses, but the masturbatory data do not support that opinion. The average male may take something between two and three minutes to reach orgasm unless he deliberately prolongs his activity, and a calculation of the median time required would probably show that he responds not more than some seconds faster than the average female. It is true that the average female responds more slowly than the average male in coitus, but this seems to be due to the ineffectiveness of the usual coital techniques."[2] In view of these statements by Kinsey *et al.* as well as those by our female subjects (which are presented below), it is clear that masturbatory activity affords most females the fastest and easiest method of sexual behavior for achieving an orgasm. One of the important implications from this observation (as was implied by the Kinsey group) is that assuming a female does not have any serious psychological problems relating to orgasm attainment, and she is able easily to experience orgasms from masturbation, her ability to achieve orgasms from sexual intercourse can be increased measurably through improved love-making techniques on the part of her mate.

From a psychological viewpoint, it is interesting to note that in reference to the nudists, the experiencing of five or more orgasms as compared with less than five, during a 24-hour period (from any form of sexual activity), was found to be significantly related to high self-esteem ($r = .33$ $P < .05$). No meaningful relationship, however, was discovered in connection with security status.

The following responses were among those reported by the participants:

[2] Kinsey, A. C., *et al.*, *Sexual Behavior in the Human Female.* (Philadelphia: Saunders Co., 1953), pp. 163–64. By permission of Dr. P. H. Gebhard and the Institute for Sex Research, Inc.

Nudists

"Thirty? No one counted. At a 'party' where a number of contacts were made—not only with my husband." "About ten. When reunited with former lover after two years absence. Met at night, in the A.M., and the next night. Felt like a bitch in heat. Developed a rash, labia swollen, legs were sore, hair in pubic area was tender, reddened—felt so ecstatic!" "Four. Once during a stimulating vacation which was like a second honeymoon and again when my husband regained his full vitality after an illness." "Eight to ten. In occasional rare times when absence of children, responsibility, etc., coincidental with a warm comfortable situation at home." "Two. Only once did I climax one right after the other. My husband wanted to see if I could." "Three. We switched mates one night and the man gave me only one orgasm. When I got home in bed with my husband he gave me two more." "Twelve. We were trying new things and attempted to see just how many I could have. Used fellatio and some masturbation, etc." "Three. Masturbation only." "Four. When I was in my early thirties and we were at a convention. Some drinking, much loving." "Can't remember but orgasm occurred several times when husband and I were alone one night at camp. It was warm but cool and we were lying nude on the grass." "Eight or nine. During one incident of intercourse. My husband is able to wait a considerable period of time before having an orgasm and I generally have several before he 'comes.' That night I guess I was particularly aroused. Intercourse probably lasted about 15–20 minutes." "About eight. This happens often." "Forty or fifty. At a party with my husband and two other couples—and all men sexed me one after another." "Fifteen. The first intercourse following the six weeks menstrual period after our baby was born." "About thirty. I was [much under age forty] at the time—I had a [very young] boy who played with my vagina and my breasts—and finally had intercourse. I went down on his penis with my mouth; we did this petting about six hours without stopping until my vagina was white with foam. I was married and my husband was present later and also had me sexually—forty orgasms over the weekend." "Approximately ten. Prolonged sex activity with many variations—orgasms both clitoral and vaginal." "Five—all day." "Fourteen. A lover early in the day and about six orgasms. Another lover in the evening and another six or more. Then my husband might choose the same twenty-four hour period to initiate sex play. Since he asks for it so rarely I never turn him down. However, he will only give me one or two orgasms because he takes only about [a few minutes] altogether." "Six—I was sitting on top doing the work and kept 'coming' one right after the other." "Four—was well rested and stimulated." "Three—during our first year of marriage we would engage in sexual relations sometimes three times a day." "Twenty? During some of the marathons with my one real lover I have had about four to five orgasms to one of his; he can 'come' as often as four times in a twenty-four hour period.—He . . . can't get an erection as frequently as he would like but he gives me time to get aroused several times (sometimes more intensely than others) before he climaxes." "Five. When we have been on vacations alone we'll play 'newly wed' and he will make me have three orgasms one day and two the next night." "Eight to ten. When I have had the opportunity to have several different sexual partners in succession." "Thirty. On a rainy day while camping." "Ten. This occurs occasionally when my husband is at home all day and night." "Six or more. I'm really not sure because I am apt to have multiple orgasms. Once when I was with my lover for five hours we climaxed together five different times; but since I am apt to have multiple orgasms it might have been more." "Twelve.—We'd been separated [subject and husband] for a few months. I went to meet him and we stayed in a hotel." "Five. With a vibrator [used in masturbation]. When being given head [cunnilingus] one time—three." "Unable to count. In a swap [of spouses] I seem to lose a sense of reality . . ." "Eight, delicious time with my husband from Saturday night through Monday morning—in many ways. A rather pleasant wild weekend—just the two of us." "Fifteen. On vacation, romantic setting." "About fifteen. On our honeymoon." "[Lesbian] Three—when I first started going with this girl. I was in school and we used to make love in the A.M., after school and at night before I went home." "Eight or nine. Husband had been gone for a period of a week." "Seven. A premarital love affair when we spent a weekend mostly in bed." "Six—seven. Given particular circumstances I find I can have a series of orgasms in a very short time. I curl up with husband in me from rear position . . . Also if sleeping with a different partner I'm often in the mood for three—four orgasms in any other position." "I'm so suggestible that I can obtain an orgasm with nothing more than verbal suggestion.—I am very suggestible and verbal approaches are quite effective with me—although it is most effective if accompanied by some type of physical contact." "Eight or so. Often, particularly after we have been separated for a night or a weekend." "Five or six. When married, a 'quickie' at lunchtime; first at night, then the big one—I would come three times during it, hitting it together on the third, then a fellatio-cunnilingus combination (or in mixed order). This was usually a twice-a-month treat." "[Lesbian]

Homosexual activity—Two or three. Occasionally I've been able to reach another orgasm within minutes after the first, when in a particularly sexy mood." "Three. One through intercourse and two from cunnilingus." "Four. Wedding night." "Three or four. One time my husband set aside a day just for the purpose of fulfilling me sexually." "Nine times during an all-night and next-day party with four other couples. Six times with males, three with females." "Seven or eight. Not married to partner. [Extramarital.] No outside influences. Neutral surroundings." "Ten–twelve. I can reach orgasm through masturbation or cunnilingus by my husband—during a 'beer spree.' I reached an orgasm ten or eleven times in about an hour or one and a half hours of his play and then one final and really *high pitched* orgasm during our intercourse." "Three times. This was recently. We had been approached for the first time in 'wife-swapping.' After my first, not so enjoyable, 'experience' with another man, I felt all the more drawn to my husband and couldn't get enough of him." "Six. Naked and in bed with lots of time."

"Potential" nudists

"Four. Cunnilingus then intercourse." "Six. Usually on weekends when both parties are more relaxed." "Three. I was really depressed over exams. I needed a release; this release was obtained during the act. (I'm always in a sexier mood when I'm depressed.)" "Three. From masturbation. Once in afternoon, one in the evening after going to bed, once more next morning upon awakening. Once for about a week and a half, I masturbated with orgasms every day twice a day; I quit when my period started." "Eight. Manual manipulation—no coitus. Lying on ground in the woods." "Three. This was the first time I ever had relations with a boy. We went to a motel for the night. I liked him more than any other boy I've met." "Four. I spent one full week living with my mate [boy friend] and one night we were both very wound up. I think I wore him out but we were at it the next morning—I had intercourse several times that evening and morning. I don't remember how many actually culminated in orgasm." "Twelve. Long weekend with lover almost twice my age." "Six. One long afternoon of intercourse and my husband masturbating with his hands." "Four. Solitary masturbation." "Approximately ten. Night in bed, partner kept going with periodic rests until he achieved six orgasms." "Four. Wedding night." "Five or six. I love rainy days." "Five. This occurred with a man other than my husband. I feel a very strong sexual attraction toward him besides liking him very much. He is experienced and a perfect sex partner for me." "Around eight. During the time we first began to live together we often spent several days sort of living in bed and since we were . . . in the lovely process of discovering and rejoicing in each other, we fucked an awful lot." "I'd estimate somewhere between six–ten. My fiancé and I occasionally have 'little sex scenes' where I have one–three orgasms at a time. Since we are currently able to see each other only on weekends we make the most of our time together." "Seven or eight. Spending a night with an extremely sexy male—after my divorce. (My first lover.) He had repeated erections and intercourse took place in a great variety of positions. I did not know I was capable of having so many in such a relatively short time." "At least twenty. During vacation when we made love several times a day (four to five). I can have a number of orgasms right after the other—once some time elapses after the first and sexual activity continues." "Three. Slept with mate in bed—while parents were out of town." "Four. Cannot really remember. Sometimes I have two climaxes per sexual contact. This may well have repeated itself on two successive nights, or a night and the next day, thus falling within the twenty-four hour period." "I have never actually counted, but I would say around five during sexual intercourse (one activity). However, I could have many more as during masturbation I have had as many as fifteen and can just continue having orgasms until there simply is no sensation left.—It usually takes a few minutes to reach the first orgasm during masturbation. (This is by manipulation of the clitoris with the finger.) The other orgasms followed after, with intervals of a couple of minutes. The time in between was not necessary to rest but to allow the sensation from one climax to ebb off so a pitch could again be built up for a following orgasm. (The fifteen orgasms took no longer than a half hour.) Once manipulation of the clitoris is begun (after intervals and first climax), orgasm is almost immediate (as compared to more time needed to reach first orgasm). These took place in bed in the morning—when I tend to become sexually excited. —Most often, when I had these many orgasms I was in a particularly high state of desire. A few orgasms would not satisfy me. I usually fantasized, about men or a man I was attracted to—usually the penis and what it would feel like—having the penis placed in my vagina. I felt certainly this would satisfy me.—I find even now a clitoral orgasm will sometimes leave me with this dissatisfied feeling—not so with the vaginal orgasm." "Thirty-five. Out of town—with some one I'm most in love with, outside of my marriage." "Twenty. I had intercourse and reached about eight to ten orgasms during sexual intromissions. My partner left; I went to sleep and had some very 'sexy' dreams about him and so I woke and through masturbation achieved twelve or thirteen orgasms (involving a lot of fantasy)." "Six. Normal circumstances, after a period of frustration, absolute privacy and deep positive feelings about partner." "Four–five. Spent weekend at lovely chalet by the sea. Made love in the afternoon, the night and early morning and achieved orgasm each time." "Three. They were achieved through masturbation." "Three. Occurs not infrequently during one act." "Two or three. During the course of a day my husband and I sometimes would have intercourse two or three (separate) times, and sometimes (not unusually) I would have an orgasm with each one." "Five. Did it in the morning upon awakening, at about noon, at about five, that night at about ten, and the next morning. No special reason except we both were very sexy." "Six or seven. Teasing to see who would achieve orgasm more often—he or I. Lost count after a while."

"Potential" nudists (lesbians)

"Fifteen." "Six. I was alone with a butch in her home. We had been drinking, not to excess, but rather consistently all weekend. I was in love with the girl." "Four. Spent the night with a girl." "Eight. My partner was performing cunnilingus on me without stopping. I climaxed four times in less than one hour. The other four times were a couple of hours apart." "Four. During mutual sexual intercourse [homosexual], in a dark room—danger of being discovered—completely naked." "Five or six. It was the third time I had gone to bed with my second lover [female]. (I had performed the act of cunnilingus with my lover, but had never been the recipient.) On this occasion I was, for the first time, on the receiving end." "One. [subject's female partner] and I were having sexual contact and I had an orgasm one night. Then I did have one sometimes; it came very quickly when she stimulated me. I preferred playing with her."

✳✳✳✳✳✳ 14 ✳✳✳

GROUP SEXUAL ACTIVITY AND WIFE-SWAPPING

Group sexual behavior and wife-swapping are indulged in much more widely in our society than most people would imagine, and they appear to be practices in which an increasing number of persons of all levels of intelligence and social status are participating.[1] While males tend to be much more in favor of these activities than are females, nevertheless, many females (as will be seen) also find them to be quite exciting and enjoyable. Although the present study did not pose any specific question in regard to wife-swapping, such information, however, was elicited by the questions which pertained to group sex activity, namely:—Have you ever engaged in any group sex activity, i.e. presence of a third, or more, persons?—If so, describe.—Does this idea appeal to you at all?

An evaluation of the responses to these questions revealed that while 38 per cent of the nudists and 17 per cent of the "potential" nudists had experienced group sex activity, the idea (thought) of group activity appealed to 39 per cent of both the nudists and "potential" nudists. Furthermore, of those nudists and "potential" nudists who had actually engaged in group sexuality, 66 per cent and 53 per cent of them, respectively, stated that this behavior appealed to them. With respect to our female Mensa subjects, the percentage which reported having participated in group activity was not only extremely lower than that of the nudists, but also slightly lower than the percentage noted in the sample of "potential" nudists. In view of the above findings, it seems fair to conclude that group sex activity was indulged in by a very large number of our nudist subjects. Moreover, it may be stated that a substantial majority of the nudists and slightly

[1] See: Wilson, T. J. B., and Meyers, E., *Wife Swapping*. (New York: Counterpoint, Inc., 1966). See also: Ellis, A., *Suppressed* (New York: New Classics House, 1965) chap. on wife-swapping.

more than half of the "potential" nudists who had experienced group sex behavior found it to their liking.

Although no significant correlation was observed between either levels of self-esteem or security and the experiencing of group sex activity by our subjects, a significant relationship was noted in the case of the nudists, between high self-esteem and an affirmative reaction to the *idea* of participating in group sexual behavior ($r = .31$ $P< .05$). At present, there is very little objective data available in the literature concerning the personality characteristics of persons who engage in group sexuality. In reference to wife-swapping, however, which often entails group activity, Ellis has remarked as follows: "Not only is mate-swapping apparently increasing in America and Europe; but there is reason to believe that fairly healthy, stable switchers, who themselves have a good sex-love marital relationship, are increasing in greater proportion than are the sick, sick, sick spouse-changers."[2]

The following responses were recorded by the participants:

Nudists

"In parties of from four to twelve persons. In some instances as many as three men were involved with me. I also have been included in 'chains' with two or more women. A.[3] Yes." "Yes. Occasionally it is enjoyable, but I prefer to concentrate on one person at a time." "Yes. It was completely unsatisfying! We went to a party without realizing it was a 'swinging affair.' We got out as soon as possible. A. No." "We've gone to 'swinging parties' but I never hit a climax. I enjoyed it at first, but then felt I was being used, so we quit. A. Not any more." "Present when another couple also engaged in sex. A.—No. Found it repugnant." "Recently when a couple and a male friend and I were drinking together. The married couple initiated it. So far as I was concerned, it was a farce that would never be repeated. I could pet and kiss in a group but would go to another room for more. A. No, I like privacy to really enjoy my loving." "We have had parallel intercourse with other couples. We have switched partners. We have shared a partner (both man and a woman). We have been in group situations. A. Yes, it seems a natural outcome *if* all parties concerned are feeling *secure* and interested." "Many times. There were two couples in one bed. While the one couple was using a vibrator on each other we were in a reverse position with our mouths on our respective part-

---

[2] Ellis, A., *Suppressed*. (New York: New Classics House, 1965), p. 68. By permission of Dr. Albert Ellis.

[3] A. stands for an abbreviation of the word Appeal.

ner's organs reaching screaming orgasms. There were nine people in various positions at this gathering—sixteen people maximum—twelve at another, etc. A., Not as a steady diet, once in a while this therapy is good. Most often, I prefer two men—first my young lover, followed by my husband." "I had my husband's brother with my husband present—several times. A. Now I like it since I got over my guilt feelings—now I do it freely without drink." "Two women and one man, myself and two men, foursomes, i.e. four couples. A. Yes, sometimes—but not always." "Two men and one girl, two girls one man. A. Yes." "When I was about fourteen years old, my girl friend and her boy friend were making love in the bed next to ours. A. No." "Twice, before marriage. Once we were two couples and played at teaching techniques. Just before my wedding the young men I knew gave me a 'bachelor's party' where three women and six men participated, together and separately. I was sore for a week, but I *loved* it! A. In the last [several] years I have had a good number of such group activities; I find them very enjoyable." "My husband and I share partners with my close personal friends. A. Yes." "Yes. (Partners were chosen by coin flips.) Positions game with another couple, intercourse on big bed with another couple and exchange of partners—in front of a fireplace on inflated mattresses (we switched partners from the start of play but I could not go through the act with other older man). A. Yes, but at times I have to fight thoughts of these acts being a threat to our marriage." "With from three to thirteen or more people. (I don't plan on it much anymore as I think I'm in love again.) A. Yes." "My husband had a friend home once and the three of us were in bed together. This came about because we had mate-swapped once, with this man and his wife. A. Not particularly." "One woman, two men; one man, two women; two men, two women; varied partners. A. Yes." "We have swapped partners four times in a six month period (with the same couple). A. No, only guilt stays with me." "Before my second marriage, two separate occasions, two different 'lovers.' On each occasion my lover and myself 'offered' me to a close friend. A. It did then. It doesn't now." "We are very attached to a nudist couple and have participated in sexual activity in their presence and they were also participating (no swapping). A. Yes." "Yes. Two women and one male. A. No." "Two men and myself; man and woman and myself; two couples together. A. Yes—but not as an obsession—or desire to engage in constantly at regular intervals." "Twice. There were three other people (two men and one woman besides my husband and I) in a hotel room. Two were on the bed and two on the floor. When one finished the other fellow started in. Very stimulating. The second time was with another couple, but went into separate rooms. Later when we were altogether we tried to start it up again, but the other couple was apathetic and went home. Not as stimulating. A. Yes, very much." "Swapping mates with one other couple. A. Yes." "Two couples in twin double beds in a hotel room. A. Yes." "In a nudist group of two other people besides husband and self. A. No.! Husband insisted." "Once. With extramarital partner and his wife. She used fellatio, while we 'necked.' A. Yes." "When my husband and I first decided that we needed the variety of extramarital sexual activities, the question was: What can we both accept and tolerate? We experimented once with mate-swapping but didn't like that because of the 'fuck now, get acquainted later' overtones. As long as we both had a full sex life we wanted outside sex to be a continuation of an already pleasant relationship. We finally decided that all outside sex would be only with third parties of either sex who were friendly and compatible to both of us. This resulted in a number of threesomes. There was no watching, there was involvement by all, although not very much contact between the two persons of the same sex . . . This continued off and on for several years but has pretty much died down now. I very much enjoyed the situation of having two men at once. It was extremely stimulating and exciting . . . I seem to like one or two men at a time and prefer to have a rather intense relationship with one, then a number of superficial ones at the same time . . . We still occasionally entertain a second woman in our bed. A. Yes." "My husband and I and another couple engaged in sexual intercourse with our own mates and then the husbands exchanged mates. This happened in our bedroom. A. Not much, it inhibited me very much." "My husband and I have swapped partners with other couples and have had intercourse in the same room with another couple—I have had two men at one time. A. I don't particularly care to have another woman around such as swapping (in the same room) but I like two men." "On two occasions only. The first time I was with my own husband, the second time he was with another woman and I was with her husband. A. I liked being with my own husband but didn't care for the other experience where we changed partners in the same room." "Favorite is to be with a man and woman, to French [perform cunnilingus] the woman while male watches and to have male seduce and French me while female watches. Also like to squat over man's face and rub it all over his face. A. Definitely." "Yes. One man and five girls were sitting around nude when it started. I left when I found out I was the one who was going to be the man's partner. Besides it was too homosexual. (I was just caressed.) I would rather have just watched. A. No." "Switched part-

ners, just four of us. A. Not as a steady thing. Once in a while . . ."
"I have engaged in activity with my husband and another woman, also
with husband and other man. Previous to being married, several times
I had been with two men at same time. Just prior to marriage I began
to engage in group activities with husband, and continued to do so
occasionally after marriage. . . . I think the most exciting experience
of my life was when I had both vaginal and anal intercourse at the
same time with two Negro men. [Subject is white.] One of the Negroes
had a gigantic penis which he inserted in my anus. One of my greatest
desires is to have three Negroes at the same time—two in dual intercourse and the third with fellatio. Also very exciting would be to be
photographed in these activities. A. Yes, provided I like the participants and we have a general rapport to start with." "My husband and
I once swapped partners during a tenting trip—using the same tent.
A. No." "No. A. Yes. Very much so. We are thinking very strongly
about it." "No. A. Sounds exciting to me but my husband objects
strongly." "No. A. It fascinates me." "No. A. It appeals to me simply
because of curiosity. Although I do not want a woman touching me
for any reason, I am curious to see the genitals of other women. And
of course, I always enjoy other men. Given the right people, place,
and with plenty of time, I think it is all right. I would not do it with
anyone just for a sexual thrill, for me, it would be wrong. As far as
being watched while engaged in coitus, I wouldn't care. If there was
me and a man and then another couple watching us, that is their affair.
When I am in the midst of this, the world beyond the bed, the car,
etc., is shut out. I do not think I would like to go into a sexual situation where this was expected of me, however. In other words, it would
just sort of happen." "No. A. Not particularly, however the thought of
watching others engage in sex is exciting; this could lead to participation." "No. A. Yes, it might— I can't dismiss it as something I positively
wouldn't do. Perhaps I might do it for a lark." "No. I have been in a
twin bed with my husband and heard another couple making love
noises in the dark, but I couldn't release inhibitions—envied them. A.
No, it terrifies me."

"Potential" nudists

"Once had intercourse with another man watching, and found it
very distracting; felt very guilty, did not have a climax. A. Have occasionally imagined myself the female in a group of men, all taking their
turns, during self-masturbation." "Before marriage. I was invited to a
party and was shocked; we were asked to take off our blouse and ex-

pose our breasts. I do not remember too much of the outcome. A. Only if they were strangers to me and unknown to the male." "Once. On a weekend with another couple. All four of us slept in one bed. I had sex only with my husband, but teased the other male. A. At the time it amused me; not particularly appealing now." "Wife swapping. A. Yes." "I've gone swimming in the nude with my husband and his friend. A. It did to me but not my husband." "Yes once. It wasn't ex- actly voluntary. I was walking downtown one night when three boys pulled me into their car and took me out to some place and they all raped me. They sort of kept taking turns. A. Under different circum- stances—I don't know, I think it might." "Engaged in intercourse with a married couple. However, the wife and I never had any physical contact during the sexual experience. At times, I preferred to be a spectator and found this very stimulating—at other times the male would either use manual stimulation on one of us while using cun- nilingus on the other, or while in the act. A. At that time, yes. Now, no." "With two men, with another girl and one man, with two men and two girls. A. Yes." "Yes. Strip poker—college graduation party— one other couple. Sexual intercourse has taken place on the bed next to me by another couple. A. Not offensive, not appealing." "Only once with a group of teenagers (I was about 14). I did not enjoy this, have never done it again. A. No, it is disgusting to me." "Two other couples also having intercourse in the same well-lit room—all close friends. None married at the time. A. Nothing special.—When I'm engaged in the sex act, I am unaware of surroundings." "With a friend and her husband. They weren't married then. It's a great way to become very close—but only if the people have no hang-ups. My friends and I haven't repeated the experience—but we love each other enormously. A. It's a difficult sort of thing to do successfully—but yes." "Two couples. A. Yes." "No. A. A little—when I feel like being very bad." "No. A. Sometimes it does. The idea of the presence of a third person (only as an observer), particularly a male, appeals to me. I have some- times daydreamed about having several men, one right after the other—it appeals to me in fantasy;—in fact I might feel too inhibited."

"Potential" nudists (lesbians)

"Once. Not very exciting. A. No." "No. A. Yes, providing it was ac- ceptable to other people involved." "No. A. Yes, I think for a 'kick' it would be exciting to try it once." "No. A. Slightly."

15

EXTRAMARITAL SEXUAL RELATIONS AND MOTIVES

Although it has long been known that numerous males in our society experience extramarital sexual relations, there still is a reluctance on the part of many (especially married males) to recognize the fact that a significant number of wives also participate in such relations. Furthermore, extramarital coital activity among females, particularly those who are "liberated" sexually, appears to be increasing. In this connection, it is interesting to observe that in response to the questions: Have you ever engaged in any extramarital sexual relations?—If so, describe the nature of the activity and indicate with how many men.— What motivated you to do this?—52 per cent of the nudists and 39 per cent of the "potential" nudists who were married or had been married at one time, revealed having done so. The percentage of Mensa females in our study who reported that they had engaged in extramarital relations was lower than that of the nudists but similar to that of the "potential" nudists. Kinsey and his associates, it will be recalled, pointed out that "Among the married females in the sample, about a quarter (26 per cent) had had extra-marital coitus by age forty. Between the ages of twenty-six and fifty, something between one in six and one in ten was having extra-marital coitus"[1] They also disclosed that "the peak of extra-marital activities of the females in the sample had come in the mid-thirties and early forties."[2] In view of these various findings, it is apparent that extramarital sexual relations were experienced by a high percentage of our nudist subjects.

Maslow, some years ago, indicated that in "higher-dominance

[1] Kinsey, A. C., *et al.*, *Sexual Behavior in the Human Female*. (Philadelphia: Saunders, Co, 1953), p. 416. By permission of Dr. P. H. Gebhard and the Institute for Sex Research, Inc.

[2] Ibid., p. 418. By permission of Dr. P. H. Gebhard and the Institute for Sex Research, Inc.

people" there are strong tendencies toward promiscuity.[3] This clinical observation was given further support by our results in that extra-marital sexual activity among the nudists was found to be significantly related to high self-esteem (r = .37 P< .05). Landis et al., in charac-terizing their female subjects who had participated in extramarital affairs, stated that "They were usually active, somewhat aggressive in-dividuals who stressed their own independence."[4] Interesting, too, from the point of view of personality dynamics is the following commentary by the Kinsey group: "Just as with pre-marital coitus, the high fre-quencies [of extramarital coitus]* were often attained by assured and socially effective individuals who had not been emotionally disturbed by their departures from the social code and who, therefore, had not gotten into difficulties because of their nonmarital sexual activities."[5] No significant relationship was noted between the security feelings of our subjects and the experiencing of extramarital relations.

MOTIVES

The main motives reported by the nudists for having entered into extramarital relations fell into two major categories: a) unpleasant marital and sexual relations, and b) at husband's suggestion—i.e. wife-swapping and group activity. Other categories of motives included: desire for variety, enjoyment of sex, desire for attention and affection, husband had been with someone else—revenge, and husband away—loneliness. Except for any reference to group activity, and an emphasis on wife-swapping, the motives related by the "potential" nudists for having experienced extramarital activity were not different from those recorded by the nudists.[6]

In describing the emotional needs and desires satisfied by the extramarital affairs of his married male and female subjects, Maslow listed the following: "desire to be sure they were still attractive, the thrill of novelty, unconscious hostility for the spouse, and often, frankly and consciously, the desire to conquer, to 'collect scalps.' "[7]

[3] Maslow, A. H., "Self-esteem (Dominance-Feeling) and Sexuality in Women." Journal of Social Psychology, 1942, 16, 259–94.
[4] Landis, C., Landis, A. T., Bolles, M. M., et al., Sex In Development. (New York: Paul B. Hoeber, Inc., 1940), p. 174. By permission of Hoeber Medical Division, Harper & Row, Publishers.
[5] Kinsey, A. C., et al., Sexual Behavior in the Human Female. (Philadelphia: Saunders Co., 1953), p. 420. By permission of Dr. P. H. Gebhard and the Institute for Sex Research, Inc.* Inserted by the writer.
[6] The lesbians were not asked any questions pertaining to extramarital sexual relations.
[7] Maslow, A. H., "Self-esteem (Dominance-Feeling)and Sexuality in Women." Journal of Social Psychology, 1942, 16, p. 279. By permission of the author and The Journal Press.

Reasons advanced by the Kinsey group in an effort to explain why their female subjects had participated in extramarital activity, included the following: a) ". . . because of the variety of experience it afforded them with new and sometimes superior sexual partners," b) ". . . a conscious or unconscious attempt to acquire social status . . ." c) ". . . as an accommodation to a respected friend, even though the female herself was not particularly interested in the relationship," d) ". . . in retaliation for the spouse's involvement in similar activity. Sometimes the extramarital activity was in retaliation for some sort of nonsexual mistreatment, real or imagined, by the other spouse," e) ". . . provided a means for the one spouse to assert . . . her independence of the other, or of the social code," f) ". . . had provided a new source of emotional satisfactions. Some of them had found it possible to develop such emotional relationships while maintaining good relationships with their husbands."[8] The following comments by Kinsey *et al.* are especially interesting, since they are directly related to the motives recorded by a number of our nudists: "There is a not inconsiderable group of cases in the sample in which the husbands had encouraged their wives to engage in extra-marital activities. . . . In some instances it represented a deliberate effort to extend the wife's opportunity to find satisfaction in sexual relations. In not a few instances the husband's attitude had originated in his desire to find an excuse for his own extra-marital activity. What is sometimes known as wife swapping usually involves this situation. In another group of cases the husband had encouraged extra-marital relations in order to secure the opportunity for the sort of group activity in which he desired to participate. . . . It should, however, be emphasized again that most of the husbands who accepted or encouraged their wives extra-marital activity had done so in an honest attempt to give them the opportunity for additional sexual satisfaction."[9]

Among the responses recorded by the participants were the following:

Nudists

"Had intercourse with six men. M.[1] An unloving marriage and responsiveness to attention of others." "Two during first marriage. Many in second marriage. All [in second marriage] have been with consent

---

[8] Kinsey, A. C., *et al.*, *Sexual Behavior in the Human Female.* (Philadelphia: Saunders, 1953), p. 432. By permission of Dr. P. H. Gebhard and the Institute for Sex Research, Inc.

[9] *Ibid.*, pp. 434–35. By permission of Dr. P. H. Gebhard and the Institute for Sex Research, Inc.

[1] M. stands for an abbreviation of the word Motivation.

and usually presence of my husband. *M*. Interest in the individuals involved—desire for variety." "During a period in my marriage when it nearly broke up after several years of faithfullness. *M*. I was looking for someone else, not just for sex." "First experience was after a few years of an unhappy marriage—led to first separation during which time I had a free-wheeling life for one year. Returned to husband and was faithful physically for a number of years, then one lover. Then faithful for one year because I tried to make the marriage better. Then we separated (a few years now). Have had eight lovers, two serious, this time." "With approximately twenty-two men—[in group sexual activity]. I did what they wanted me to but they couldn't seem to hold out long enough for me. *M*.—My husband." "Several times, isolated occasions during a previous marriage. *M*.—Dissatisfaction at home. Bravado." "One man on two occasions. Wife-swapping arrangement on an experimental basis. I decided I didn't particularly enjoy it even though I reached an orgasm. It could have been the man involved. *M*.—Interest in the Oneida Community philosophy created interest in some experimenting on our own after also reading about instances of wife-swapping." "A few times—when my husband was wandering or we were on conventions when there was some mixing—but I never really enjoyed it. He was my man and the only one who could really satisfy me." "With fourteen men. The activities involved intercourse and petting, by prearrangement, usually. Several different occasions over a long period of time. Some meetings were clandestine; others not. Some a result of group activity. *M*. I enjoy love-making. It seems to be the natural outcome of affection between two people. Sometimes sheer chemistry. I like variety." "In our group sex activity, singly, and in groups of a total of twenty-seven different males and nine women have participated in all phases of sex play with me to full intercourse. With some once and some multiple times. *M*. The desire for added thrills and to relieve the boredom of ordinary marriage—to renew our marriage." "With sixteen men. *M*. My marriage was shakey and my husband suggested sex with other men and me. I did not want to but did so for him. My husband and his friend got me drunk, otherwise I would not have done it. Afterwards, I came to like this—and now my marriage is very firm." "Yes. *M*. Some call it love." "As in group activity. This and extramarital relations—also with husband present in foursome. Approximately fifty men over a period of twenty years. Up until five years ago the men were one at a time. After that there was group activity and several different 'affairs' going simultaneously. *M*. Enjoyment of sex—and sex as a culmination of an expression of other types of relationships such as emotional or intellectual." "Forty men. M. Need and curiosity." "Yes. M. I was breaking up with my husband. My boy friend and I would make love in the car or a motel room." "Yes, [with many]. Normally, I will have one important lover for one year—or two or three—or sometimes a man remains important to me up to ten years. However, after a few years I will seek a new man, or be receptive to advances. There will be a number of trials before finding a man who pleases me in every way— or nearly every way. M. On the day after our honeymoon, my husband announced he would have but *one* orgasm per week and that should do for me. Also, when he returned from overseas duty, he was impotent for a long period and it was his suggestion that I resume the 'friendships' I had made during his absence, in order that I might have patience and tolerance of his fumblings while he regained his health. This I did." "We have several couples with whom we share experiences from time to time—with about five men. M. Search for added variety after eight years of marriage—but I am still happily married." "Once, for a few times with one man. M. Husband was in the service and I just seemed to need the other man." "With one man—in the first year of my marriage. I wanted to try another man for comparison. It wasn't worth it. He didn't know the importance of the clitoris—so I was left unsatisfied. M. Inquisitiveness." "I've been married [many times]. Have had others during and in-between. I have been uninhibited most of my life. M. Sometimes, spite. Usually, just because I like variety. (Haven't found 'that one' to keep me satisfied.)" "Intercourse with ten men in eight years. M. Boredom, search for excitement." "Mate-swapping. Also with a man which . . . lasted several years. . . . We were friends before it started. I knew that if I had an affair, the man would have to be discreet and live up to my ideals of love. We both knew in advance that we would not break up our marriages. M. My husband had been going through a very passive sexual stage [which strained the relationship]. This might have been one reason. I felt that I really loved this man. . . . I think that I was always looking for the perfect love." "Sometimes separately, sometimes in groups. M. [Husband and subject feel that extramarital sex enhances their capabilities for living together]." "When my former husband was [seriously ill]—with one man, twice. I became quite ill at the thought of it and discontinued the practice. I did not reach a climax. M. [Husband was an invalid]." "Many years ago I had extramarital relations with two men. I have nothing pleasant to remember from the relations. I have since told my husband. M. The first was due to flattery, with the second I was looking for something lacking in the first. I did not find it." "Intercourse with four men. M. Agreement with my husband and attraction to partner." "With two men—on a bet. *M*. The bettor." "No and yes. I have never had intercourse with another man, although I have been in bed naked with one. I 'chickened' out because he did not appeal to me when he was naked—he had no body hair, except pubic hair, and I found his hairlessness repulsive. *M*. I had not seen my husband for sometime—and I was horny." "This was with one man only. I thought I loved him. He was wonderfully understanding, gentle, persuasive, masterful, sensitive—intellectually stimulating as well as sexually. *M*. Undue pressure at home, misunderstandings and misplaced feelings." "With one man over a period of [several] years in my first marriage. Once while away from home in another city. Picked him up at a bar. *M*. Was depressed and as a bet to myself to see if I could do it." "With one man. We went to a motel, used the usual position with me on the bottom. *M*. My husband had been with someone before, so I wanted to also." "Yes. *M*. Opportunity and practicality—also consent of husband." "Wife-swapping, three times. *M*. My husband, group situation. Attractiveness of other males." "With one, a recently widowed friend of my husband, who has had his eye on me for years. My husband made the offer himself and delivered me to his home. We prefer to meet on a neutral territory (a hotel) for dancing, and sex in my overnight room, which he leaves around midnight to return to his [home]." "With the same man we engaged in group sex with. We had intercourse alone one time. This was the first and only man. The whole episode was unsatisfactory. *M*. I was slightly attracted to him physically. I found my husband and his wife were having sex." "Swinging (swapping partners), four different men. *M*. I had a crush on another man and could have him only through swapping." "We had been approached to 'swap' wives. We went to their home one evening, nude dancing started the evening and sexual intercourse with exchanged mates ended the evening; only with one man. *M*. My husband was very much interested and after weeks of talking it over I decided to try it. . . . Out of an [over ten-year marriage] and 5 years of being nudists—only recently were we ever approached to 'swap wives.' This seems to be the 'thing' now. Honestly speaking I don't know if I am for or against it." "The last year before I was divorced my husband went home to his parents and I had two affairs, one following the other. Both were delightful, refreshing, exciting and good for my ego at a pretty shattering moment. *M*. After the emotional jolt of a broken marriage had worn off I really think it was curiosity to see into a man's world after the sheltered and unsatisfied life of marriage." "Had relations with one consisting of basic position—bottom and top—and cunnilingus. *M*. He was one of the two or three most sexually attractive men I have ever seen." "Six men (both ways) and four women, being submissive and aggressively active, alternately. M. My strong bi-sexual interests." "Only switching partners [with husband present]. M. Appealed to me." "My husband and I went to Tijuana and hired a woman for him and an eighteen-year-old boy for me. After he was done an older man had me . . . M. I've always wanted to try other men. Mostly I think in hope of them bringing me to a climax." "I had relations with four or five men, with two or three of them on more than one occasion. Nature of activity included fellatio, cunnilingus, and intercourse. M. In nearly every instance, it was the result of a quarrel with my husband." "Intercourse—fellatio, cunnilingus—masturbation—five men. M. Sexual drives." "Three separate 'affairs' and one mate-swapping. M. My husband and I agree that we have other attractions, so we 'let' each other have other relationships. . . . We decided that sex with only one person was unrealistic and debilitating so we've practiced our 'freedom' for six years and it works!" "Intercourse, very short periods, six men. M. Dislike of sex with husband." "One man. Roman position. Exploration with touch and sensuality currently. M. Current 'open door' policy—sexual depression initiated by husband."

"Potential" nudists

"Fellatio, cunnilingus, masturbation, and intercourse with three men. M. Attraction, plus friction in the home. Curiosity, to see what sex would be like with other men." "Wife-swapping about seven or eight times. M. Because of just only having had my husband." "During a previous marriage, four men. Practices—fellatio, cunnilingus, and various positions. M. Sex relations with husband were unsatisfactory, causing me to seek satisfaction from other men. Gradual realization that I did not really love my husband." "With several men. Only after separation from my husband." "With one person. I recently met an old friend I was engaged to before marriage. M. I guess to see what or if I felt anything." "Once. M. The result of much affection and absence of our own partners, good opportunity, and sensual-setting situation. Very pleasant." "With two men. M. One was for fun." "During a previous marriage. Having consecutive affairs with at least six different men—lasting from a couple of times to many months. M. Unhappy marriage, feeling trapped and needing escape, poor contact with reality." "With several men. M. Disinterest in husband." "During my marriage I was completely faithful. Since my separation I have had affairs of varying duration with six people, ranging from old friends I knew before marriage to a man I picked up at a club. I have always seen them many times, sometimes overnight. *M*. I wanted to have sex relations. Since I have not been emotionally attached to any of them, I seem to want variety." "When separated and just before separation from first husband, but with his knowledge. Had relations a couple of times each with three men, then with future husband. *M*. Immaturity, curiosity, infatuation with one of the three men, dissatisfaction with first husband's passiveness." "Former marriage was extremely unhappy. I had several love affairs, each lasted over several months. *M*. Looking for love as much as sexual gratification; wanted more 'ideal' relationship." "Switching mates—two others. *M*. No two people fulfill each other completely—agreed to mutually." "Two. Number one saved my marriage at an early stage when I needed to be admired. Sex took place over five years, when we were able to meet and satisfy each other. On bottom reached climax occasionally. Number two—all known methods—reach climax frequently. *M*. #1. Need for knowing I was attractive to others—husband was indifferent. #2. I fell in love."

EXTRAMARITAL RELATIONS IN THE FUTURE

In response to the question: Do you think it is possible that you may engage in extramarital sex relations sometime in the future?—of those nudists and "potential" nudists who were married or separated (divorced, single, and widowed subjects were excluded), 63 per cent and 65 per cent, respectively, answered in the affirmative. More specifically, of those nudists and "potential" nudists who had experienced extramarital activity and were either married or separated at the time they participated in our study, 90 per cent and 71 per cent, respectively, gave a positive response to the above question.[2] Kinsey and his co-workers in this regard reported that "among the married females in the sample who had not had extra-marital experience, some 83 per cent indicated that they did not intend to have it, but in a sample of those who had had extra-marital experience, only 44 per cent indicated that they did not intend to renew their experience . . . . among those who had already had extra-marital coital experience, some 56 per cent indicated that they intended to have more or would consider the possibility of having more."[3]

Consistent with the findings noted at the beginning of this chapter

---

[2] Single, divorced, and widowed subjects were not included, since it was felt that their exclusion would insure more accurate results.

[3] Kinsey, A. C., *et al.*, *Sexual Behavior in the Human Female.* (Philadelphia: Saunders, 1953), p. 431. By permission of Dr. P. H. Gebhard and the Institute for Sex Research, Inc.

concerning nudists, the factor of high self-esteem was also found to be strongly related to the possibility of experiencing extramarital sexual behavior in the future (r = .55 P < .05).[4] No such meaningful relationship was disclosed in regard to the security feelings of the subjects.

Extramarital sexuality and premarital coitus

With respect to the nudists, our findings revealed that extramarital sexual relations were experienced significantly more by those females who had engaged in premarital coitus (nonvirgins) than by those who were virgins at the time of marriage (r = .42 P < .05). No similar relationship, however, was observed in connection with the "potential" nudists (r = .02 N.S.). Kinsey et al., in discussing the relationship between extramarital and premarital coitus commented as follows: "It would appear that the premaritally experienced females were somewhat more inclined to accept coitus with males other than their husbands after marriage. To put it another way, 29 per cent of the females with histories of pre-marital coitus had had extra-marital coitus by the time they contributed their histories to this study, but only 13 per cent of those who had not had pre-marital coital experience."[5]

Comments by the subjects included the following:

Nudists

"Possible under certain circumstances." "Yes. I no longer believe in monogomy. Men seem to respond better to a woman who is not docile." "I hope so!" "Certainly." "We may try to have a similar arrangement with another couple. At this time we have decided it would only be on a mate-exchange basis. We may change our minds about the idea. It [extramarital relations] has been stimulating to our own relations in amount of times of behavior as well as variety in the experiences." "Yes. As long as I live or am able. It is beautiful and beneficial to our marriage. I have had my young lover three times a week for over three years in my own home in my own bed (plus other men less frequently) with my husband present in the house. Sometimes my husband is busy and sometimes I reach an orgasm loudly and he comes in and caresses me while my lover continues." "Yes. If I meet a man I find attractive as a person and physically. My

[4] This finding was based only on nudists who were married or separated. Single, divorced, and widowed females were not included.

[5] Kinsey, A. C., et al., op. cit., p. 427. By permission of Dr. P. H. Gebhard and the Institute for Sex Research, Inc.

husband and I agree that marriage should not shut one off from loving relationships with other people. Neither of us would be interested
in a simply sexual relationship, but we are open to a loving relationship, communicating and making love. . . ." "I hope not. It would
have to be a very strong physical urge or else with someone I feel
I loved more than my husband." "Sure—because I want to." "Frankly,
I don't know what my decision would be if such an occasion ever
arose." "No, not unless it would be a group affair with my husband
involved." "If I thought it would be mutually enjoyable—but so far
no one has appealed to me to be worth the effort or the risk of being
'caught.'" "As often as possible." "I think it's possible, but I haven't
yet found a man that appeals to me." "Only with my husband's consent, not behind his back. My husband doesn't find anything wrong
with switching partners but I don't see sense in it, and I feel I would
be unfavorably compared to other women." "(Group sex relations).
Not unless my husband and I both agree that it would be a beautiful
and meaningful thing to do. We have discussed this very deeply. We
both feel, as a result of our experiences with LSD, that there is an
undeniable desire in human beings to be closer to each other. We
feel that if there ever was occasion to express this desire to be closer,
in a sexual way, with other people for whom we had deep feelings
of tenderness, love and trust, we would seriously consider doing it
together. But it would never be anything like the popular pastime of
'swinging.' Neither of us have a taste for that, because we feel that
such sexual contact is meaningless. Those persons are simply looking
for something to fuck, and I believe that it is more of an escape from
real feelings than anything else." "Yes, there is always that possibility
but it's a very slim one." "Perhaps. Although I would not feel comfortable with anyone else. I am too used to my husband. He knows
what I want. I am, however, attracted to certain men and find that
those to whom I am I could also enter into sexual activity (in many
instances)." "Yes—but would prefer to do it in a group with all parties
aware of what was going on." "Maybe, if I can make myself do it."
"Yes, if the person is sufficiently attractive and I can do so without
becoming sordid and sneaky about it." "Yes, if the chance occurs."
"Yes. Both my husband and I. We feel it will help our marriage by
helping to relieve some of our personal tensions. Simply because we
will both know about it instead of trying to hide these inner feelings
that everyone has—whether they want to admit it or not." "Yes
(switching partners only) [with husband involved]." "It would depend on my feelings toward the man I would marry [Subject is a
widow], as well as his attitudes toward sex. If he favored group ac-

tivity then I would also. If he were unaware of group activity, and if my feelings toward him were strong enough, then I probably would not desire extramarital sex relations. However, if I really desired extramarital sex I probably would engage in it." "Yes. I feel that my inclinations are for polyandry." "I am pretty sure I will; however, I must add I am not one hundred per-cent sold on this idea." "[Widow over 60 years of age.] I still enjoy sex relations when an appealing man is available."

"Potential" nudists

"I think every normal honest woman contemplates this no matter how happy her marriage. I've been tempted especially when someone I find sexually attractive and who indicates an interest in me. However, if I ever did engage in extramarital relations, I think it would have to be with the full knowledge and consent of my husband. I would want to be sure that it would not damage our marriage in any way. Under these conditions the chances are probably rather slim." "Yes, when I marry again." "No—unless my mate proves incompatible as far as sex relations are concerned." "Perhaps in far future in the form of wife-swapping." "If my husband would go along with the idea." "It is possible but I have so many fears of this idea I doubt it. It is the emotional involvement which comes with such a relationship that frightens me; not the physical." "Absolutely." "Yes. I think it's possible, if my relationship with my husband were to become quite unsatisfying." "Yes, as long as I am unable to live with the man I'm in love with." "[Single.] Yes. If I marry. I don't think I can stay tied down to one man. I like variety." "No, very definitely not—it is appealing to me but there are many dangers involved. I couldn't stand the thought of my husband engaging in extramarital affairs." "I think if my husband wanted to, I would go along with it, but it must be a frank, known act between us." "Yes, probably . . . We are very well suited to each other. I do not think I am in love with him but he is a good and dependable friend also. It may be wrong but it compensates for my unhappy sex relations with my husband. I think secretly I get even with him in this way." "[Single.] If I marry—very probable. I'm too curious to ever be 100 per cent faithful—I think." "Yes. My husband and I have discussed the possibility."

****** **16** ***

SEXUAL ACTIVITY WITH ANOTHER WOMAN

While homosexuality among females may not be as prevalent as it is among males, it is much more so than the average person in our society is aware of. Moreover, lesbians (female homosexuals) in America, like male homosexuals, are very well organized. For example, there is a national organization of lesbians known as the Daughters of Bilitis (formed in 1955) whose purpose is to promote "the integration of the homosexual into society," and which publishes a high level and informative monthly "Lesbian Review" called *The Ladder*. The national headquarters of the Daughters of Bilitis is located in San Francisco, and there are chapters in Los Angeles, New York City, and Chicago. There is also a homosexual group (includes lesbians) known as the Janus Society, which is located in Philadelphia, Pennsylvania.

During the preadolescent and early adolescent years, many females as well as males experience some degree of homosexual activity. When such behavior is transitory, it is usually regarded as being inconsequential. It is only when homosexuality becomes the *sole* or main form of sexual expression, particularly during adulthood, that it is viewed with some concern. In order to determine the preponderance and nature of homosexual activity on the part of our subjects, the following questions were posed: At any time during your life have you ever engaged in any sexual activities with another woman?— If so, describe (i.e. nature of activities, with how many women, at what age, etc.).—Were you the active or passive one?—What motivated you to do this?—If never, do you think it is possible you may in the future?

Incidence

Some 36 per cent of the nudists and 49 per cent of the "potential" nudists[1] disclosed having engaged in some form of sexual behavior

---

[1] Included in this group, as was indicated earlier, were several females (lesbians) who belonged to the Daughters of Bilitis organization.

with another female at some time during their life. The percentage of Mensa females (those of very high intelligence) who indicated having experienced homosexual contacts was substantially lower than either that of the "potential" nudists or nudists. The Kinsey group, it will be recalled, stated that "The number of females in the sample who had made specifically sexual contacts with other females . . . rose gradually . . . without any abrupt development, from the age of ten to about thirty. By then some 17 per cent of the females had had such experience. By age forty, 19 per cent of the females in the total sample had had some physical contact with other females which was deliberately and consciously, at least on the part of one of the partners, intended to be sexual."[2] It is very clear, therefore, that compared with the Mensa finding and those reported by Kinsey *et al.* concerning the incidence of sexuality with other females the percentages noted in the cases of both the "potential" nudists and nudists are quite high.

Homosexual behavior on the part of the nudists was found to be significantly related to high self-esteem ($r = .55$ $P< .05$). No significant correlation, however, was revealed in connection with the security-insecurity feelings of our subjects. Maslow, in his illuminating study, pointed out that "In women with *very* high dominance-feeling, the probability is much higher than it is in the general population that investigation will find either active homosexual episodes in the history or else conscious tendencies, desires, or curiosity."[3]

Nature of activities

As will be observed from the responses presented below, the homosexual acts described by our subjects were varied and included touching different parts of the body, fondling and kissing of breasts, rubbing against one another, embracing, kissing, hand-genital contacts, mutual hand-genital contacts (mutual masturbation), cunnilingus, and mutual cunnilingus.

Ages and degree of participation

The earliest age at which homosexual activity was experienced by the nudists was six years and the oldest age was thirty-two years.

[2] Kinsey, A. C., *et al.*, *Sexual Behavior in the Human Female.* (Philadelphia: Saunders, 1953), p. 453. By permission of Dr. P. H. Gebhard and the Institute for Sex Research, Inc.

[3] Maslow, A. H., "Self-esteem (Dominance-Feeling) and Sexuality in Women." *Journal of Social Psychology*, 1942, *16*, p. 275. By permission of the author and The Journal Press.

Since a number of the nudists did not give a specific age in regard to the occurrence of their homosexual behavior, no meaningful median age of first occurrence could be derived. In several instances homosexuality was practiced over a span of time. While a few more of the nudists indicated having played a passive rather than active role, the majority reported having been both passive and active.

In the case of the "potential" nudists (nonlesbians), the earliest age at which homosexual behavior occurred was three or four years and the oldest age was thirty-one years. The median age of the first homosexual experience was thirteen years and for the most part it was of relatively short duration. Similar to the nudists, slightly more subjects were passive than active, and the majority of them were both active and passive.

Unlike either the nudists or "potential" nudists (nonlesbians), in the instance of the "lesbian" group of "potential" nudists, the majority of the females assumed an active role during their homosexual behavior. None were just passive and only a few were both active and passive. (See Chapter 10—verbatim comments.) The age of the occurrence of homosexuality was not asked of these subjects.

Motives

The primary motives expressed by the nudists for having participated in homosexual behavior were: Curiosity, a positive feeling for the female, as part of "group activity," and a desire to experiment. The major motives given by the "potential nudists" (nonlesbians) for having experienced homosexual activity were the same as those mentioned by the nudists except for the influence of "group activity." It is interesting to observe that the two predominant motives recorded by the "lesbians" for having engaged in homosexuality were a liking for women, and a dislike for men. Fear of pregnancy was also denoted by a few of the "lesbians."

Homosexuality in the Future

While 16 per cent of the nudists and 11 per cent of the "potential" nudists[4] signified that it was possible that they would engage in homosexual activity in the future, 3 per cent and 8 per cent of them, re-

---

[4] The "lesbians" in this group were not asked about their future intentions. (They were given a different questionnaire.) If they had been asked, it is very probable that the total percentage for the group of "potential" nudists would have been much higher than 11 per cent.

spectively, stated that they were uncertain (or doubtful) concerning such a possibility.

The following were among the comments recorded by the respondents:

Nudists

"Mutual frenching [cunnilingus]—about four different women—both active and passive. M.[5]—Appreciation of the woman or for my husband's entertainment. F.[6]—" "Five lovers and an occasional momentary passion. At present I am in the midst of the fifth affair. At age 22, I was 'brought out' [first overt homosexual experience]. Both active and passive. M. Curiosity at first, which then developed into a deep feeling. F.—" "Age 10, rubbing against each other while clothed —embraced—one occasion. Passive. M. She wanted to play 'Hawaiian Honeymoon.' F. Not possible in the future. Lesbians repel me." "With one girl friend. We just masturbated one another but not to orgasm. Both active and passive. M. It was pleasurable. F.—" "Age 12, kissing, possibly some masturbation but I can only say this looking back, because at the time I was not really aware of what I was doing. Passive. M. Don't know. Looking back I believe that the girl involved (same age) is a homosexual or a latent homosexual. F. Not again." "This was in connection with a parallel activity and switching of partners described in [a previous answer]. With three women—within the last five years.—Fondling, especially of breasts. Touching each other's genitals and body. Both active and passive. M. It was partly the situation [group activity], also an extension of our very close feelings and high excitement with all involved. F.—" "During college and one year after graduation. Two older women (no real sexual contact—just being held). With another student as inexperienced as I was—kissing, some genital touching but no orgasms. With one experienced lesbian who made love to me but didn't let me touch her. No orgasm was experienced. Passive. M. I was going through a period of rejecting men, feeling they were just using me for my body. . . . My homosexual relationships were more crushes than sexual. I was insecure and immature—wanting to be cuddled more than aroused. F.—" "With a total of nine women, started at the age of 23. When I was first married I was unable to reach an orgasm, so I played with a girl of 19 years of age—caressing her breasts, touching her vagina, going down and kiss-

[5] M. stands for the word Motivation.
[6] F. stands for the word Future.

ing her pubic hair.—I met a lesbian who made love to me and I to her—this lasted about two years until she found another partner. This was tender and thrilling. My husband agreed it [homosexuality] would pass and I found it increased my desire for males. [I've experienced] female on female to help get aroused for the climax. My first orgasm was a result of being kissed on the pubic hair area by another female—before marriage. M. The great need to reach sexual satisfaction which a man could not do at the time. My religion had put fear in me so that I could not react normally. F.—" "She started rubbing my cunt with her fingers and did everything one woman can do to another. I kissed her breasts and put my fingers in her cunt. My husband was enjoying this. I was passive—then became active somewhat. M. My husband and she cooked up this idea and I got hot and didn't care. I enjoyed it. F. I might do it again." "During high school—kissing and caressing. Recently, as part of group activity just for kicks and out of curiosity. In the main, I was the passive one, but I reciprocated also out of curiosity—and since it was sort of part of the game. M.— Curiosity and because it seemed a natural part of group sex activity. F.—" "Yes. I was the active one. M. Desire. F. Yes." "In 19—— I met a WAVE who was a 'dike' and courted me, e.g. with candy, flowers, dinner and drinks, ballet and theater—until the time came that I could think of her as a man and the idea of a woman as a lover seemed no longer very ridiculous. She was the 'man' at all times. However, I am never passive for long! I found her exciting and learned to enjoy our love-making. We lived together about two years and remained lovers for another three years. F. There is no other woman in my life, but in group sex play I will give and receive such tongue play with another woman when it is acceptable." "Teenage, experimenting with pencils in vagina—also when both couples were on the bed recently [group activity] I reached out and touched the other woman's clitoris as she was not 'coming' and I thought it might help her. I was active. M. In teenage, curiosity.—I got no kick from touching the other women [when an adult]. F.—" "In boarding school, in our senior year in high school—we were 18 and discussing orgasm. There were three of us in our room—two of us were describing what it felt like to the third girl—it was just easier to manipulate her clitoris. Just one instance. I was the active one. M. Enlightenment and sharing the joys of sex—or rather the clitoris. F.—" "At 6 or so I exchanged 'play' with girls and at 12 I really made love to one or two. I didn't do much after 13 until I was around 22. I have had several real affairs and numerous 'one timers.' Active. M. It 'just came naturally.' F—." "Hugging and kissing. I was around 10 years of age. Was both active and passive. M. We were staying overnight with each other and sleeping in the same bed. *F.*—" "Mutual masturbation at 10 years old. *M.* Experiment. *F.*—" "At 12 or 13 years old—masturbation—fantasy. Was both active and passive. *M.* Curiosity. *F.*—" "With the ex-wife of my present husband. She set out to 'lead me down the garden path' to quote her. 'Our' husband was also there [present]. Was passive. *M.* Her desire to do it to me. Also, my desire to open myself up. *F.* I would say that it is possible. However, I'm not looking." "With one girl at age 13—hand manipulation. Passive. *M.* Experimenting. *F.*—" "With girls at boarding school—but not 'women.' Was both active and passive. *M.* It was in style in the 8th grade. *F.* No." "About age 20, five women, mutual masturbation. Passive. *M.* Curiosity. *F.*—" "With one woman. We started when I was 16 years old. We are still together. Passive one. *M.* I got VD from sex with men. *F.*—" "With two different women at different times. Both times with men [present]—the woman's husband was in the room. One was in her forties, the other in her late twenties.—Cunnilingus on the part of myself and the other female, caressing, mouth kissing, body touching, and kissing. I was active with one and passive with the other. *M.* Interest of others having me join them.—Curiosity of how it felt to touch a woman. I feel that I actually know how a man feels when he touches a woman. . . . Many women know how they should be caressed, etc., to become aroused, and in making love to another woman they have an idea of what would make the other woman excited (men know, also); this is one aspect of being with another woman that is fascinating. I think my experiences in this area were good; I learned from them. I am not obsessed with the idea of sleeping with a woman, but am glad I experienced it. . . . *F.*—" "With one lesbian, at age 32. I was curious and she showed me what girls do together. Strictly physical on my part; no emotion. Was passive. *M.* Curiosity. *F.*—No, not unless I can get some emotional involvement." "At puberty, mutual masturbation with female friend same age. (On top of one another, not with hands.) Both were active. *M.* Awakening of sex reality in both of us. *F.*—" "When I was about 12 my sister and I laid foot to foot in bed and interlocked our legs so that we exerted pressure on each other's labia, like two pairs of scissors opened and put together so the hinges were in contact. There was no hand contact and it lasted only a few minutes. There was not any other stimulation, even with motion. *F.* It is extremely unlikely that I will ever engage in any homosexual activity in the future." "With perhaps a couple of dozen women—in each instance one or more men were present. Nature of activities included mouth to genital with other woman while engaging in fellatio or intercourse, or in fellatio and cunnilingus at same time with man both women. Active—passive. Took turns. *M.* A general desire to engage in many forms of activity. *F.*—" "I was only caressed on my bust and thighs. I was nude and so was she. She was a Negress and I let her pick me up. I wasn't sure what was going to happen. She was kind and I wasn't afraid. *M.* My first husband was so unsatisfactory that I thought I must be queer—I was a bit inexperienced. *F.*—No more, thank you." [Lesbian. Subject responded to questionnaire designed for Lesbians] . . . with six females. In making love with another female, passionate kissing and petting always precede consumation of the sexual act which might end in mutual masturbation, oral-genital contact or other acts satisfying both partners.—All homosexual practices are satisfying to me if there is a mutual love. Sex without love satisfies the physical body while doing little to create emotional and mental satisfaction. The type of act is not so important as the receptiveness of both partners to the act at that particular time. *Kind of Female Found Sexually Most Appealing:* Most appealing is an intelligent girl with at least moderate good looks, athletic, healthy build, neither fat nor thin, with blue eyes and fair complexion. I don't know why. *Main Reasons for Engaging in Homosexual Behavior:* When I used to date boys I could never get really interested in them except as friends. When they made passes I froze up. When I learned about lesbians, I not only responded eagerly but made advances myself. I was delighted to find I wasn't cold as I had thought. I felt I had 'found' myself. I never regretted the choice I made. [No guilt feeling] . . . I have gone with three women for considerable lengths of time. In each case I was in love and thought it was going to last. After five years with my present lover we are both very happy, very much in love and hope it will be forever." "With women ranging in age from 18 to 30—as previously described. (To be with a man and woman, to 'French' the woman while man watches. Also like to lie face down while other female places her breast nipple against my anus and moves it around.) *Active—passive.* Both. *M.* My desire to please women who wish their pleasure in that way. *F.*—" "When I was in high school a girl friend and I fingered each other a little. *Active—passive.* Equal. *M.* Inquisitiveness. *F*—" "Age 13 or 14. Mutual masturbation and cunnilingus. One girl same age. Passive. *M.* Curiosity. *F.*—" "Yes, one, when 19 and 20. Some sort of physical contact whenever possible. Rubbing leg muscles to relax contraction. Sleeping next to. *M.* Love of another woman. *F.* Yes." "No. *F.* Yes. I would like to try it." "No. *F.* It's possible I might. I've always been very curious about it."

"Potential" nudists

"Mutual masturbation with closest friend at age 10.—Group activities at Girl Scout Camp at age of 10. Was both active and passive. M. Everyone else was doing it. F.—" "I was upset about finals, so I went alone to a bar and some woman took me to her apartment after I got drunk. I was about 18 and she was about 30. I remember her taking all my clothes off—but after that I passed out. I was completely passive. M. I didn't know what I was doing. F. No. I don't exactly care for other women." "With one girl, a definite lesbian. I was 14 or 15, she was a very close friend and I felt sorry for her—being naturally affectionate, I was completely 'innocent' for a long while. I was passive most of the time—active only on her insistence. M. Pity and friendship, lack of understanding because of age, etc. F. Never again." "Age 18, two experiences. The first, I was passive, the second I was aggressive (at age 25). M. The first experience—curiosity. Experience at age of 25 was with a girl during a group of four—a little orgy. M. Curiosity and drunk. F. It is possible, but I doubt it. (Don't like the emotional involvement.)" "I played strip poker with two friends at age 13. I also was soul kissed by a friend at the same age. She forced this upon me as a means of demonstrating how someone had kissed her. I was passive inasmuch as I was taken completely by surprise. F.—" "With one, during the two weeks I was separated from my husband. She wrote notes, sang songs—we courted, cuddled; she used her hands and mouth on my genitals. I used my hands on hers—kisses on the mouth. (Active-passive), fifty-fifty in sex. She began the courting. M. I loved and desired her; I could help her and she me, I enjoyed it intensely, felt free. F.—" "Between myself and a mostly heterosexual girl at college. Occasional affairs with two lesbians. Perhaps five girls in all. Most relations were outgrowths of friendships. I was both active and passive at times (reciprocal). M. I *liked* the girls and our affection eventually reached physical expression. F.—" "With my cousin and on other occasions with a girl friend—at about ages 8–10—we would manipulate and spank each other. We changed roles but most often I was passive. M. I think I was seeking punishment. F.—" "At approximately 8 years—mutual masturbation with another 8-year-old girl. Passive. M. Curiosity. F.—" "As a young girl—with a girl friend when we were first beginning to develop. We were both active. M. Just simple curiosity. F.—" "Only with a girl who taught me masturbation at 10 years of age. Passive. M. Just learning. F. No." "When I was 12, a girl friend of mine and myself decided to pretend we were being seduced. We inserted a clothespin in each other and tried to 'pretend.' Neither of us achieved any satis-faction. (We kissed each other also.) M. Desire for experimentation. F.—" "Ages 9–11, with cousin, exploration of each other's body. Both active and passive. M. Curiosity. F. No." "About 7–8 years of age. Feeling each other—exploring in a sense. *Active—passive*—compro-mised. M. Wanted to find out more I guess—I've forgotten. F.—Not again." "Age 18, with a close friend—having at present—have a rela-tionship with another woman. Active. M. Tired of suppressing desires to make love to women. F. Most definitely yes." "One woman. Girl made the approach with expectations of being taught how to kiss. She was 18 and I was 30. *Active—passive*, both. M. Felt nice. F.—" "When I was a child I played 'doctor' with my closest friend.—At about 12 a girl friend and I liked to dance closely to slow music. Nothing since then. Both passive and active. M. I never thought about it. F.—" "Ages 8–9, dual masturbation. Active. M. Curiosity. F. No." "At age 19, for two and a half to three years I was 'in love.' We mas-turbated each other, with mutual caressing during foreplay, digital manipulation of genitals. Since then, one contact with one girl I did not love—not repeated. *Active—passive*. I felt myself to be the woman, but was fairly active. M. I was living with the girl, sharing a bed, and she had previous homosexual experience. I felt I loved her. F. Doubt very much that I could with a same-sex partner again." "A friend is a lesbian—although married (her husband is a voyeur.) I was curious —so we made love one evening. Was passive. M. Curiosity—which was satisfied. I guess I wondered if it would appeal. It doesn't. F.—" "Kissing only, with one woman. I was 31 or so. This was during the same unhappy marriage already mentioned.—Both active and passive. M. Unhappiness and curiosity. F.—" "1) When about 12—we felt each other's breasts, 2) also when 3 or 4 a girl used to take me to her room and touch me. *Active—passive* 1) both, 2) passive. M. 1) curi-ous about growth of our bodies and the interesting feelings we had. 2) fun. F. No." "No. F. No, but I am aware of the possible feelings to the degree that I would rather not have my daughters sleep with me when I was a widow." "No. F. If approached properly." "No. F. Perhaps."

"Potential" nudists (lesbians)

The responses presented below were recorded by lesbians, in refer-ence to one of the questions included in the questionnaire designed specifically for lesbians. The question read as follows: Do you (did you) ever engage in any sexual activity with another female, e.g.

passionate kissing, petting, mutual masturbation, mouth-genital contacts, sexual intercourse, etc.?—If so, please describe in detail the nature of these acts.

"Kissed breasts, neck, ears, hair, mouth; felt all parts of the women. Fingered vagina." "Passionate kissing, petting, sucking the breast and inserting finger into vagina. Have not had mouth-genital contact with another woman (but I'd like it)." "First experience in late teens—no genital contact, only gentle touching, kissing, hugging; in my twenties I had to do mouth-genital to an older woman (I disliked this very much); in thirties had one female with an extra large clitoris who could use it like a penis. In my forties attempted my mouth to her clitoris, sucking—didn't work. Never did like this. . . ." "Open-mouth 'French' kissing. Caressing—mutually. My partner's mouth on my genitals. Mutual kissing and sucking of each other's breasts. Kissing each other's necks—bodies, shoulders, etc. Both being completely nude." "I have never been with a man to the point of orgasm, but have with many women. The methods used were mouth-genital contacts, digital manipulation and fusion of genitals. I have found the first to be most satisfying. With one exception, I have been the passive partner. With a woman, I prefer her to be on top." "Kissing, 'French' included. Mutual petting. Oral-breast contact. Simultaneous cunnilingus. Digital penetration." "I am a female homosexual. This is practiced by mouth-genital contact, petting, kissing, touching, holding and any other way which is enjoyable to both parties. I have always been the more aggressive and much more often enjoy making love to my partner, than being loved." "Kissing, caressing, manually exciting other person and vice versa—once tried mouth-genital contact with other woman— it was unsatisfactory."

Main Reasons for Having Engaged in Homosexual Behavior[7]

". . . I am physically and mentally attracted to other females. I enjoy sex with other females. I dislike the brutalness of men and their loss of insight. . . ." "Heterosexual behavior leaves me cold—even if I like the male. Lesbian activity excites me—don't really know why. Have always enjoyed being with females—close contacts, etc." "Because I love women. Heterosexual activity seems animal-like. There is rarely much love involved, just some physical craving." "Men are just generally disgusting to me. All they seem to be interested in is getting

---

[7] The lesbian questionnaire also included the following questions: What are (were) your main reasons for engaging in homosexual behavior; i.e., why do you prefer this kind of sexual behavior over heterosexual behavior?

into bed. . . . I would never want to be pregnant and have a child. This seems to be the worst possible thing that could happen. Women are so much softer, gentler, more understanding." "I have a basic aversion to men due to an early emotional rejection by my cold father. I also attended girls' boarding schools for 5 years and was not used to seeing men. Homosexuality came naturally and easily for me for this reason. The first person I ever loved or had sex with was a woman, and my only experience with a man was incomplete, degenerate and frightening. . . ." "Perhaps I prefer this kind of sexual behavior over heterosexual behavior because the only heterosexual experience I experienced was being violated by my brother." "I enjoy it. Women are more gentle than men. No fear of pregnancy. I like women and am very attracted to them. I can talk to men but am still a virgin as I am afraid of them in a way. I just like women. I have ever since I was 11 or 12 years old. I used to dream about them—picture myself kissing them—have erotic fantasies about them—especially teachers." "It's desirable—I do not have any desire for sex with a man, although the idea excites me. There is none of the warmth or closeness I find in homosexual relationships. The actuality of heterosexual sex leaves me cold." "It is sweet, gentle, tender, romantic, and thrilling."

17

MAIN SOURCES OF SEXUAL STIMULATION:
EROGENOUS ZONES, AND IN THE ENVIRONMENT

MAIN EROGENOUS ZONES

While almost any part of the human body, if stimulated appropriately, by the "right" person, can produce erotic sensations, there are certain bodily structures or regions which are more responsive sexually to tactile stimulation than others. To ascertain the primary erogenous zones of our subjects, the following question was asked: Which are your main sources of sexual stimulation on your body? (i.e. breasts, clitoris, etc.). The most frequently mentioned anatomical structure by both the nudists (85 per cent) and "potential" nudists (79 per cent) was the clitoris, and the second most prevalent response by both groups was the breasts—nipples (nudists 63 per cent), ("potential" nudists 58 per cent). Kinsey et al., in discussing the sensitivity of the clitoris, stated that "there is considerable evidence that most females respond erotically, often with considerable intensity and immediacy, whenever the clitoris is tactilely stimulated."[1] In regard to female breasts as sources of sexual excitement, they commented as follows: "There are some females who appear to find no erotic satisfaction in having their breasts manipulated; perhaps half of them do derive some distinct satisfaction, but not more than a very small percentage ever respond intensely enough to reach orgasm as a result of such stimulation."[2] Among the other more prominently mentioned erogenous zones by the nudists were the vagina (genital area, labia, vulva), but-

[1] Kinsey, A. C., et al., Sexual Behavior in the Human Female. (Philadelphia: Saunders, 1953), p. 574. By permission of Dr. P. H. Gebhard and the Institute for Sex Research, Inc.
See also: Masters, W. H., and Johnson, V. E., Human Sexual Response. (Boston: Little, Brown & Co., 1966).
[2] Ibid., p. 587. By permission of Dr. P. H. Gebhard and the Institute for Sex Research, Inc.

tock—anus, neck, ears, mouth-tongue, lips-kissing, and thighs—inner. A number of nudists reported their sources of sexual stimulation to be all over their body. Responses noted by only a few of the nudists included: the stomach-tummy, back, armpits, shoulders, upper arm, hair, hair line, eyes, nose, skin behind knees, and toes. In general the erogenous zones designated by the "potential" nudists were very much like those recorded by the nudists.

Responses recorded by the subjects included the following:

Nudists

"Clitoris vulva, breasts." "Eyes, ears, nose, toes, etc., and mental stimulation." "Neck, hair, clitoris." "Mouth, clitoris, love to have hair stroked." "Clitoris, labia, skin behind knees, armpits, around stomach." "In this order: clitoris, breasts, lips, vagina." "1. Clitoris, 2. Breasts. Caressing of body." "Breasts—especially nipples.—Sometimes overall. Clitoris, lips and mouth. Neck at about the jugular vein." "Clitoris and breasts simultaneously." "Clitoris—although breasts are very responsive to husband's lips and tongue." "Breasts (nipples) and clitoris." "My cunt." "*All over*, but tongue kissing, stimulation of nipples and clitoris are especially sensitive." "Clitoris—not the breasts too much." "The breasts are the starting point.—But I enjoy all contact." "With the right man I quiver all over—everything he might do stimulates me—but surely the clitoris and vagina are most sensitive." "Clitoris, breasts, vagina, neck, below jaws, lower back when rubbed, buttock." "Kissing breasts and clitoris." "Clitoris to reach orgasm, breasts are part of foreplay." "In order—clitoris, back of neck, ears then breasts. Also the anus." "Clitoris and upper thighs." "Breasts, mouth, clitoris, back, hairline." "Breasts, clitoris, ass." "My nipples, my breasts, clitoris, buttock (that order)." "Breasts, clitoris, and like to have my buttock stroked." "Clitoris, anus and breasts. Stimulation of these are not, however, necessary for orgasm. The penis entering and moving in the vagina is the most frequently used stimulation." "Sucking on breasts, rubbing clitoris, pinching buttock." "[Lesbian] Clitoris, inner thighs, sometimes breasts, light stroking all over body." "Ears, nipples and clitoris." "Breasts and clitoris. Blowing on my neck and ears." "Breasts, armpits, inside of thighs, ears sometimes, clitoris sometimes is oversensitive." "Breasts, clitoris, and tickling of the anus with other finger on penis. I also like to lie face down while other female places her breast nipple against my anus and moves it around." "First kissing of mouths, then kissing and stroking of breasts, finally the clitoris." "My breasts, my whole genital area and the insides of my upper thighs. But I become aroused more by caressing and touching a man than I do by being touched myself." "Mouth, vagina, nipples, ears, anus, everything to some extent." "Breasts, clitoris, insides of thighs. Firm pressure of a hand on my belly. Under upper arm. Anus." "Lips, breasts, clitoris, and insertion of fingers into vagina." "Entrance to the vagina, ears, tongue and clitoris." "My neck and stomach and inner thighs when kissed gently are extremely sensitive—but breasts and clitoris are *most* sensitive." "Breasts and clitoris most sensitive, but entire body is very sensitive." "My nipples are very subject to stimulation."

"Potential" nudists

"This depends so much on my mood. When easily aroused—neck, ears, very fond of being kissed on my eyelids, breasts (especially nipples), around the pubic area, inside of thighs, clitoris (highly sensitive) and sometimes behind." "Breasts, clitoris, neck and shoulders, ears, stomach—if in the mood, all over." "In early stages breasts, then clitoris." "Breasts, clitoris, ears, armpits, buttock, feet, thighs." "Clitoris." "Ears, clitoris, thighs, arms, back, stomach, neck." "Breasts, clitoris." "Main source is my clitoris. However, my neck is extremely sensitive (kissing my neck) and the fondling of my breasts also stimulates me." "Breasts, neck, ears, clitoris, anus, buttock, back, arms, thighs." "Breasts (especially nipples), clitoris, vaginal area—secondary: stomach, buttock, inner thighs—having a man working his hand's on my back is very stimulating." "Breasts and clitoris and sometimes when in certain moods, all over my body." "My breasts." "I am extremely sensitive to sexual stimulation on any part of my body—especially neck, breasts, abdomen, clitoris and thighs." "Inner genital area, clitoris, breasts, tummy, anus; anywhere if handled appropriately, usually softly and gently, teasingly." "Inner thighs, nipples, clitoris, stomach, insides of my arms and my neck." "Breasts, clitoris, insides of legs, back of knees, neck, inside of arms." "1) clitoris, 2) breasts 3) inner thighs 4) mouth." "Breasts, thighs, waist, back of the neck, tummy. Actually, just about everywhere!!!" "It varies, sometimes my breasts and sometimes my clitoris, usually I am most greatly stimulated by deep penetration into my vagina." "Very direct stimulation in vagina is best, but I like clitoris stimulated also." "Clitoris and deep vagina." "The breasts—direct clitoral stimulation can have a numbing effect." "From kissing to breasts." "Breasts, ears, fingertips, clitoris, inside of thighs, vaginal opening, lower abdomen, of course mouth." "My back, stomach and the entire genital area." "Vagina. Secondary—clitoris, neck and anus; breasts are not as sensitive since birth of my child." "Breasts, clitoris, vagina, anus." "Clitoris, nipples, small of back, inside of thighs." "Clitoris, ears, everything, I guess."

"Potential" nudists (lesbians)

"All—clitoris and vagina most intensely." "Lips." "Breasts, buttock, clitoris and strangely enough, ears. S. used to nibble my ears and it nearly drove me wild." "Clitoris, armpits, ears, feet." "Back, inside upper arms, inside thighs, breasts, clitoris." "My neck is very sensitive. My shoulders, breasts, abdomen, genitals (clitoris especially)—inner thighs. Also my lips, tongue and face." "Breasts, clitoris, lips-vagina, ears."

MAIN SOURCES OF SEXUAL STIMULATION
IN THE ENVIRONMENT

With the aim of learning which stimuli in the environment our subjects find to be most stimulating sexually, the following question was asked: Which are your main sources of sexual stimulation in the environment? (i.e. reading, movies, TV, etc.) The source which was reported most by both the nudists (63 per cent) and "potential" nudists (67 per cent) was: reading. Other of the more frequently specified sources by the nudists included: movies, music, "my husband," men, and sexy talk (conversation).

Except for the fact that only two of the "potential" nudists alluded to their husbands in responding, and no specific reference was made to sexy talk (three subjects used the terms: conversations—discussions), the responses of these subjects (nonlesbians) were quite similar to those of the nudists. It is especially interesting to observe that the primary environmental source of sexual stimulation recorded by the "potential" nudists (lesbians) (80 per cent) was: other females. The Kinsey group in this connection has remarked as follows: "The recognition of erotic arousal upon observing other individuals of one's own sex is, of course, a basically homosexual phenomenon."[3]

In general (except for the importance of music), the above overall findings were in line with those revealed by the Kinsey researchers. For example, they discovered that 60 per cent of their female subjects had responded in an erotic manner during the reading of literary works, and that "Twice as many of the females in the sample had responded to literary materials as had ever responded to the observa-

[3] Kinsey, A. C., et al., Sexual Behavior in the Human Female. (Philadelphia: Saunders, 1953), p. 652. By permission of Dr. P. H. Gebhard and the Institute for Sex Research, Inc.

tion of portrayals of sexual action, and five times as many as had responded to photographs or other portrayals of nude human figures."[4] They also noted that 48 per cent of the females found "moving pictures erotically stimulating,"[5] while 17 per cent of them "reported that they were particularly aroused upon observing males, whether they were their husbands, boy friends or other males, and another 41 per cent recorded some response."[6] These investigators also reported the following: "For most males, discussions of sex often provide some sort of erotic stimulation. They do not provide anything like the same sort of stimulation for the average female, and in consequence she does not have the same inspiration for engaging in such conversations."[7]

The following were among the responses noted by the subjects:

Nudists

"Reading, music." "Personal contact and my own interest." "Reading, talking, seeing, hearing, breathing, living." "Music, sight of beautiful eyes, looking, smell of a man." "I have seen sex movies that have stimulated me." "Reading and movies." "People I am attracted to are the most important. Once in a while, reading pornography, also music." "Reading. I have never seen any so-called pornographic movies or pictures, but I suppose I would be most aroused by them." "Reading very sexy stories. But mostly my fantasies while in the act of reaching an orgasm." "My husband." "Men, talk which is directly sex talk designed to stimulate." "Reading, adult movies, movies of natives and island living." "Reading somewhat—good music like symphony or opera, if wild—throbbing and abandoned." "Late candlelight dinner—dark room with fire in fireplace. Talking about sex and sex play. If I read a book describing enjoyable sex, I'll become stimulated." "TV and reading." "Nature—moonlight nights, a walk in the woods (winter or summer). A romantic story, romantic music." "The sight of a naked man keeps me in a pleasant relaxed state of readiness for sex. This may contribute to my not requiring any extensive build-up for sexual enjoyment." "Swimming in the nude, 'French kissing.'" "Some looks, also talking about sex with my husband." "Just thinking about my husband and how much I love him." "Men." "The beauty of my hus-

[4] *Ibid.*, p. 670. By permission of Dr. P. H. Gebhard and the Institute for Sex Research, Inc.

[5] *Ibid.*, p. 659. By permission of Dr. P. H. Gebhard and the Institute for Sex Research, Inc.

[6] *Ibid.*, p. 651. By permission of Dr. P. H. Gebhard and the Institute for Sex Research, Inc.

[7] *Ibid.*, p. 676. By permission of Dr. P. H. Gebhard and the Institute for Sex Research, Inc.

band's nude body, sometimes his torso, sometimes just his presence." "Reading, touching, kissing, massaging, sucking." "I can get drunk and all sexed up from music." "Reading. Just reading this form [questionnaire] bothers me." "Reading dirty books—or jokes." "My boy friend." "Reading sexy novels alone or to each other." "Memory of previous occasions and reading." "[Lesbian] I enjoy all of these, like to read 'gay' books, see 'gay' movies, go to 'gay' parties, bars, etc. on occasion." "My husband wanting to have sex and telling me so." "Reading, *uninterrupted* romantic music, drive-in movies (adult plots); naughty pictures, suggestive language from husband." "Sometimes pornographic movies, although not always. The maximum environmental stimulation would be derived from a situation such as an artist's costume ball, where I would be wearing a nearly nude costume and be exposed to fondling by various men, and by dancing very close so that I would feel their penises pressing into me and being told how and in what manner they would desire me." "Anything shared can be stimulating if I'm in the mood." "I find men more stimulating than anything I have found in books, pictures, movies, etc. It has nothing to do with whether he is clothed or unclothed, or what he is doing. My biggest pet peeve is men who dress so that you can't tell if they have anything more than any woman does under their clothes. Men have something to be proud of in being men, and it seems ridiculous to not be able to tell unless they're undressed. You don't find very many women pretending they don't have any breasts by binding them up or wearing baggy blouses, and a man shouldn't harness himself in either. I like men whose sex is in evidence." "Verbalization of men, reading, thinking." "Usually reading, but sometimes lines from a play. —A deep contralto voice—and sometimes Dietrich's gowns will do it. But usually it is the actual presence of a person." "Reading and adult movies. However, in these movies it is not the nudity, but the situations that excite me." "Good-looking men." "Reading, movies, pictures, music."

"Potential" nudists

"Reading stimulates me more than anything—a well-written book. As a teenager, reading was one of my highest sources of stimulation (besides fantasizing). On occasion, viewing pictures of nude males (art books) will stimulate me. I have wondered why they don't have good books out solely with pictures of nude males that would appeal to females (rather than the homosexual). Those which I have seen consisted of pretty young boys, really not directed to some women in our society, I felt. A good love story (movie) will sometimes stimulate me, depending on how well it is. Actually it really doesn't have to be a love story: if the male or males in the film are appealing in some way, I become sexually aroused. On a couple of occasions, just talking or looking at a person I was extremely attracted to would excite me to the point where I would actually feel throbbing in the clitoral area. This happens very, very seldom though (darn). Regarding the 'throbbing in the clitoral area,' it is of the same pleasurable nature I experience during the beginning of sexual foreplay on and around the clitoris. The throbbing is akin to pulsation. I felt a warm sensation as well, much as I do when I begin to get excited during foreplay. . . . I think it was actually the feeling of physical closeness which brought about this sensation; the warmth of the other person's body, the expression of the eyes, while we were talking." "Having the man I love with me." "People." "Reading—I am able to place myself into the character's position." "Reading, thinking about or doing something forbidden." "Reading and TV." "Music." "Reading books and certain movies." "Foreign movies." "Most romanticism (reading, pictures, movies, not 'sexy' but romantic) and seeing someone I'm attached to." "Reading—I also find a trip to the beach stimulating—seeing healthy happy people enjoying life." "Reading, beautiful bodies, car rides, store windows with pretty things. Any good idea (not necessarily sexy). Making things, beautiful scenery, drawing nudes, nonverbal exchange of awareness via eyes and energy with an aroused partner— sometimes with my husband, often with [another female]. Occasionally seeing either my husband's or [another female's] body; especially when I feel strong rapport." "Erotic literature, occasionally erotic photos." "Reading, daydreams, kidding around about sex with guys— some casual physical contact with guys, e.g. brushing shoulders as we walk." "Movies or TV, occasionally. Prurient material usually strikes me as amusing." "Movies, if it is a good love story—reading a descriptive sexy novel." "Presence of physically attractive men—reading." "Music, swimming, hot baths, or just time enough." "Feeling of closeness and being understood." "Reading and imagination." "Being with an attractive male! (Sexy movie scenes are *poor* second.)" "Reading. Different surroundings can be stimulating, spending the night in a different room or camping outdoors." "Most definitely literature—it's detailed and descriptive." "Some music; blues, jazz." "Reading, movies, dancing." "Reading and discussions, and watching a beautiful man move.—One who is in top physical shape and mentally acute." "Visual —the sight of an attractive male, sexual activity in movies or real life; reading sometimes." "Proximity to, or thoughts of my husband."

"Thinking." "Books, movies, TV can be stimulating." "All." "Reading, movies, some men."

"Potential" nudists (lesbians)

"Reading and other females." "Other women and reading." "Other females because they're real." "Reading a sexy book—pictures—sometimes just touching another woman of the type I like (as in an elevator) upsets me terribly."

✳✳✳✳✳ 18 ✳✳✳

REACTION TO THE SIGHT OF A PENILE ERECTION

Studies have shown that males as compared to females are much more responsive to, and stimulated by, visual sensual and sexual stimuli. The findings of the present study add further support to the existence of such a basic sex difference. This was denoted by the fact that while in response to the question: How would you describe your reaction to the sight of the penis in a state of erection? (i.e. exciting, attractive, ugly, neutral, etc.?) the large majority of the nudists (71 per cent) and more than half the "potential" nudists (58 per cent) responded in positive terms, e.g., attractive, exciting, beautiful; 18 per cent of the nudists and 21 per cent of the "potential" nudists indicated their main reaction to be neutral. Moreover, several nudists in responding used the adjective ugly (in some instances certain circumstances were described in which this reaction would be experienced), and a few employed the words: frightening, embarrassing (embarrassed), disgusting, and repulsive. Descriptions such as slightly shocked, and humorous were also reported. In the case of the "potential" nudists a few used the adjectives: ugly, frightening, and repulsive. Other responses included the terms: humorous, funny, ludicrous, and envious. The percentage of Mensa females who responded in an essentially positive manner to the above question was noticeably lower than that of the nudists but similar to that of the "potential" nudists.

No significant relationship was found between either the levels of self-esteem or security feelings of our participants and a reaction to the sight of the penis in a state of erection.

With respect to the way in which most females tend to react to the sight of the penis, Maslow has stated that "Generally, the higher the dominance (with ego-security held constant) the greater the attractiveness the penis has for handling, looking at, and thinking about. High-dominance women ordinarily think it to be a very beautiful object in a truly aesthetic sense. To most of the rest of the population

163

it is considered to be either ugly or neutral in appearance."[1] Kinsey
and his associates disclosed that 48 per cent of their female subjects
(of whom the question was asked) "reported erotic arousal as a product of their observation of male genitalia, and more than half (52
per cent) reported that they had never been aroused by observing
male genitalia."[2] They also pointed out that "Many females are surprised to learn that there is anyone who finds the observation of male
genitalia erotically stimulating. Many females consider that male
genitalia are ugly and repulsive in appearance, and the observation
of male genitalia may actually inhibit their erotic responses."[3] The
present writer, in a previous study of female sexuality, reported that
"In the main, the subjects tended to view the penis as being rather
neutral in appearance."[4]

In terms of the various findings and comments presented above
concerning the reactions of females to the sight of the penis, it seems
quite probable that, as a group, our sample of female nudists tends
to perceive the penis (in a state of erection) in a much more positive
(healthy) manner than do most females in our society.

Among the responses recorded by the participants were the following:

Nudists

"Both attractive and exciting." "Exciting at times, neutral or ugly
at others." "Exciting and attractive—beautiful in fact!" "Exciting. I
can't resist the thought of sex, even if I tried or had not been in the
mood before." "Neutral." "Embarrassed, even by husband's." "Depends. If it is for my pleasure—exciting. If against my will—ugly."
"Neutral, unless accompanied by advances. Repulsive, if advances
were made by someone not desired." "In someone I care for—exciting.
Otherwise, neutral—but interesting." "No reaction." "To see my husband's penis in a state of erection is *very, very* exciting to me." "Exciting. I like a cock about eight inches long." "I am stimulated by the
sight." "Exciting and beautiful—I am a nudist." "Attractive, exciting,

[1] Maslow, A. H., "Self-esteem (Dominance-Feeling) and Sexuality in Women."
Journal of Social Psychology, 1942, *16*, p. 286. By permission of the author and
The Journal Press.
[2] Kinsey, A. C., *et al., Sexual Behavior in the Human Female.* (Philadelphia:
Saunders, 1953), p. 655. By permission of Dr. P. H. Gebhard and the Institute
for Sex Research, Inc.
[3] *Ibid.,* p. 655. By permission of Dr. P. H. Gebhard and the Institute for Sex
Research, Inc.
[4] DeMartino, M. F. (ed.), *Sexual Behavior and Personality Characteristics.*
(New York: Grove Press, 1966), p. 130. By permission of the Citadel Press, Inc.

and most desirable." "I find it exciting and wish to fondle it." "If someone walked by with an erect penis I'd find it humorous. In bed I find it exciting—but I think it's more fun to agitate it from a limp stage to an erect stage. Just to look at it, I think it is a source of amusement." "Beautiful! ! !" "Depends on to whom the penis is attached. Reactions are from exciting to disgusting." "Just to see a man or a picture would be nothing. But the man I love—it would please me to see it that way—even if it meant that it would lead to nothing;—like in the morning." "It used to repel me when first married but now its quite exciting." "Very ambiguous. Sometimes beautiful!! Sometimes frightening!!! Reaction is increasingly more positive." "To me the sight of the penis in a state of erection is not only attractive but absolutely beautiful. My husband's circumcised penis and the velvet-like foreskin is a part of God's image, created for reproduction through marriage for the good . . . physical and mental well-being of family, husband and wife, living and loving each other through life together." "Exciting. I also enjoy the beauty of the male genitalia in a relaxed state and find them very exciting." "Attractive and does excite me somewhat." "[Lesbian] Disgusting and ugly." "That does help bring on the urge." "It's the most—it thrills me through and I'm hot in a second." "It is exciting only if I know intercourse will follow. Neutral otherwise—as when he awakens with an erection and we are both going to work." "I have never seen an ugly erect penis. There are some more attractive than others, but I have never found any that fail to excite me to some degree. I like sex, and I like sexiness, and there is nothing sexier than a man who wants to make love to me, whoever he is and whether he does." "Attractive; if aroused—exciting." "Fascination—admiration." "Generally neutral. Depends a little upon the penis." "Very exciting, enticing, provocative—actually quite attractive-looking." "Depending on mood, my reaction could range from exciting to neutral (never ugly, though)." "Before I was married, I found it rather ugly, but my husband's is beautiful, even perhaps magnificent! It does not excite me but I admire it." "If its aroused because of me I find it very exciting. If because of another woman I might feel revulsion." "Exciting, inviting, and a stimulus to oral participation." "[Lesbian] it would be ugly and very frightening. I've never seen one in a state of erection." "Very pleasing, desirable." "What I think of the man determines what I think of his erection. My husband's is beautiful and exciting. However, I've seen very ugly ones." "Occasionally, slightly shocked at first, but later I become either neutral or even slightly attracted, though sometimes I don't realize it at the time." "Attractive." "Attractive and exciting." "It is a beautiful sight . . .

I do not particularly enjoy the raised organ outside of the proper place and time. And never in social nudism. . . . Social nudism, of course, has no sexual overtones and I am not aware of the penis as a sexual organ at these times." "Under the right circumstances, exciting; wouldn't care to see one on main street." "This would excite me greatly."

"Potential" nudists

"Neutral." "My excitement is reduced if I look at it." "It is extremely exciting (even more so when I watch it 'grow'). Also, I do have a bit of penis envy." "Exciting and attractive." "Seeing it erect under clothing is mildly interesting or neutral." "Attractive or neutral." "Assuming the situation to be one of close intimacy, it is somewhat exciting (feeling, more than sight)—not particularly attractive.—Can be repulsive if intimate relationship is lacking." "It depends on whose, when, and why." "Exciting and artistically interesting." "Natural, sometimes faintly ugly—depends on rapport." "Generally pleasant in a warm, agreeable sense. Occasionally, exciting. General interest in it as an aesthetic object. Usually, a desire to feel the smoothness, etc." "Very exiciting to me. I become very much aroused." "This depends on how aroused I am. I would call it neutral—but often exciting if I have begun to be aroused." "Depends on circumstances—if sex partner—its attractive. If person whom I am not attracted to—frightening, ugly." "Exciting to the point of wanting intercourse immediately." "I think they are cute. There is nothing ugly about it at all—plus very fascinating." "Assuming it is during an intimacy—exciting, although not really attractive; somehow very sobering; depends on the situation —a man on a subway is pretty repulsive." "Funny as can be." "Pleased at the fact it indicates strong desire, foretells pleasure." "On my husband when I am interested, I find it very pleasant and I want to show my affection by touching." "Exciting, attractive, stimulating, want to touch." "Neutral, although it's *use* interests me." "During sexual intercourse—stimulating mentally—other times—indifferent." "Very exciting and attractive." "I find this extremely exciting and more so the longer I am around a penis. I am fascinated by the penis; I enjoy looking at it, feeling it, and watching it as it becomes erect. I think it is a delightful part of the body. I sometimes have tried to imagine what sensations the male experiences; what intercourse feels like to them and the handling of the penis." "Exciting if I think of what it can do and where it can go—otherwise not pretty." "With husband, negative—with lover exciting." "I think the penis is very, very exciting and attractive—expecially in a state of erection which is extremely desirable and stimulating. I love to look at it and feel it." "Exciting and motivating—gives me somewhat of a sensual sense of power for having brought about the erection." "In the past ugly, now exciting." "Awe, exciting, frightening, beautiful." "It looks nice to me if I like who is wearing it." "When excited I find it *very* appealing. At other times I am very curious, almost envious—I like to examine it." "Exciting and aesthetically appealing." "Exciting if the man is not otherwise repulsive." "Neutral, but curious." "If you're [I'm] emotionally involved—very exciting. Otherwise I suppose anywhere from 'wild' to ludicrous."

"Potential" nudists (lesbians)

"Exciting." "Neutral or exciting, according to circumstance." "It didn't do a thing for me—neutral. (Is that a Freudian slip? It *did* do one thing and it was disgusting.)" "Neutral—it's kind of funny." "Sometimes exciting, sometimes ugly." "Repulsive" "Exciting to look at and fondle only."

✸✸✸✸✸ 19 ✸✸✸

MAIN REASONS FOR BECOMING A NUDIST

In an attempt to learn some of the reasons why females become social nudists, or would like to become nudists, the following questions were asked of the subjects: Would you like to become a member of a nudist group?—Why?—What were your main reasons for becoming a nudist?[1]

Before some of the responses to these questions are presented, it should be emphasized that in most important situations the true motives which govern the behavior of an individual frequently are unconscious or unknown to him or her. Quite often, in such instances, the reasons given by a person in an effort to explain his actions are incorrect and are mainly rationalizations. To get at unconscious or "true" motives or reasons, frequently requires that an individual be subjected to projective techniques, or depth-psychotherapy, clinical analysis, hypnosis, etc. At the same time, however, it should be observed that conscious motives are not necessarily *always* inaccurate. For as Dr. Gordon W. Allport has stated: "the direct responses of the psychoneurotic cannot be taken at their face value. The defenses are high, the true motives are hidden and are betrayed only by a projective technique. The normal subjects, on the other hand, tell you by the direct method precisely what they tell you by the projective method. They are all of a piece. You may, therefore, take their motivational statements at their face value, for even if you probe you will not find

---

[1] These questions are only part of those relating to social nudism. The other questions which were designed to identify nudists were: Are you a member of a nudist group? Have you ever spent time at a nudist camp? The present sample of nudist subjects included: a) members of nudist camps; b) those who practice social nudism in private groups; c) independent social nudists (nonjoiners); and d) a few females who gave every indication of being social nudists, but who as yet were not formally attached to any nudist group.

anything substantially different."[2] Since depth approaches were not feasible in the present study, and since all the subjects were not "normal" (free from neuroses), in evaluating the comments noted by the participants, it should be borne in mind that there *may be* more important personal and different (unconscious) reasons why these females became nudists or might like to become nudists.

An analysis of the protocols revealed that in many instances there were a combination of reasons (several) which motivated the subjects to become social nudists. Nevertheless, certain motivating forces appeared to be stronger than others. The reason which was recorded by far the greatest number of respondents for having become a nudist was one which indicated that the subject had become such because of her *husband's* desire, interest or incitement. (This was noted by 26 per cent of the nudists.) Kinsey *et al.*, it will be remembered, found that many more males than females were aroused erotically from observing the genitalia of the opposite sex.[3] Among the other more prominently mentioned reasons by the nudists were the following: a) desire to sun-bathe and get a tan all over the body; b) pleasure derived from a sense of freedom; c) feeling of relaxation, naturalness and comfort; d) dislike of wearing clothes; e) curiosity; f) sensual aspects, i.e. enjoyment from being seen nude and seeing others nude, way of experiencing sensuality, desire to meet people interested in group sex; g) good and healthy atmosphere in which to raise children—i.e. they can grow up without acquiring neurotic attitudes about their bodies and sex; h) carry-over from the practice of private nudism; i) desire to swim in the nude. Reasons given by relatively few of the nudists included the following: a) desire to meet other people with similar beliefs concerning nudity and the like; b) to be in a healthy atmosphere with respect to attitudes toward sex and the human body; c) to improve one's physical health; and d) because of friends being nudists.

In general, the above findings are similar to those reported by previous investigators. It is of some interest, however, to note that a greater number of our participants (9 per cent) designated specifically sexual motives for having become nudists than did those females on which prior studies were based. Although this difference may have been due to the nature of the present sample, it is believed that it was

[2] Allport, G. W., "The Trend in Motivational Theory." *The American Journal of Orthopsychiatry*, 1953, 23, p. 110. Copyright, the American Orthopsychiatric Association, Inc., reproduced by permission.

[3] Kinsey, A. C., *et al.*, *Sexual Behavior in the Human Female.* (Philadelphia: Saunders, 1953).

170 | THE NEW FEMALE SEXUALITY

primarily the result of the fact that almost all our subjects responded anonymously to a questionnaire, while the other studies involved face to face contacts between the researchers and the respondents.[4]

The reasons indicated by the "potential" nudists for wanting to *become* a member of a nudist group were somewhat different from those stated by the nudists, in that no reference was made to their husbands or children as motivating influences, a desire to meet other people with like beliefs, the urging by friends, or a desire for group sexual activity. Particularly noteworthy in relation to the responses disclosed by the lesbian group of "potential" nudists, as will be seen, was the relatively strong emphasis placed on sexual or sensual reasons for desiring to become a social nudist.

Reasons given by the subjects for having become a social nudist, and wanting to become a member of a nudist group, included the following:

Nudists

"Friends' proselytizing, curiosity." "Being an exhibitionist, as are most nudists, I have ample opportunity to let others see me. This I love." "I had been going to solariums for nude sun baths for about ten years; also had sought out isolated beaches, but this became difficult and I became curious about trying a nudist park. Therefore, I sought one out as soon as I could locate one [many years ago]." "My husband and I feel that the human body is at its most beautiful in its completely natural state. We do not feel that the body is so shameful that we have to hide beneath layers of clothing, as evidently so many people feel. We became nudists mostly so our children would have the privilege of growing up being rightly proud of their bodies. Consequently, being proud of one's self. You can not be proud of yourself if you've been taught to feel ashamed of your own true self." "My husband wanted to be a nudist, so I became one to keep peace between us." "Husband's desire to do so, then belief on my part in the nudist way of life." "My husband wanted it very much and I didn't mind becoming a nudist. Now I enjoy it very much." "I like the comfort and ease of nudist life (regarding clothing); it is an excellent form of recreation (when we can afford it); I would like a chance to advance the nudist movement; and when we have children I want them brought up without shame of their bodies or morbid curiosities which

[4] See the following: a) Ilfeld, F. Jr., and Lauer, R., *Social Nudism in America.* (New Haven, Connecticut: College and University Press, 1964). b) Casler, L., "Some Sociopsychological Observations in a Nudist Camp: A Preliminary Study," *Journal of Social Psychology,* 1964, *64,* 307–23. c) Weinberg, M. S., "Becoming a Nudist," *Psychiatry,* 1966, *29.* 15–24.

may make trouble later." "I hadn't any reasons to begin with except to fit in. (All my friends are nudists.) Then as I got older I had to think about it, my whys, etc. It's not as easy as 'it's free' and all that bull shit. Many nudists will tell you that, but I believe it involves more. As compared to draft-card burning, freedom marches, beards, etc. (now don't mistake nudist *group* with a *camp;* there is a great difference), the people belonging to a camp are being 'liberal' in (usually) only one aspect—running around without anything on. But just try to discuss the bible with them or the Birch Society. Yeah! A nudist group is a follow-through of ideas, be they right or wrong. The idea in itself is good and I believe in releasing ourselves from most of our sexual taboos. But it usually tends always to be in a group with equality on their minds. That lets us women in as well as the Negro (but not quite as well). I take off my clothes when I'm able and the temperature is right. I like the freedom I got used to when I was being like everyone else. I'm glad I am free that way. But I would no longer use the fact that I am one as a shock value or a 'step up' on my neighbor. I'll take off my clothes whenever it is comfortable for me and the people around me." "I enjoy the freedom, belonging to a group of good people; a variety of people. Lots of good enjoyment. Feeling of everyone being equal. The idea of becoming a nudist appealed to me for a long time. But I never knew how to join or even if it was legal. I heard very few good things about it. I began to wonder if I wasn't nuts, until my husband finally got a nudist magazine with a directory.—I also like the outdoors and company." "Husband's idea in beginning. I enjoy swimming in nude and having an all-over tan. And I guess I'm a show-off, since I have a nice figure." "It seems natural and beneficial to the people involved." "It is very good for getting over the shame you feel about your body. In the beginning, my husband nagged me into going. After my first thirty minutes I felt so relaxed, so relieved of some unknown heavy load, I was anxious to join a camp. The effect on our kids was another reason for becoming an 'organized' nudist. There is no misinformation and nasty, sly remarks that my kids can't handle about the nude body. They've seen human beings from one week to ninety-three years old completely nude. They've seen amputees, overweight and underweight people. In a nudist camp there is no sneaking and wondering and trying to get a peek up some girl's dress. You see somebody, you look at them, every inch of them if you want; and there's nothing covered up or taboo to look at.—It's so very hard to explain the good feeling you get when you throw off those garments and that heavy, heavy load of guilt and shame we've been carrying since we were three or four years old." "On a dare by a male friend—my husband had talked about it for years but I had no desire to go." "My husband was interested. He has been a home nudist ever since we were married [over ten years ago]. We both would usually be nude before bedtime and have always slept in the nude, so becoming a nudist was just one step more." "I have always been interested in the human body, as an artist and as a person. I never could believe in the doctrine of original sin. I rebel at the stupid taboos society imposes on human beings because of false religious ideas handed down to us. I wanted to see people as they really are. In years of life classes, when I was learning to draw, I never saw the male genitals; they were always covered. In a nudist society, I learned about the great variety. I also came to appreciate our particular endowment and our youthful appearance at ages—and—. Behold two happy people." "I enjoy seeing and being seen." "The comfort of being nude and a desire to swim in the nude." "I like to sun-bathe without fear of peeping Toms. Open-minded people. Good for children. Healthy atmosphere." "Like natural way of life, elimination of prudery. Friends showed me sense it made— was curious and had been a private nudist all my life (mother sun-bathed nude, family bathed together; I swam nude with boy friends and some girl friends; fits in with yoga, natural childbirth, and other interests)." "My husband wanted to go [become a nudist]." "My husband felt it would help me come out of my 'shell' and it has." "To be able to play in the nude and also to see what other people looked like." "My husband wanted to become a nudist and he finally convinced me of the physical health benefits of sunshine and fresh air. I actually joined to keep peace and harmony at home. We do not practice nudism any place but at a nudist camp." "For freedom of activities and health and well-being." "Not sure; before we were married, we saw a nudist movie together and were intrigued by the philosophy and just the acceptance of such an idea. We kidded about it for some time and joined as soon as we were married. Since then we think our reasons are relaxation, advantages for our children, abolishing some taboos about body. Why should we continue to accept things because that's the way they are. Try to better ourselves and nudism helps." "To please my husband. I joined almost under protest but now I like it and wouldn't consider leaving." "Being able to get a sun tan all over the body." "Appreciation of physical culture and human body. Desire of well-being and natural living. More desirable than dress, sophistication. Love of outdoors, sun." "Husband interested. Now I like the feel of air and sun on my skin, seeing others in natural state. Skin is a very useful organ and we want our children to use it. Also want our children to grow up without neurotic ideas about the body and sex." "Being a sun worshipper, I naturally wanted my complete body to receive the sun." "My man at the time wanted to become one. I love it and wouldn't change for anyone." "I like all-over suntans and swimming in the nude. 2) I was eager to meet people who could see above the arbitrary and sometimes silly rules of society.—I thought they should be people who think for themselves. 3) I am curious about new experiences and this was one I hadn't tried." "I became a nudist because my husband desired it. He was looking for sexual companionship but was discouraged by the nude-prudes." "My husband wanted to." "A sense of physical and spiritual freedom. It seemed natural. A way of experiencing sensuality in a total, direct, open and natural way." "Freedom of feeling." "Nudism is something I've known all my life. My parents were nudists and through the years I have grown to love the freedom I felt while being nude." "Through nudist magazines, I became convinced of the wholesomeness and the dignity of the entire nude human body. I enjoy the freedom from clothing and the feeling of youthfulness in romping outdoors unrestricted. I enjoy visiting with others who hold the same nudist beliefs." "I am part of a group of people who are nudists, but have never spent any time at a nudist camp. I have some friends who are nudists; one couple have a pool with a high fence around their property and another couple have a garden with a high fence. We spend as much time as we can with them; we are also nude in our home quite often. *Reasons.* I'm a nudist because I'm not ashamed of my body or anyone else's, and it's the most natural thing to do when you get up in the morning, or go to bed, or if it's hot. Clothes are to wear if it's cold and you don't have any other way to keep warm—and to keep from getting thrown in jail by other people who haven't got any sense." "A doctor first recommended nudism to my mother as a means of counteracting a tendency toward TB in me. I took it gladly. I believe that all families should go nude within their homes." "My husband is physically disabled and sunshine and exercise help him. We joined because of this and now we enjoy nudism and practice it at home." "Curiosity. My husband was interested." "Because we both dislike feeling bound down by clothes —so we tried a camp. We like the feeling of freedom and now after meeting other nudists also find we like the people because in the nude people seem to learn to be more themselves—and do not put on airs or show off as people tend to do with clothes on." "I enjoy being seen naked and also enjoy seeing both men and women and children without clothes—this without wanting to 'touch'—but only see." "Husband initiated after years of private nudism. To expose body and mind and live naturally with the opposite sex." "We recommend Nudist Club membership to parents who want to bring up their children without curiosity and in clean and decent surroundings." "Freedom of body and mind." "My husband talked me into it." "My husband wanted to—good for our girls to see others nude as they are growing up so they will have a healthy attitude toward the nude body and the bodies of men and boys. Now I enjoy feeling the sun and air on my body very much and love swimming nude." "Our young boys were showing an interest in girls—e.g. hiding nude pictures of girls in their dresser, discussing girls and their bodies. I had never considered nudism before, although my husband had discussed the desire to visit a camp for the past ten years. I felt I didn't need *social* nudism—but I agreed with my husband that the children could certainly benefit from social nudism. Now I regret not having joined a camp ten years ago when my husband suggested it. I find being a nudist has not made any great change in our sex lives." "Sun is health-growing—outdoors is healthful. I like swimming nude and especially sun-bathing. A tan looks good and 'feels good.' I find clothes *most uncomfortable*." "My husband wanted to go so I went to please him and now I enjoy it as much as he." "It is difficult to go nude outdoors in the area where we are living—a camp could provide this service.—I've been a nudist since I was born. I like the feeling of freeness." "I don't like to wear clothes! Also, I'm somewhat overweight and find it hard getting attractive clothes to fit. At nudist clubs I don't have to worry about what to wear. At home I wear very loose casual clothes." "I always liked the freedom of my body without clothes. I always wanted to be able to swim in the nude, but never had the opportunity. I wanted to be able to walk with nature and have the gentle breezes caress my body. Partly curiosity. I wondered how you could be unembarrassed. I found out you are not embarrassed. I'm glad I became a nudist because I've experienced a sense of freedom I've never known." "I wanted the opportunity to meet other people who were acting in accordance with some aspects of our philosophy." "Being completely natural and at ease; the high caliber of the type of people that are nudists." "We had practiced it in the home for years. We wanted to lose our bathing suit line." "At first to please my husband. Later, I became convinced of the mental and physical benefits of social nudism and its normalizing effect on the relationship between the sexes." "I originally joined because I am a professional figure model and I needed an all-over tan. Now I enjoy nudism so much I would continue even though I ceased being a model." "My husband felt so strongly about going that I finally had to give in. At first I hated it, but now, I want to be a nudist forever —as long as my body stays in decent shape!" "To be able to go to a place where I could not only sun-bathe, but swim, play games, meet people, eat, talk, etc., all without my clothes on." "Because of the health of my son." "The freedom of being able to get out of heavy, cumbersome clothing in the out-of-doors, and the good attitude toward sex that people have. We also feel it is a very good atmosphere in which to bring up children and to provide them with a good attitude toward sex." "Cloth is for protection of the body only." "Curiosity at first. This aspect vanished after the first afternoon spent as visitors to a camp. The unclothed environment then becomes a natural every-day living atmosphere. . . ." "Primarily, to please my present husband who wished to join and wouldn't go without me. Otherwise, I would never have thought of it. Actually, we wander around nude whenever practical and whenever we have privacy." "(None of my friends know I am a practicing nudist. I have never met anyone I ever knew before, in a camp I've been to. I have met only the one nudist that I have formed a sexual alliance with). Maybe curiosity—maybe something to do with sex. I wanted to meet other people who think like I do about nudity. I think it is silly to have to wear bathing suits to sun or swim. I am sort of Greek in my regard for the dignity and beauty of the human body. I have always practiced nudism in my home—after by divorce—and a marvelous sense of freedom followed. I read an article in a newspaper on nudism and decided to try it. Very satis-fying, makes me feel healthy—free, unencumbered. Very close to nature and all outdoors." "Primarily physical reasons (at age —), i.e. to relieve my emphysema and asthmatic condition and reduce the volume of medication required to cope with the condition. Effects: very satisfactory and most beneficial via nude sun-bathing to expel phlegm, retain clear lungs and good easy breathing. I shall continue nudism for good health to body and mind. . . ." "I have always hated to wear clothes and loved to swim nude and sun-bathe nude. Love the feeling of freedom and of being completely separated from a normal environment. Love the unselfconsciousness of the children at nudist camps. The children are darling." "Enjoy sun-bathing and being nude. Total freedom." "Because they [others] share our beliefs of the body being wholesome—it's healthy—friendly, nice people. I like the open-ness and freedom about it. Good for kids too, fresh air and sunshine and see all sexes, making for no mystery about it." "Being able to swim, participate in sports and activities or just relax without clothes fascinated me and I wanted to experience it. Now that I have, I hope I never have to give it up. It gives me a special and good feeling."

"My family are also members.—The freedom in taking off my clothes when I want to. After being there [at camp]—feeling of exhilaration from sun on my entire body and just being able not to wear clothes. The freeness also leads many times to freeness of expression in other areas, i.e. sex, intellectual conversation, etc." "I like the freedom of no clothes. It also excites me to see other people nude. Because I like the outdoors and the feel of the sun and water on my bare skin, and also had hoped to meet people who were interested in group sex." "Wanted to meet broad-minded people, get an even tan; don't believe in clothes when not necessary—such as swimming, etc. I feel we already wear too many restricting clothes." "To raise our planned children in a more healthy sex environment was our motive for trying them [nudist camps] out. But now we also enjoy the naturalness and relaxed persons we have met." "I enjoy the natural way of life and the people because everyone is on the same level. With nothing to hide they are more sincere friends than any people you can meet anywhere." "To get a tan with *no lines*, so I would no longer get sunburned. My father was a careful beach nudist. My family used to swim nude when possible on camping trips. I am not much interested in the social side of nudism—mainly the physical sensations." ". . . I like to dance and am conscious of good body movement. Walking, swimming, all body movements have a delightful freedom about them when nude. My main reason for going the first time was to overcome self-consciousness about being quite flat-chested. I have never been concerned sexually, since none of the men I slept with seemed to care about my small breasts—but I cared. I wanted to test myself in a situation with all kinds of females and see if I still felt inadequate. I found to my surprise I was unconcerned. I liked the experience and would go back for the pleasure of it."

"Potential" nudists

"I think it is a healthy form of recreation for a family." "I don't like clothes. I feel too restricted in them. Also, I feel less inhibited when not in clothes." "I like going nude but am always afraid someone will knock at the door." "I feel that it is healthier for your body not to be clothed and also I am a sun worshipper." "I enjoy being nude and I think it would be a wonderful feeling." "I think there is nothing greater than the clean and natural body being exposed." "I hate clothes." "Clothes are too much trouble, expense, etc.—besides everyone looks about alike—so what's the difference." "Perhaps to overcome my feelings about my body and also feel it would be healthy." "Temporarily for the experience—would be very interesting as I expect there would be a lot less sexual perversion." "I will admit I'm curious." "I would enjoy the freedom of moving about without the restrictions clothing usually imposes on one's physical agility." "Might enjoy seeing the bodies artistically and/or sexually; might like the freedom from clothes. I have used nudist camps in fantasies." "I enjoy nude sun-bathing and its difficult to find private places. Also, I like to swim nude, but get queasy at the thought of fish and slimy plants to touch: this means a private pool." "Interested in nudism. . . ." "I'm not sure. I enjoy being nude, and I don't object to seeing others nude. I think this is a healthy thing." "Perhaps . . . Temporarily. It would be very interesting to experience such openness. I can't imagine feeling comfortable but I imagine I could get used to it. Actually nudist camps have very strict restrictions on sex. I wouldn't be interested in terms of sex. I would like to see what people are like so unclothed all the time." "Because people would really be themselves without the hindrance of clothing. The human body is beautiful if taken care of." "I enjoy being nude— would like to see whether I would enjoy being nude in public." "I feel very happy in the nude. As long as everyone took it for granted I do not think it would embarrass me in the least. I might take better care of my figure, however." "I don't know if I'd like to or not. I love lying in the sun with as little on as possible and am not at all modest. . ." "I feel many of the fears and defensivenesses are hurtful in our culture. More openness and trust and acceptance of ourselves and others would lead to a happier and more fulfilling life." "Being without clothes is comfortable and free-feeling." "Think of all the free models! In my life sketching class, the model fee is almost as much as the instructor's fee. Having spent a number of years drawing and painting nudes, my reaction to the nude body is only under certain circumstances sexual." "I have a skin condition that might be cleared if all the skin could be exposed to sun rays. First I will try a vacation in a sunny climate with a bikini." "Curiosity." "Perhaps if I thought my body was more attractive—I don't known." "I would enjoy the 'freedom,' but I think I'm too inhibited to join." "Nudity seems more a natural state." "To see how people react when nude constantly. Not for sexual reasons." "Would be lovely to be nude outdoors. Nice to see enough bodies to lose sense of embarrassment." "Would like to be in a sexually relaxed atmosphere; also sometimes I'm proud of my body and would like it to be seen." "It would be most pleasant not to be bothered about what to wear—cheaper, too. I enjoy the sun." "Experience and renewed excitement. It gives one the feeling of freedom and I think bodies are objects of beauty. That is, some of them." "Very honest and healthy—not such a tendency for parts of the body to be considered 'nasty' which they definitely aren't." "Might be interesting—a lark." "I like to swim nude, to have the sun on my entire body. I think that people should treat nudity more casually." "I sat in with a nudist couple for the first time in my life, naked; it was great. I like the familiarity they have with the body, seeing it as a body and not a status symbol. I found out that being flat-chested is not an earth-shattering thing." "I think it would be erotic if it weren't for the overdone 'pureness' and almost religious air that goes with it." "I'd like to examine my reactions to such an environment—I think I'd like it." "Seemed very natural [subject visited one in the past]." "To see what everybody else looks like, both male and female —also to expose myself. I never would join one, however."

"Potential" nudists (lesbians)

"It's nice to run around nude." "I think it is a healthy way to live. However, I would be physically uncomfortable without a bra. Also, I tend to be shy about anyone viewing my backside, which is scarred." "I don't particularly like clothes. I like the feel of sun, wind, rain, water on all parts of my body—like free feeling of body." "To see women. They excite me. And because I think there is nothing more beautiful than a nicely formed human body." "Love being nude and seeing nudes." "To take off the façade and show myself as I am. To be free. Also to see lots of nude women. A female nudist colony would be nice." "I adore beauty." "I think it's just curiosity to see what it is like. I'd like a female nudist camp." "I have no voyeuristic tendencies. I would just enjoy the freedom of walking around in the sun unclothed and becoming tanned. I also think it would free me of what inhibitions I have." "Seems like I would be able to be more honest with myself and other people."

✳✳✳✳✳ 20 ✳✳✳

KIND OF KISSING FOUND MOST EXCITING SEXUALLY

Based on the responses to the question: Which kind of kissing do you find most exciting sexually?—it may be said that both the nudists (60 per cent) and "potential" nudists (56 per cent), view "french" or "deep soul" kissing, which involves the active use of the tongue and mouth, to be the most exciting and stimulating sexually. It is particularly interesting to observe that genital kissing (cunnilingus) was reported as the second most sexually exciting kind of kissing by the nudists (15 per cent). This form of kissing ranked a very close third in the case of the "potential" nudists (8 per cent); ordinary kissing—lips to lips—ranked second. Among the other more frequently mentioned forms of kissing regarded as exciting by the nudists included: kissing on the breasts and nipples, kissing all over the body and kissing on the neck.[1] Similar responses were also noted by the "potential" nudists.

Kinsey *et al.* found that "Deep kissing was in the petting experience of approximately 70 per cent of the females in the sample who had not had pre-marital coitus. The incidences, however, rose with increased coital experience, and deep kissing was in the histories of something between 80 and 93 per cent of those who had had coitus before marriage. There were some differences between the educational levels on this point. For instance, among those who had had coitus some twenty-five times or more, deep kissing occurred in 83 per cent of the high school sample, and in 98 per cent of the graduate sample."[2] It was also reported by these investigators that "Among the females in the sample who had not had pre-marital coitus, only 30 per cent had accepted mouth breast contacts. . . among the females who had even

[1] For an interesting commentary on the kissing techniques practiced in different cultures, see: Opler, M. K., "Cross-cultural Aspects of Kissing," *Medical Aspects of Human Sexuality*, 1969, 3, 11–21.

[2] Kinsey, A. C., *et al.*, *Sexual Behavior in the Human Female*. (Philadelphia: Saunders, 1953), p. 252. By permission of Dr. P. H. Gebhard and the Institute for Sex Research, Inc.

limited amounts of pre-marital coitus, such contacts had occurred in 68 per cent of the histories, and in 87 per cent of the histories of those who had more extensive coitus. The acceptance was greatest among the females of the younger generation, particularly in the better educated groups."[3]

Some of the responses reported by the subjects were as follows:

Nudists

"Mutual kissing as in '69'—fellatio and cunnilingus engaged in simultaneously or the lips without thrusts of the tongue." "Passionate." "Deep French kissing (use of tongue)." "Any kind, depending on who's doing it with me." "Kissing with the mouth open." "Tongue and exploring, then deep tongue kissing." "Soft and easy and loving." "French kiss except with my husband." "Open mouth, and oral—genital." "Soft, slightly moist, gentle kisses." "Slow, gentle, but firm." "A hard-firm, clinging kiss—no so-called French kiss." "French kiss and in the ear." "On cheek or eye rather than mouth." "1) Cunnilingus, 2) mouth to mouth, 3) on the nipples. All are equal in different moods." "Deep (tongue in and out), slow, soft movements; kissing all over body." "Body kisses, open-mouth kisses." "Oral sexual in the pubic area, but not the rectum, this is repulsive to me." "Any but soul-kissing." "French kissing—deep and long." "I don't find kissing exciting sexually—only pleasant." "Cunnilingus." "Tongue on tongue, tongue on lips." "Open-mouth and clitoral." "French kissing, kissing neck and back." "All kinds! Deep kisses on the mouth—and all over the body—giving and taking." "Genital and mouth-tongue kisses." "Enjoy all kinds—everywhere. Tonguing, 'blowing'—sucking. In every crevice with the right partner." "French kissing, and I like to be kissed on the neck." "Lip to lip and cunnilingus." "Light kisses, first on the neck and ear or arm —then breast, then firm kisses on the mouth for a long period—then French kisses—then clitoral kisses." "Gently on the neck and on the lips—with a 'gentle' Frenching (tongue)" "Gentle and slow." "On my vagina and clitoris." "Tongue to tongue; if properly stimulated, breast kissing." "I like tender, little kisses, but in the heat of passion the deep soul kiss." "Deep penetration with tongue." "None really, I'm not too fond of kissing." "The way my husband kisses (or licks) me all over. French kissing, too." "A soft, gentle, lingering kiss." "Lips to lips, tongue to tongue; kissing of my breasts and nipples; and of course, kissing my vulva." "I like my husband to wear a mustache. Like him to

---

[3] *Ibid.*, p. 254. By permission of Dr. P. H. Gebhard and the Institute for Sex Research, Inc.

bite my lip—easily." "A 'regular' kiss and I like to be kissed all over very gently." "Rubbing moist lips together and tonguing." "To kiss his 'balls'—(Excuse the vernacular)—and to have him kiss my tits.' " "Almost any kiss beyond a goodby kiss in the morning—I like it on the palm of my hand with his tongue." "I find slow, sensual kissing, with lips somewhat apart though not 'French' kissing to be the most exciting. I like kissing because I enjoy the way bodies and any parts of them, fit together." "They're all exciting if the invitation is there." "Any kind. I like to touch as much of my partner as I can." "Soft, tickling, teasing kisses." "None." "Breast kissing." "Hot, wet, 'sloppy' kisses, with much use of the tongue." "I think I would enjoy the French kiss, but the men I've kissed don't seem inclined to try it." "A gentle caressing, not—too—moist kiss, more lip action than pressure; teasing. A sudden forceful one at the right point is effective. French kiss sometimes is o.k." "French kissing with partner's tongue moving in and out rather rapidly, or else opposite—just barely touching or brushing partner's lips." "Kisses around ears, neck, breast, and vaginal area." "Soft with only the lips, working into a French kiss—still soft." "Sucking of tongues." "Kisses on lips, throat, breast, and clitoris." "Kissing of each other's bodies." "Open-mouth kissing." "I enjoy a plain kiss but a 'French' kiss arouses me more."

"Potential" nudists

"Cunnilingus." "Tongue and lips." "Wet, forceful, French kissing." "His tongue in my cheek." "Ordinary. I do not like French kissing, but I like having my closed lips licked by the other person." "Soft kisses—sometimes French—mouth, neck, ears." "Any kind of kissing." "Soul-kissing." "Very gentle 'French' kissing—also kissing of my neck and tummy." "When kissed as if I was really needed by my partner or with true emotion." "Mouth closed." "French kissing, feeling the tongue all over my face and body." "Light kissing not only on the lips but on the neck, breasts, thighs, and vagina." "Tongue kissing, but I don't like that unless I'm already aroused." "Very gentle French kissing—extended! To be kissed on the breasts and on the neck." "When tongue caresses any part of me." "Genital kissing." "Only as foreplay, otherwise deep kissing is distracting." "It's not so much a matter of how I'm kissed as it is of where." "Mouth to mouth gentle kissing." "French—mate's tongue in my mouth." "French kissing—soft—passionate." "French or deep kissing, simulation of intromission with the tongue, mouths closed and moving around causing friction. Kissing on various parts of the body. Simulation of intromission with the tongue in the ear is very stimulating." "Slow and gentle moving of lips and/or tongue, with mouths loosely together." "Kisses on breasts— genitals." "Very light—'tantalizing' kisses—mouth kisses." "Tongue in mouth." "Soft, open-mouthed—not too much tongue."

"Potential" nudists (lesbians)

"Tongue kissing." "Gentle, non-wet, and only if great affection accompanies." "Mouth—genital contact." "Deep 'French kissing'." "Open-mouth 'French' kissing—necks, much tonguing, etc." "Any kind if it is executed well."

✸✸✸✸✸✸ 21 ✸✸✸

SEXUAL CONTACTS WITH ANIMALS, AND INCESTUOUS BEHAVIOR

SEXUAL CONTACTS WITH ANIMALS

In response to the question: Have you ever engaged in any sexual behavior with animals? If so, describe—13 per cent of the nudists and 12 per cent of the "potential" nudists indicated that they had done so. The percentage of Mensa females who revealed that they had engaged in sexual behavior with animals was noticeably lower than that of either the nudists or "potential" nudists. Kinsey and his associates reported that during pre-adolescence 1.5 per cent of the females in their study had experienced some kind of sexual relation with animals and that after becoming an adolescent 3.6 per cent of their female subjects had had some sort of sexual contact with animals.[1] It is apparent, therefore, that the female nudists as well as the "potential" nudists in our samples experienced significantly more sexual contacts with animals than did the sample of females studied by Kinsey, *et al.*

Although to most people in our society the thought of any form of human sexual contact with an animal is repulsive, it should not be assumed that every person who indulges in such behavior is abnormal. Rather, in evaluating this form of behavior as well as many other kinds, the underlying, governing motives of the participant must be taken into account before any major conclusions may be drawn concerning his or her level of psychological health. For, as Dr. A. H. Maslow has remarked: "It would appear that no single act can *per se* be called abnormal or perverted. It is only abnormal or perverted individuals who can commit abnormal or perverted acts. That is, the dynamic

[1] Kinsey, A. C., *et al., Sexual Behavior in the Human Female.* (Philadelphia: Saunders, 1953), p. 505.

meaning of the act is far more important than the act itself."[2] With respect to both the nudists and "potential" nudists, it seems that among the primary motives for their sexual contacts with animals, were their strong sexual drives (the great majority of these subjects reported their drives to be above average, strong, or very strong), and their desires to experiment and experience new sensations.

Of the female nudists who had sexual contact with animals, six (42 per cent) had dominance scores which were in the top three deciles: Very high, High, Tendency to be high. Two subjects had dominance scores which were in the Average range and one was of Low dominance (decile 9). Five of the nudists who experienced sexual contacts, for some reason did not respond to the self-esteem (dominance) inventory. Unfortunately, because of these omissions, it is not possible to make any definitive statements concerning the relationship between dominance-feeling and sexual contacts with animals.

In the case of the "potential" nudists, four were of Very high dominance and three had dominance scores which were in the 8th and 9th deciles: Tendency to be low and Low. Two subjects were of Average dominance.

No significant relationship was found between the security levels of our subjects and the experiencing of sexual behavior with animals.

The following responses were noted by the subjects:

Nudists

"I have masturbated a small dog." "Encouraged a dog to lick me out of curiosity because of a joke I'd heard—didn't like it but no disgust." "Once. I would allow the dog to lick my pubic area until I reached an orgasm—while at the same time I would fondle his penis. This happened when I was 14 years old." "Yes. Licking." "Yes. Screwed by a boxer. A friend's boxer 'ate' me a number of times and once or twice I jacked him off. Had a Great Dane that liked to eat my pussy, too." "Yes. My dog likes to lick my genitals when my partner and I are engaged in intercourse." "Yes. Cats, dogs (I tried). I let cats or dogs lick my clitoris. I could not get to make love to a male dog but I tried." "Yes. Once I was cuddling a kitten and it started to suck my nipple which aroused me." "Yes. Experimental." "Yes. Once had a dog lick me but I didn't like it." "Yes. Once, in my early teens, I allowed a

[2] Maslow, A. H., "Self-esteem (Dominance-Feeling) and Sexuality in Women." *Journal of Social Psychology*, 1942, *16*, p. 286. Reprinted by permission of the author and The Journal Press.

dog to lick my vaginal area. Have sometimes had a desire to try intercourse with a dog or pony, but never attempted it." "I have let a dog lick my vagina." "I tried to get our Weimeraner (dog) interested one time, but he wouldn't have anything to do with me.—Oh, yes. I got a kitten to lick honey off my inner labia once." "Once or twice. My dog licked my vagina after I had intercourse. But I felt 'dirty' afterwards."

"Potential" nudists

"No, except for touching clitoris and testicles on dogs." "Sometimes my toy poodle snoops around while I'm having relations and likes to give me a little lick on my genitals;—it tickles." "Yes. Having a dog licking me between my legs." "Yes. Dog licking my clitoris, age approximately eight." "A little. In my teens. I allowed a kitten to suck my breasts. I have been tempted to see what a German Shepherd would do, but never actually tried." "Yes. Having a dog lick my genitals; that was one way in which I first discovered my sensitive area." "No, unless you count having a dog lick my privates when I was little."

"Potential" nudists (lesbians)

"Yes. I once tried to masturbate my dog. I was disgusted with myself and still am." "Yes. Masturbated a male dog." "Yes and no. Used to own a dog—very attached to animal—it was exciting to watch it masturbate."

INCESTUOUS BEHAVIOR

The one form of sexual behavior which is tabooed or outlawed in most societies whether they be primitive or civilized, is incest. To elicit information concerning incestuous behavior on the part of our subjects and the possible lasting effects of such experiences, the following questions were asked: At any time during your life have you ever engaged in any incestuous behavior?—If so, describe with whom, etc.—Do you feel it has had any effect on your overall sexual life?

An analysis of the responses to these questions disclosed that 13 per cent of the nudists and "potential" nudists, respectively, at one time or another, did participate in incestuous relations.[3] For the most part, these acts occurred during the years just prior to and those of adolescence. While 42 per cent of the nudists and 50 per cent of the

[3] Incestuous relations as viewed herein pertain to sexual activity between the subject and her father, step-father, grandfather, brother, sister, or uncle.

"potential" nudists reported that the incestuous experiences had a negative effect in some way, on their overall sexual life, 57 per cent of the nudists and 50 per cent of the "potential" nudists stated that these activities did not effect their sexual life in anyway.

The following responses were recorded by the participants:

Nudists

"Mild mutual masturbation with a sister two years my senior. No effect." "I tried to masturbate my sister when I was about five. No effect." "When about twelve and thirteen my grandfather seduced me. We shared a bed every night when I visited for summer vacation, etc. The rest of the family seemed unaware of the implications. I was afraid of him, but cannot remember feeling aroused. He would fondle me, enter me. I presumed he had orgasm. I do not remember any sensations. After, he would have me hold his penis and we would go to sleep. I did not talk with anyone as he said they would punish him and I didn't want that. I wanted to please him but became anxious about recurrences. E.[4] Yes. It was one factor in my not going all the way in high school despite excitement. Also, I was shy about handling and kissing a penis until after marriage." "My uncle masturbated on my leg once, both of us were clothed; I in bed in my pajamas. E. No." "Yes. First cousin when he was eighteen and I was twenty-one. With father when I was nineteen—both were normal intercourse, I think— maybe not. E. No." "With step-father when a young girl. E. None." "With father, brother, and cousin. E. No." "Against my will with my father. I hated it. E. Yes—made me freeze up quite a bit." "With older brother who was at puberty and was curious. E. Yes—served as a source of information and guilt at the time of occurrence." "When I was about twelve I slept in the same room with my brothers. One tried to have intercourse with me. This happened [several] times. I now realize he didn't achieve it but at the time I thought he had. E. Yes, definitely. It seems to have set up some sexual blocks. I get to a high state of excitement and then it seems I am just switched off." "My brother forced me into it. Nobody was at home. Although I screamed I felt dirty. E. No." "When I was about 12, my sister and I laid foot to foot in bed and interlocked our legs so that we exerted pressure on each others labia, like two pairs of scissors opened and put together so the hinges were in contact. There was no hand contact and it lasted only a few minutes. There was not any other stimulation, even with motion. E. I don't know if it has had any overall effect on my sex life,

---

[4] *E.* stands for the word Effect.

but I suppose I have some guilt feelings about it, and the effect may be there even though I don't reailze it." "Yes. My brother, one experience. His age was nine; mine eleven. *E.* No." "Yes. At age twelve; my uncle would find me alone and play with my breasts (what little I had) and rub my clitoris through my clothes. I hated it but did not know how I could reject it as he was my uncle. *E.* Yes." "No. Certainly never interested in either father or sons. But wonder what would have happened if I'd had any brothers." "No. But I am aware of incestuous feelings."

"Potential" nudists

"Once. When I was fifteen and my brother was eighteen. *E.* No." "Around the age of eight I engaged in a very limited amount of sexual behavior with my older brother (twelve years of age). *E.*—" "A kind of mutual masturbation with my younger brother. *E.* I am not sure, I have always felt guilty about this." "Yes. Age thirteen first cousin, twice removed (male). *E.* Yes—subconsciously embarrassed, disgusted with myself." "Yes. When I was about eight and my little brother was five. It was useless, no interest on my brother's part. *E.* No." "This occurred with my brother. There was no actual intercourse but more of an investigation of our anatomy and a few awkward attempts at inserting the penis. My brother was around six or seven and I was about nine or ten. *E.* None whatsoever." "Genital manipulation by father at age three–four. One painful attempt at penetration. Intercourse twice with father at age nine. Rather innocent sexual play with my brother, at ten–eleven. *E.* Of course. Much treatment has not dispelled completely the complicated reactions I had to my sexual experiences with my father."

"Potential" nudists (lesbians)

"I was violated by my brother. *E.* Yes." "Used to with younger sister when younger—it was a game she and I made up where I would be the prince and she the princess. *E.* No—maybe contributed to my homosexuality." "No. My brother-in-law *tried* to rape me, so did an uncle. *E.* No."

REACTION TO THE THOUGHT OF BEING RAPED
IN A NONVIOLENT BUT FORCEFUL MANNER

Since it is well known that there are a number of women who, at times, enjoy the feeling of being "taken" and "overpowered" during the sexual act, the following question was asked of our subjects: What is your reaction to the thought of being raped, in a nonviolent, but forceful manner?—It should be emphasized that while the term rape was used, actually, as worded, this question does not refer to the typical violent and criminal assault type rape situation in which the victim's life is threatened severely. Rather, it pertains to a sexual experience in which the female is overwhelmed and forced to submit, but *without* any threat to her of bodily harm.

In response to the above question, 27 per cent of the nudists and 42 per cent of the "potential" nudists indicated that they viewed such an occurrence in a positive manner. No significant relationship, however, was noted between either the levels of self-esteem or security feelings of the respondents and a favorable reaction to the thought of being raped in a nonviolent, but forceful manner.

As will be seen from the statements presented below, there were several factors which played a prominent role in motivating the subjects to respond favorably to the aforementioned question. Among these were: the fantasying of an attractive and sexually appealing male, and the conscious or unconscious realization that such an experience would automatically resolve ambivalent feelings and personal conflicts concerning certain sexual desires, and at the same time absolve the "victim" of any feelings of responsibility or guilt.

Some of the comments reported by the subjects were as follows:

Nudists

"Fantasy—sounds great—must try it sometime." "Attractive idea." "Once I might have feared it—for fear of becoming pregnant by other than my husband. Now it wouldn't phase me." "I used to think I'd rather die than go through rape, now I don't honestly know." "It would depend on the man. In general, it seems rather boring." "Very attracted to thought, but would probably make me sick unless the man was attractive to me." "If the man was appealing, clean, and my desire for sex just right, I would enjoy it very much." "It would depend by whom—I prefer a little intellectual rapport with my sex." "I would love it if he did not want to stab me or hurt me or kill me." "Desirable." "Normally, I'd say no—but if I were love starved and the man was attractive to me, it would be different." "Possibly exciting and different." "Would be exciting." "I like to have my husband be very forceful with me at times. I suppose this forcefulness satisfies an inner desire to be raped." "Interesting." "There are several men I've known whom I'd like to make love with, but won't because I believe in being faithful to my husband—but if they raped me, my husband couldn't object. I like the idea." "I don't think that I would care to be raped—unless possibly I was strongly attracted to him and there would be no other way." "Pleasant, but a fear of pregnancy might override other reactions." "By a stranger, I'd probably pass out— if it was someone I knew it wouldn't be so bad." "I think I would like it." "It used to be a main ingredient in my adolescent fantasies. It is still exciting to a degree." "Exciting. My boy friend wants to tie me but so far we haven't done this." "Would depend on circumstances. Probably exciting if I was attracted to the person to begin with; otherwise probably repulsive." "It does not bother me except that I am afraid of VD. Otherwise, it has happened to me many times by men who were in a hurry. I enjoyed it." "Very exciting; in fact it is a frequent part of my fantasies." "I think I would probably enjoy it very much." "At times (usually fantasy) the thought seems pleasant; at other times it seems childish and as if the results of such an encounter would be insufficient." "I like it. But only by my husband." "It would surely tax my ingenuity! Relax and enjoy myself? Knee him in the balls? Cooperate, then bite him? Let yourself be led astray while you are still worth leading?" "Before pills I would have been terrified. Now, I think it would be quite an experience—once." "Depends on who rapes me. Someone tried once and I found it disgusting and frightening (this only happened a few months ago so fear was not because of lack of experience)." "Repulsive." "[Lesbian] I would be so frightened I wouldn't know what to do and so ashamed I'd feel dirty and unfit to touch." "I don't like it. Wouldn't enjoy being forced into it. I would put a mental block and would not reach a climax. Would pretend to enjoy it so he'd hurry and get off." "I would not like it, since I feel that I have to like the man before I would have intercourse with him." "I don't think I would like being raped, violently or any other way. I don't have to be forced into sex to relieve any guilt about doing it, and I like being a consenting active partner. The only forcefulness I want is for the man to be assertive instead of hesitant."

"Potential" nudists

"I think I'd like it." "I wouldn't mind it at all as long as I wouldn't get pregnant. I feel I would feel honored that somebody loves my body." "Sounds interesting." "Would like it, I think." "Might not be bad if done by the right person." "I get intensely excited by it and aroused in the gut—but I could socially 'turn off' the awareness and simply not react." "Sounds exciting, if it were by someone to whom I was attracted, yet I know I'd not like the idea at all at the time. Curious ambivalence, can't explain it." "I like the idea." "Although I don't think I really would like to be raped, at times I do find the idea exciting." "Great—once in a while. After I have known him for a time." "I don't approve of this—but I think I'd like it." "If I knew I was protected against pregnancy and liked the partner, I might not resist too much." "It would depend who was doing the raping." "Sounds interesting." "It's exciting—but only by an attractive man—one I would want as a lover anyway. It resolves the conflict of wanting sex but feeling obligated to say no because of social conventions or personal superego restrictions." "It's a nice fantasy." "I don't really think I'd mind." "When I was frigid I would have loved it—but now I enjoy knowing and understanding people and being understood. The physical aspect isn't so important." "It is very appealing. Forceful, dominant, and sexually strong men are very exciting—though I don't desire a passive role. Mostly, it sounds very appealing to be taken and used (nonviolently) by a man of great sexual prowess." "I would like it." "By husband? Great!" "I don't find this thought unpleasant." "Yes. Go get em!" "If you are referring to being 'raped' by someone attractive to you, then I no longer consider this rape but probably something you wanted to happen. The thought of being 'taken' in a forceful manner by someone very appealing is stimulating to me. However, I wouldn't consider it rape." "Kind of favorable and then again—don't really know. It would be interesting to find out." "I don't really think I'd mind." "If in a nonviolent but forceful manner and with someone I cared to be with, it might be feasible, but undesirable if otherwise." "Kind of exciting, but depends on the person. I mean, if you asked,

How would you react to being raped by so-and-so? I could answer more definitely." "I just might like it, but only if I already knew and liked the man." "Fun—exciting." "Most unpleasant, but not frightening." "I wouldn't ever want it to happen if I was sober. (If I was drunk I don't know)."

"Potential" nudists (lesbians)

"Like idea very much—depends much on whether I knew the person and if I like him or she." "Slightly interesting." "Depends on the attractiveness and attitudes of the male.—Could enjoy it under some circumstances—if given opportunity for orgasm." "Violently negative." "Scares the hell out of me.—I'd probably kill the bastard." "Horrible." "He'd have to kill me to do it."

✶✶✶✶✶ 23 ✶✶✶

MAJOR MISTAKES MADE BY MALES IN THEIR LOVE-MAKING AND SUGGESTIONS OFFERED BY SUBJECTS

To be adept at the highly delicate art of love-making requires, among other things, that one possess much sensitivity, skill, ingenuity, and sexual knowledge, as well as an appreciation and awareness of the needs, desires, and idiosyncrasies of one's sexual mate. Since these are attributes which have to be learned and developed, and there are no institutions where they are taught formally, it is not surprising that as lovers, many males (and females) in our society leave much to be desired. In the hope, therefore, of eliciting information which eventually could serve as a source of reeducation, the following question was asked of the subjects: In your opinion what is the major mistake men make with respect to their love-making and sexual expression?

The most predominant mistakes committed by males, as described by the nudists, included the following themes: a) They are too selfish, b) They do not engage in enough sexual foreplay and do not prepare the woman sufficiently for the act, c) They are too much in a hurry— too fast, d) They do not make certain that the woman has been satisfied, e) They are not gentle enough—too forceful and crude, f) They lack imagination in love-making techniques. Among the other mistakes made by males in their love-making and sexual expressions, as recorded by the nudists, were as follows: g) They are not aggressive enough, h) They are not romantic enough and don't tell the woman often enough that they love her, i) They are overly concerned about satisfying the woman, j) They do not sense their partner's mood, k) They do not communicate verbally during the sexual act, 1) They are inexperienced and ignorant (especially concerning the importance of the clitoris), m) They are too vulgar and profane, n) They think females don't know anything about sex. In general, the comments of the "potential" nudists were very similar to those of the nudists.[1]

Thus, it can be seen from the above summary of responses (as well as the protocols presented below) that while there are certain aspects of behavior relating to sexual expression which are generally viewed by females as objectionable, as stated earlier in Chapter 11, there is no *one* style or form of love-making which all females always find desirable or undesirable. Rather, different females prefer different approaches and techniques at different times.

Comments related by the respondents included the following:

Nudists

"Not sensing their partner's mood." "They do not relax and make certain that the woman involved has satisfaction. Also, they are reluctant to discuss the act either before, during, or after." "I like to be kissed and held for a while and aroused! With sex I have to be the aggressor almost always and I don't like it. I feel most men are not aggressive enough." "Not preparing the woman enough in advance. They should build up the event by being kind and gentle, loving and thoughtful. Take her out to dinner, show her you love her. Create a need and desire on her part." "They think that their penis is God's gift. When in reality many women (like me) need masturbation [manipulation by male] during or after intercourse to reach a climax." "Men are too rough, they should be more gentle and use clean hands. Follow directions of the woman." "Some men get hung up on being sure the woman is 'satisfied.' I find this inhibiting at times. I think there is a point at which a man should let his own sensations take over—when this happens my own response can be freer." "Vulgarity." "Move too fast; for me not enough gentle caressing of skin." "Their greatest mistake is reaching a climax too soon. Very little love play before, being too clumsy and in most cases letting the woman do most of the preliminaries." "Men without imagination in love-making—men who say that sucking a cunt is distasteful." "His demand for *frequency* makes it commonplace instead of a rare experience to crave and look forward to. I am constantly being accused of not loving him enough because I don't display the intense interest in sex that he does. Social criticisms destroy the feeling of love during intercourse. He insists that I must reach an orgasm regardless how I feel about it." "Not enough foreplay. Some are narrow-minded about a woman expressing the way she feels by doing whatever she feels. They feel it is up to the man to start the love-making." "Failing to caress the clitoris gently and

[1] The lesbians were not asked any question relating to mistakes made by males.

steadily during intercourse." "I dislike men who are very unromantic, crude and violent." "Using the woman as a thing instead of a human being. Being interested only in his own needs, not giving the woman time to build up to full participation. Getting in a rut with the same old sexual habits and not exploring new ways. Having no sense of humor (this is one of the most important needs). Thinking of sexual activities as something sort of evil or forbidden—but necessary to get rid of a biological urge.—Thinking that one round of sexual inter-course should serve to clear up and extinguish forever any major dis-agreements or differences the couple might have." "Sometimes men force themselves on women—thinking only of satisfying themselves instead of satisfying the woman. If she is satisfied she will try harder to satisfy him." "My one objection is to men who must make con-versation while making love. There are men who need to use profane talk—I can tolerate that, but do not wish to respond.—Others must always describe what they are doing or describe other acts and situa-tions during their activities. I need to concentrate on what I am doing and feeling, and find conversation unnecessary and distracting. This presumes that otherwise I have found a lover to my taste, i.e. no inhibitions." "Men in general are not apt to tell a woman that he loves her often enough." "When a couple get married, the man should try a woman out to see which way is best." "They don't take enough time to stimulate women—they leave women up in the air. They want women to be as easily aroused as they. They want women to be like sex-crazy novel and movie heroines—ready for bed instantly." "They dot not realize that sometimes sex is inconvenient and women need time to untense from the day's household activities. They also cannot seem to read the level of excitement in a woman if it isn't black and white." "There are too many things they 'hate'—perhaps they haven't found someone to love. Love brings out a lot of dormant expression." "Most men are too anxious about each individual sexual experience, like each one is a matter of life or death. That turns me off. You can only be compassionate with men like this—not passionate." "They don't take long enough for love play. They don't whisper sweet noth-ings. I like a man to talk to me when he's making love." "Lack of tenderness." "Premature ejaculation. Selfish." "Ignorance—not know-ing about a woman's body and finding the areas from which pleasure is derived most; especially the clitoris. Many men don't realize the sensitivity of this area and if manipulated well, how much pleasure it can give. . . . Another mistake may be that many men still don't recognize the equality between men and women in terms of sexuality. Also, a lack of communication between both persons about what exactly their relationship is, especially in regard to premarital sexual relationships." "Their lack of real interest in what is exciting to women. Also they are overly concerned with the connection between a woman's climax and their masculinity." "Most men are too concerned with the image of masculinity which they feel they must maintain to properly experience first-hand love-making. They worry more about the image than they do the love-making; consequently they are generally one-sided and unresponsive, inhibited, and as mechanical as if they were reading a sex manual as they went along. Thus, they create their own fears of not being considered a 'good lover' (masculine) and try to justify their fears by becoming 'more' masculine. (A vicious circle.)" "They expect a girl to warm up quickly to the touch alone; often they advance things too soon when a little patience would have the girl waiting for more. A few well-chosen words at the right time and in the right place will put almost any girl in the mood, especially if he takes the trouble to know the girl's preferences. She likes to be surprised to find out how much he *does* know about her." "Some men are only interested in satisfying themselves and don't take time to help their wives enjoy sex. I think this plays an important part in so many divorces and running out on husbands." "Some are overly aggressive and some are overly concerned with the obligation to please the female." "Men don't seem to use sex as an emotional thing as much as I do, and while they take adequate care of the physical side of satisfaction, they too often fail to satisfy me emotionally. I don't necessarily believe that they have to love me (nothing irritates me more than to have a man tell me he loves me because he thinks that's the only way to get me in bed), but I don't like being looked on only as a sexual being. I'm not saying that most men are cold emotionally. They just don't know that there is more to sex than just physical satisfaction for a woman. They too often assume that just because they are adequately turned on, I am too." "Too much talk with no physical contact. An assumption that my clitoris is all important. It doesn't take much manipulation to completely numb my clitoris. Physical roughness. I know this is difficult to judge because some women require a heavy touch. I require a very gentle lover. . . . I demand verbalization of what is going on, particularly at the time of ejaculation; but I don't always verbalize what I feel unless specifically asked to do so . . . I think that the assumption that sex is the only important thing is a mistake men make with me. Sex is quite important but communication is more so. Sexual relations are a form of communication." "They are too distant after sex. Some of them jump on their wives without thinking of kissing and caressing them." "They only think of themselves—they do not try to make the woman have an orgasm or are not even aware as to whether she had an orgasm or not. My husband is the rare exception, probably because I have made him aware of this, as I have so much trouble obtaining an orgasm." "Inconsiderateness. They often don't care if you are 'with them' . . . I hate men who indulge in sex and then apologize. It should be a mutual pleasure and that is all. (That is, outside of marriage.)" "Most American men are disgustingly stupid. They need to have the dirt washed out of their minds and mouths. They need to have less 'Mama' and more of male companionship as children. They take for granted that a girl knows all about it when usually she knows nothing at all. They are too smug; too superior. They have no respect for their partner and start pawing her before she gives her permission to be pawed. An individual is the temple of the Holy Spirit and no one has the right to touch another without expressed permission. They do not know the meaning of the words sensitive and gentle." "There is too big a rush to have sex and not make love." "I don't think most men know enough about manual manipulation of the clitoris." "I think they forget the importance of using pet names and praise to their wives—just an 'I love you' seems to become sufficient. I think 'I love you,' '[pet name]' or whatever he used when you dated would show that old 'spark' from before marriage."

"Potential" nudists

"Too rough, in too much of a hurry, forget the needs of partner." "Men, on the whole, are too concerned with themselves. They seem to forget that we also have to be satisfied. Many times they forget little but important things like nibbling on the neck, 'Frenching' the ear, stroking the body in general." "Too hard, too fast." "Insufficeint sex play before intercourse; failing to put the woman at ease so she can enjoy herself; failing to use a variety of positions; not satisfying the woman before having his own orgasm; treating the woman in too delicate a manner; showing little or no affection after intercourse; failing to respond to a woman's sexual desires when his own are not keen." "Many are afraid to touch me. They think I am glass or something fragile. They are afraid to express their real feelings and wishes." "Not taking enough time on foreplay or the effect of love talk (not necessarily obscene) on the sex act." "Lack of consideration as to his partner's satisfaction (reaching orgasm). This could be a mistake on the part of the woman also—selfishness." "I refuse to be 'used' and dislike obvious lines, also disrespect, indiscretion—sexual activity is very personal and private and should never be broadcasted." "Not enough foreplay to where a woman is aroused and the ignorance of how to have sexual relations—or knowing how to play with a woman correctly to get her aroused." "They are too hurried in their love-making. They also assume that a woman is frigid if she does not have an orgasm during intercourse. I find intercourse pleasurable even without a climax. Also, too few men make inquiries as to what their partner finds pleasurable." "They fail to honor the *love* needed, don't protect and care for body and emotions of partner, too direct an assault on the clitoris; they 'hop on and hop off.'" "They seem to feel that affection is reserved for love-making alone; most are very timid about using a variety of sexual techniques; most men are abysmally ignorant about the female body." Most often they are unaware of a woman's need for *emotional* (rather than physical) arousal and satisfaction." "They forget that a girl can also wish to take and increase her pleasure through response and active caresses, etc. Too often I have been told, 'You just relax, you don't need to do anything.'" "They forget caresses and fondling once entrance has been achieved. They overevaluate their ability to satisfy." "Many are too quick and don't pay any attention to the woman's needs; not enough foreplay or after play; too conventional and rigid." "Not being free and spontaneous—afraid to enjoy themselves without restrictions and not being aware enough of the woman to know whether she is being satisfied enough. Or feeling that technique is an adequate substitute for a warm feeling —it isn't." "Worry too much about the woman's reaction to their love-making." "Husbands seem to make sex too foremost in the marriage. I love and enjoy sex very much but I hate to have my husband show affection constantly toward the sexual organs just in passing. They should also learn their partner's moods." "They don't perfect techniques of arousal and don't want to exert themselves to satisfy the woman." "I feel that I am being used as merely a body. Generally, they are too fast—sometimes too slow in that they get so involved in kissing they forget the rest of the body (this comes from inexperience). A girl loves to be fondled. Often a boy is too rough because he is excited when approaching my genitals, which are fantastically sensitive. Because boys are often rough I don't enjoy having my genitals stroked." "I feel the major mistake men make is that they seem to have little respect for women as individuals with minds to think, with emotions much as their own. They see women as sex objects or 'the ole lady.' . . . The male whom I find sexually attractive is one who is sensitive to a woman's feelings, who likes to 'kick' an idea back and forth with her, sharing a relationship on a one-to-one basis.—I worked [a number of years]. I spent more time around men than women. I found that the ideal type men were those who had better attitudes toward sex and could talk about it freely, without guilt, and who were sincere in their compliments, and not embarrassed to let you know in a direct manner that they would like to go to bed with you. . . . In actual love-making, I feel communication is the greatest failing. I want to be able to tell my partner what I like and what I don't like, just as I want the same from him. I want the most pleasurable experience I can get, just as I want to give the most pleasure. . . ." "One man I'm involved with at present (almost over) is strange. He's said he resents the fact that almost every time we've made love I've wanted to. He wishes I wouldn't want him so he can force me or something, I guess—or feel he's completely dominant and I'm at his mercy." "Rolling over and going to sleep after reaching climax. Too often satisfying own needs and ignoring mate." "They assume that women want to be and should be passive and often don't understand what it takes for a woman to achieve orgasm. I think too that premarital sex is no more wrong for a woman than it is for a man (she just has to be careful). I think men often think women who've had sex have already been had and don't want to marry them —I think this idea is ignorance displayed." "Often they seem not to really enjoy it—rather they go into it as though they are driven and must accomplish the ejaculation act as quickly as possible. With some thought and concern about making the union a sharing experience, things would be improved. Sometimes they're in such a hurry to have their orgasm they don't spend enough time in foreplay—in getting their whole body rather than just their penis ready to make love." "The lack of some verbal expression, showing a lack of aggressiveness on the part of partner." "A lot of them are awfully casual . . . not enough of a leader . . . too cooperative." "They want to be satisfied and they don't give a fuck how they do it. I have run into many blundering, lame men, and it makes me think I will more than likely be masturbating for the rest of my life, unless you come up with something that will snap those creeps into believing that they don't know a thing about it." "Men in a casual relationship are often too shy—they seem to be afraid to offend. In a more intimate, long-lasting relationship they seem to lose interest but are not willing to make the effort to keep variety and excitement in the sexual act itself." "Not attempting to learn to meet needs of partner. Also, not realizing that the emotional aspect (expression of love) is of major importance to women." "Lack of consideration for woman's fulfillment—purely 'animal' attitude toward sex.—No finesse." "Unbelievably enough—the thing I dislike most is 'over concern,' 'Did you have an orgasm, Honey?' makes me furious—mostly because it's such an un-male way to react. So—sort of weak-kneed. Most men just aren't loose enough or relaxed enough."

SUGGESTIONS OFFERED

So that the participants could be given a chance to make constructive suggestions as to ways in which males may enhance their love-making approaches and techniques, the following statement was included in the questionnaire: Make any suggestions that you would like to in regard to Question 27 on preceding page 7. (Q 27 read: In your opinion what is the major mistake men make with respect to their love-making and sexual expression?)[2]

The suggestions recorded by the nudists were diversified and included the following themes: a) Men should take more time in their love-making and engage in more extended sexual foreplay. b) Men should educate themselves (through reading) in matters relating to love-making techniques and heterosexual expression. c) Men should be more considerate of the emotional needs and desires of women. d) Men should express their love for women more often (before, during, and after the sexual act). e) Men should be more romantic and seductive. f) Men should learn more about the emotional aspects of women. g) Men should make sure that the woman achieves an orgasm. h) Men should compliment women with respect to their love-making techniques. i) Men (husbands) should be more passionate in their love-making. j) Men should realize that a woman does not always have to reach a climax in order to enjoy the sexual act. (Women take great pleasure from pleasing men.) k) Women should tell men what they want done and how to do it.—The suggestions offered by the "potential" nudists were very much like those of the nudists.[3]

Suggestions made by the subjects included the following:

Nudists

"Go slowly; explore sexually together; put your mate first; use variety." "Men usually seem to approach intercourse as just sex instead of *making love*. I like to think of it as more than just physical fulfillment—but as a deep mutual fulfillment also. The joy of being

[2] This question is repeated here for the benefit of the readers of this book. It was not repeated as such in the questionnaire.
[3] The above question was not included in the questionnaire designed for lesbians. Consequently, no such suggestions were obtained from the group of "potential" nudists (lesbians).

needed and loved is one of the dearest emotions possible." "Men should come to an agreement with themselves, believe in themselves, and realize they don't have to appear anyway but the way they are, to be 'masculine.' They should learn that 'masculinity' is no substitute for consideration, awareness of other people (especially in sex), ability to express one's feelings without shame or fear of being reproved, and sufficient lack of inhibition to be able to give oneself openly to provide mutual rapport." "I would like to have a man make love to me as if it were the first time (that he and I had been out together) and he wasn't sure I'd accept going all the way until I finally said yes." "If men would really try to know the woman and her body (this also works the other way) he would know how to give her the greatest pleasure. Also, I think women should be able to talk to their partners and tell them where to touch, kiss, etc., without being embarrassed. An open mindedness must be developed. Respect also must be developed—a true communication and honesty between two people—sometimes even or first on a sexual level." "More sex education is necessary in order that males and females understand their general differences in reaching orgasm—society should not create self-centered persons." "A girl likes to receive gifts such as candy, flowers, etc., provided she is sure of a man's intentions. She may respond to a phony build-up, but if she ever finds out about it, she is likely to feel like a prostitute or a fool. The best advice to give any man is 'be sincere.' . . ." "Be gentle, make sure the woman achieves an orgasm." "I wish he [husband] would be more like he was when we were first married. Then, he held me in his arms and kissed me and caressed me and was slow and gentle." "I suggest every man give his wife full attention and help her enjoy sex." "I think if a husband showed he was happy to be home, greeted his wife lovingly, enjoyed his meals, and wasn't afraid to say he appreciated you [his wife]—the average woman would fall over herself to please him." ". . . I like to be important in the sexual activity. When my hubsand is 'doing his duty,' just doing it because he thinks he should, I feel put out. At the same time, I want him to enjoy the act to the fullest. I think he does if he knows I do." "Only that men be aware of the woman's response and see that she obtains an orgasm. I have been left so tense and ready to climb the walls and my partner not even aware of how I felt." "That men swallow their inborn pride and get down to the business of reading some good *modern* books on sex. It doesn't all just 'come naturally.'" "Husband should approach when wife is in the right mood. Ensure with kind words and caressing; don't overlook 'The charm of Love.' Lovemaking and love-playing should be evening long." "Women like to be told how good it was and that it was appreciated—and followed by a little more love to taper her off." "Men should understand better the emotional aspects of females." "I like to be told that I am loved as well as physically desirable." "I like to be approached slow and gentle and be stimulated before intercourse." "Use of wine, candlelight, and romance beforehand. The element of seduction once in a while, *even* in marriage—otherwise what reason would there be for a person to keep up his appearance, etc." "I've found that men will do many things to please a woman—but most don't know how. It's up to the women to tell them . . ." "Men who are 'hip' sometimes make you feel that you are like LSD—an experience, not a woman. And some men get possessive—one lay and you have to be in love. While others act as if they had done you a favor." "I find that the man who takes time to caress and arouse his partner can usually get her to respond in such a way that he enjoys it more too. Also, if he lets her know that he really wants her to let go her reservations and give her all—it helps. . . ." "Husbands often make love with too much 'love' and 'respect,' rather than with passion as lovers." "My ideal in love-making is first a clean body to start with, a cocktail to mellow one, then the love play between the man and woman—the going down on the penis or vagina for arousing one's desires—fondling his testicles, sweet tender mouth kisses—then intercourse in the beautiful female with the most satisfying of orgasms." "Some men ignore the possibility that it gives a woman great pleasure to please them—and that she does not have to reach a climax every time. It should not be totally either way, of course." "Men should be taught that sex can be the most beautiful and complete form of communication with a woman . . ." "If women could stop using their sex as a threat, a hold-out, or a weapon, and stop exchanging their sex for material security—"

"Potential" nudists

"I think that a little prompting on the woman's part is necessary. I noticed that once a male catches on he becomes even more satisfied just from satisfying his partner (it becomes more mutual, as it should be.)" "If husbands or bed partners would try to take it easy and satisfy their mates a little before they get their satisfaction, there probably wouldn't be so many frustrated women around and maybe fewer divorces." "Change the double standard in the U. S. We are very narrow minded in this country. Sex should be taught in schools, and I think It would be a good idea if men were taught how to make love. So few men have consideration for the women." "Act yourself—be all *male.*" "Men should be honest and tactful—very caring; this would lead naturally to attributes most valued by women in their lovers." "Sex education for the younger generation so that they will be able to enter into a relationship free from prudish attitudes and guilt feelings." "Sex education classes might be a good idea, and should play down the 'conquering he-man' tradition." "I would like men to be forceful and firm in love-making without immobilizing me or putting me in a position where I can do nothing to actively give them pleasure." "I should like to see more affection shown by men before and after actual love-making. Education: I find men much more puritanical than women in their attitudes. The female body is really not all *that* mysterious." "If men would try to make the sexual experience as exciting as they can—and not be afraid to express warm, tender feelings for women as well as sexual feelings. They should experiment until they are good lovers—and should fully accept both themselves and their women as sexual beings and as individuals." "They are too careful." "Men should be willing to learn from a woman; they should feel free to talk about what each person likes and excites them; should realize that great as his cock is, it's not the only thing involved." "Husbands and wives should discuss their feeling toward sex and get to understand each other." "I think men and women should be more inventive and nontraditional, trying a variety of positions. Men should learn about a woman's sexual feelings—they should learn to achieve orgasm together. Women could reach climaxes earlier if men knew more about their physiological structure. I think instead of thinking they know everything about sex (our society promotes this 'legend'), men should try ridding themselves of many of their misconceptions and realize that women have a sexual drive, too. They should be willing to learn." "I have to masturbate in order to have an orgasm, so if men (there are some underground) would take the time to find these things out and wouldn't hop on like a sack of cement and think that you should really be going for it, it could be nice. But I think my problem is that I have never cared for anyone who cared enough for me to make it worthwhile." "Bone up on subject. Discuss with partner from time to time. Be romantic." "Teach boys reverence for the human body and sex act, that intercourse is an act, sex is worship in the temple of the body—not a gutter graveling or gymnastics in the back seat of a car." "Female needs affection after intercourse." "I feel that men who could still be loving (not love-making) after relations, would not make women feel so alone and unnecessary. It is the fast withdrawal and sudden rejection on the part of a lot of men that can make a women feel used instead of desired."

MARITAL HAPPINESS AND DOMINANT MATE

MARITAL HAPPINESS

According to recent reports, about one in every four marriages in the United States ends in a divorce.[1] When this figure is added to the number of separations which occur and the many unhappy marriages which exist, it becomes very apparent that in our society happy marriages are relatively rare. In view of this backdrop, therefore, it is particularly significant that in response to the question: How would you describe your marriage with respect to your feelings of happiness? a substantial majority of the nudists (76 per cent) employed such positive terms as happy, very happy, extraordinarily happy, exceptionally happy, extremely happy, good, very good, great, complete, etc. Only 19 per cent of the nudists described their marriages as being (or having been) unhappy. A few of the responses by these subjects were unscorable. (As was indicated in Chapter 2, 80 per cent of the nudists were married, three were separated, two were widows, 9 per cent were divorced, and five were single.)

In the case of the "potential" nudists, 50 per cent of the participants characterized their marriages as being (or having been) basically happy and 27 per cent viewed their marriages as being (or having been) unhappy.[2] Some of the responses were not scorable. The percentage of Mensa females who indicated that their marriages were (or had been) fundamentally happy was significantly lower than that of the nudists, but quite similar to that of the "potential" nudists.

While the very high percentage of essentially happy marriages among the nudists may, in part, be a reflection of the somewhat selective nature of our sample of subjects, it is also quite possible that actually there are significantly more happy marriages among "lib-

---

[1] Mace, D. R., "The Present Status of Marriage in the United States," *Medical Aspects of Human Sexuality*, 1968, 2, 14–26.
[2] The lesbians were not asked any question relating to marital happiness.

erated" social nudists than nonnudists. Although this is a question which may be answered conclusively only in terms of future controlled studies, in light of the overall findings of the present study, and especially those discussed in the latter part of this chapter (in regard to the relative dominance status of the marital partners), it is felt that there is a good possibility that such a difference exists.

Among the comments recorded by the respondents were the following:

Nudists

"I feel my marriage is unusually successful and we are both happy, creative people. I do not possess. I want to help my husband become the man he was intended to be." "I was happiest when it [the marriage] was over." "I have never felt more self-assured, confident, and happy in my life." "In comparison to most marriages we are happy. My husband *wants* to come home at the day's end. He is king and we all show him our love." "My only satisfaction in my marriage was in my children. I felt lonesome, degraded, bullied, humiliated. He was cold, unfriendly, bad tempered—and completely charming to the outside world." "My marriage at one time was very happy. My husband spent many years trying to get me to join group sex activity. I rebelled so bad. My happiness now comes from our children and my work." "I love my husband very deeply. I respect, appreciate, and need him. But he doesn't arouse me at all. I'm very happy when sex is not involved." "Very good. I am quite often delighted to feel myself thoroughly loving and 'in love' with my husband." "I'm very, very happy." "Very happy." "Very good." "Happy, we have a few areas of disagreements but we do not allow them to affect our overall happiness. Our ideas and philosophy are well-integrated." "Average to above average." "To the extent of sexual life, it is happy." "Complete." "I can't imagine being happier with anyone else. I consider our marriage unique in many ways and feel very lucky." "My husband is the only one who can satisfy my sexual desires to the fullest. This, to me, is the greatest happiness a man can offer. Material things become secondary. Being loved completely makes for a feeling of happiness. I have been married to the same man for [over twenty years]. We do not feel we cheat on each other—because we discuss every aspect of our sex lives—and assist each other." "My marriage ended before it began." "My marriage is the beginning of my happiness—all other happinesses stem from it." "My marriage is the major cause of my happiness in its every aspect." "Because we have such opposing views on many subjects including his insistence that I *must* reach orgasm even though I have more vitality without it, we make each other miserable." "Now I have a happy marriage—we are now sexually adjusted." "In general I am happily married, but not wholly in the sex relationship. I don't think a strictly exclusive sex relationship with one's husband leads to fulfillment of either spouse's sexual potential." "We are very happy and madly in love with each other." "I feel we are pretty happy. Sex is about the only thing I would like to change. My husband wants to let go but he doesn't know how. I feel that if I can be patient, with my help, he'll learn." "Had an unsuccessful marriage." "I am happy generally but worry about whether newly acquired ideas and experimentation will damage the marriage; but I feel more and more that same are making our relationship even stronger." "We have been married [over ten years] and each year is better than the last." "If I could live life over, I would want to live it exactly as I have. Everyday is happier than the preceeding one. We have been married [over fifteen years]." "As far as sex is concerned all [previous] husbands were terrific at first. I'd like to be 'happily married' if I could find the right man." "In bed, indifferent, although attracted to my husband physically—married life good—happy with husband." "We feel that we have a very happy relationship. The reasons we live together are many, including several mutual interests and an active sexual life. We feel it is important that we do not try to force each other into a mold, sexual (one partner) or otherwise." "I've been married and divorced twice. My ex-husbands were both very satisfactory lovers. I was not happy with their personalties. Physically, I was very happy." "An overall feeling of serene peace and happiness." "The Greatest: extraordinarily happy. Living and loving and enjoying the same things to make over twenty-five years of married bliss one continuous honeymoon." "I am not completely happy." "My marriage was unhappy. My love affair, now in its –th year, has brought me much happiness, given me confidence in my femininity, and added zest to my life." "Great." "Happiness is not relevant. We want to be together. Both of us tend to be miserable twenty-five to fifty per cent of the time—because we are not doing what we want, i.e. working in or at our respective [desired] endeavors." "I like and respect my husband. He is the most ethical person I know. We try to retain as democratic a relationship as possible considering that we're both individualists. We do not engage in deceit. What more could I ask? I'm not sure what happiness it." "Pleased with marriage situation." "We think we're exceptionally happy, fortunate, lucky, and clever." "When I was married I was quite contented. I wonder now if after three years of marriage a little variety on a mutual basis would not have been good for us though." "Happily married, satisfied, contented." "My husband and I were perfectly mated and very happy . . . We shared everything together, sorrows and fun." "Was terribly unhappy the last two years of my [short] marriage. Am much happier free." "I am happy except my husband likes sex too much and is a nudist." ". . . Generally . . . I am most happy with him. He is kind to me and loves me." "Generally happy and secure; mutually enjoyable. I sometimes get restless and would like to have a chance to do more on my own, sometimes feel frustrated but this is due largely to the situation, not my husband . . ." "I feel I have a better than average marriage. I was very lucky in marrying the man I did. He's a very good and understanding man. Everything is discussed between us—including sexual disagreements." "Happy as long as I can acquire sexual satisfaction. When I can't do this, I find sexual satisfaction extramaritally." "[Widow] I consider that my marriage was happier than average. Sexually, we were completely compatible; attitudes were generally compatible and love for each other was very strong." "By and large we are very happy together. I wish I could respond to his touch more often, for I enjoy sex only then and it makes him happier than when I just passively comply with his wishes. He understands my needs very well, but I wish he'd learn a few tricks I didn't teach him." "I feel that marriage-type love is a blanket excuse for possession. I am not happy with my marriage. I think it is detrimental to the individual. We feel we have destroyed each other." "Most of the time I'm very happy. My marriage is a very good one. I'm happier now than I've ever been." "I feel I am beginning to make an adjustment and be happy with my husband. I love my husband; however, I periodically desire an emotional and physical relationship with another man." "I feel satisfied with my marriage most of the time. We are still learning and growing together." "I believe we are happier than most couples. I am sure there are others more sexually active but we are pretty well adjusted—*both* have made sacrifices in trying to adjust, so it isn't a one-way relationship." "My husband and I have been married [over ten years]. This is a first marriage for both of us. I have no doubts here at all. I am very happy and love my husband very much." "I feel that my marriage is as happy as one is entitled to expect."

"Potential" nudists

"My feeling of happiness comes through success in my personal endeavors. I try not to depend on my husband for happiness—but try to develop this feeling within myself." "I am happier living alone." "With my sex life, I'm very happy. But there is something I'm not happy about—nothing is perfect." "I have never been as content and happy as I feel now." "I feel happy, comfortable, secure, and very well loved." "Marriage has made me happy, emotionally secure, and pregnant." "Moderate, fluctuating, less challenging than my affair [with another female] was sexually, often very fulfilling. Improving rapidly." "I'm not really happy. I've only stayed [married] because of the children." "My marriage was a bore. Sexually, it was so-so. The sexual part neither contributed to the marriage nor broke it up. It was one of those things that just should not have happened." "My marriage has been happy except for the sex angle, my husband and I have many things in common." "I wasn't happy while I was married." "Quite happy—general contentment with periods of great joy." "I can truthfully say that I am happier than being along, and miss my husband very much when he is traveling [but have problems]." "Happily married, with plenty of bumps." "Right now my sexual life with my husband is most unsatisfying. We have had 'good spells' in the past, and I hope for improvement. During the times when we satisfied each other the glow of happiness carried into everything in my life." "Unhappy. My marriage was very unhappy for so many reasons—sexually as well as physically. Immature marriage." "The relationship between my husband and myself is the most important thing with regard to feelings of happiness. We both feel we have a unique marriage. We really like one another, first of all, plus being attracted. We respect and are proud of each other. We give feelings of security to one another. This didn't just happen; we have worked at it. We simply work and play together and like being in each others presence." "Awful—it was hell and I felt guilty because I was miserable [divorced]." "My marriage provides little happiness." "Compared to most, it is very happy. We are both quite neurotic and depend a lot on each other." "[Widow] He was wonderfully tender and replete with understanding and consideration." "I know of none happier." "Am not always happy, but have a most satisfying relationship on all levels that I have ever encountered."

DOMINANT MATE

Based on clinical and empirical evidence, Maslow has stated that "The best marriages in our society (unless both husband and wife are definitely secure individuals) seem to be those in which the husband and wife are at about the same level of dominance-feeling or in which the husband is *somewhat* higher in dominance-feeling than the wife. In terms of status this means that marriages with equality status or 'split-dominance' status, or the husband in dominant status (but not markedly so) are most conducive to happiness and good adjustment for both husband and wife. In those marriages in which the wife is definitely dominant over her husband, trouble is very likely to ensue in the form of both social and sexual maladjustment unless they are both very secure individuals."[3] In view of these comments and the findings presented at the beginning of this chapter concerning the preponderance of happy marriages among our nudist subjects, it is especially significant that in response to the question: Whom do you feel is more dominant psychologically (in general), you or your husband? 61 per cent of the nudists indicated that their husbands are (or were) more dominant, 12 per cent reported that no one marital partner was the more dominant, while only 20 per cent described themselves as being (or having been) more dominant. A few of the responses were unscorable.

With respect to the "potential" nudists, 36 per cent disclosed that their husbands are (or were) more dominant, while 13 per cent stated that neither spouse was more dominant and 36 per cent described themselves as being (or having been) more dominant.[4] Several of the responses were not scorable.

Apropos to the observations made by Maslow pertaining to the relationship between marital happiness and the dominance levels of husband and wife, it is of further importance to note that of those nudists who stated that their husbands were more dominant than themselves, 86 per cent characterized their marriages as being essentially happy,[5] while only 65 per cent of those who viewed themselves as being more dominant described their marriages as being happy. Particularly impressive was the finding that all the nudists who stated that neither mate was more dominant rated their marriages as being basically happy. A similar pattern was observed in connection with the results obtained from the group of "potential" nudists. For instance, of those subjects who reported that their husbands were more dominant, 71 per cent signified that their marriages were happy, and of those who described themselves as being more dominant, 42 per cent

[3] Maslow, A. H., "Self-esteem (Dominance-Feeling) and Sexuality in Women." *Journal of Social Psychology*, 1964, *16*, p. 278. Reprinted by permission of the author and The Journal Press.

[4] The lesbians were not asked any question pertaining to the factor of dominance in marriage.

[5] A few of the responses involved in this relationship were not scorable.

indicated that their marriages were happy. Moreover, of those subjects who revealed that neither marital partner was the more dominant, 80 per cent characterized their marriages as being basically happy. The results derived from the study of Mensa females (those with very high I.Q.'s) lend further support to the remarks made above by Maslow.

Responses reported by the subjects included the following:

Nudists

"My husband—but not in the sense of overbearing—just a leader and doer." "I am, but not happily so. There are times when I wish he were dominant." "My husband—I don't feel strongly enough about things to argue, so I give in easily to his ideas." "My husband—I am sexually dominant with my husband." "My husband. I couldn't respect a man I could dominate. He is both leader and collaborator and my most constructive critic." "My husband is because I feel he should be." "Husband. I cannot deny his wisdom." "My husband, I suppose, but I like him to feel that way so I don't really know." "My mate. I also feel that if he weren't dominant, I couldn't respect him or respond to him sexually." "My husband definitely. While this disturbs me at times, I don't think I could respect a man that wasn't dominant." "Husband. I suspect that as I acquire more education I will approach him in psychological dominance. We understand and see through each other pretty well." "It's a tossup. He's stubborn and I'm mean." "Husband probably, although we each make concessions and adjustments in specific situations." "I am definitely the dominant personality in our household. I am outspoken to a fault. I am gregarious; I make all decisions; I am opinionated, decisive, and generally the guiding factor in our home." "About equal. Usually if I initiate action he becomes dominant toward the end of the evening. (After I have had sufficient number of orgasms and he reaches his climax.)" "Neither." "We are pretty well even." "About equal, sometimes he, sometimes I."

"Potential" nudists

"Me. I had to teach him to 'insist' on being a male I could look up to." "I was definitely. My husband's sex drive was extremely low even for a man twice his age (he was 21). He wanted to be dominated at home and at his work. I heartily disliked his dependence." "Husband in some things—myself in others." "Neither is more dominant; however, because of my husband's higher degree of education and age, he frequently takes the leading part in conversations or personal situations." "I was and didn't realize it then." "I think we break about even." "Husband was when alive. I am now with my lover. Prefer former relationship." "My lovers—otherwise they wouldn't be in that position." "[Single] I would want a more dominant male [when subject marries]."

✳✳✳✳✳ 25 ✳✳✳

ADDITIONAL COMMENTS BY SUBJECTS

In order to afford the subjects an opportunity to express themselves in any way desired, concerning our study, the following statement was placed at the end of the questionnaire: Please add any additional information or comments which you feel will enhance the nature of this study.

Although the comments noted by the participants were quite varied, for the most part they pertained to nudism, nudists, and nudist camps, their reactions to the study, their attitudes about sex and marriage, and their feelings toward other females. The responses of the "potential" nudists (lesbians) dealt mainly with their homosexuality and thus were especially enlightening in this regard.

Among the additional points of information and comments recorded by the participants were the following:

Nudists

"Nudist couples seem to be happier because they are nonconformists (together with others) looking for happiness. Your study should not emphasize marriage; there are those of us who have had (and prefer) different types of relationships which are as meaningful (or possibly more) than matrimony. An intelligent affair with a sensible man can renew a woman's faith in herself and life." ". . . You have made me think. Good luck in your work." ". . . Sexual activity is very intense during pregnancy. (No fear of pregnancy.) I would be interested in the results of this study." "My husband will read this before I send it in. (He has asked me and I gladly let him.) This has not influenced my answers. We are open with each other as much as possible. [Subject was quite frank in her responses.]" "It would seem to me that the present-day girl could learn more enjoyment of sex—everything is much freer. In my day it wasn't 'nice' to talk sex and give away to

211

emotions. I never even undressed in front of my sister. It took a bit of doing to come to the state where I could get real satisfaction and pleasure for myself. Till then it was mainly the desire to please the man I loved. I am filling this out to represent the older generation. . . . Thought I'd fill it out to show that the older ones liked sex too."[1] "Your survey will no doubt prove the great *diversity* of female sexuality—we are all different individuals. Even after reviewing my answers I keep wondering about the degree of honesty in each. Anyway, lets at least say your questionnaire made it necessary for me to *think* and to face myself and my sex life as clearly as I possibly could in trying to explain it to another. My first reaction was that it's none of your damn business, but you really did me a great big favor in forcing me to see myself as I *think* I am. I'm so sorry I didn't type this material." "I'd like to see the results. When they are published, I hope you will make the findings or the reference to the findings available to the nudist magazines." "The freedom of fear of pregnancy is very important in sex." ". . . I can't notice any difference in our sexual life since becoming nudists. We always slept bare and made love bare." ". . . I would like to find out the results of this study. I hope the American Sunbathing Association will be notified when it is completed . . ." ". . . I dislike most women, they are gossips. I do not trust other women, even my closest friends. I am liked by most men, I dress for men. I knew both of my husbands before marriage and if I was ever in the circumstance where I was without a husband, I would definitely know a man before I would marry him, because I feel that the sex life has more to do with compatibility, respect, and the making of happiness than anything else; without a good sex life, true love leaves." "I was raised a Catholic and I think that this was very detrimental to my sexual outlook until I started to think for myself. How fortunate the children of nudists are; they won't grow up in ignorance of the human anatomy. They will have respect for the human body and no curiosity because they will know." "I have answered these questions very truthfully and enjoyed writing down my personal feelings. I feel that sex is really fun—the more you can learn about it and try, the more fun it is. I hope I have contributed to your study." ". . . I am a nudist and a figure model. I believe in free love for unmarried people. I do not believe in free love for married people." "It is ironic that most people associate nudity or nudism

---

[1] In the writer's book, *Sexual Behavior and Personality Characteristics,* Grove Press, 1966, there is a study which reveals that some persons of over ninety years of age are still active sexually.

with all sorts of moral and sexual excesses. In reality, the average 'organized nudist,' or 'true-blue,' as we sarcastically refer to them, is the most asexual human being alive. It is too bad that the general public can't be shown that a visit to a nudist camp would not result in their being immediately raped, etc.; and that a nudist camp is absolutely the safest place in the world you could possible be—short of a convent—if you are worried about being confronted with sex. We find the welter of rules so constricting and the majority of the people so conventional (psychologically, emotionally, spiritually,) that we rarely visit camps anymore. We have our own secluded little house, and we go nude there, or on the beach, on the desert, in the mountains—anywhere to get away from 'offendable' people." "I wish more people could regard nudists as average (apart from nudism). I have met some of the finest people I know at nudist camps. Most nudists do not drink or swear, and divorces and juvenile delinquents are rare. In our club of [over 100 couples], I know of only one divorce—no juvenile problems and . . . two of our teenagers were national merit scholars. With no clothing you must refuse to lie to yourself about yourself physically—and this seems to carry over psychologically. Everyone must then become more relaxed and at home with himself and with others." "My husband and I are very happily married and I accredit this mostly to our active and successful sex life. My husband lets it be known he doesn't desire any other woman and I definitely don't desire another man." "I don't feel that having become a nudist has affected our sex life; it is still enjoyable and probably a little more wholesome." "Perhaps a few questions on the female's attitude about pornography—Is it stimulating? Is it used? Is it thought to be dirty? Are pornographic pictures or reading matter used to stimulate? I regard pornographic pictures I have seen as antisexual; they turn me off. Reading pornography is sometimes exciting. . . . Something that is very important to me is the way my husband's skin smells. I find that very stimulating. In general, I do not like him to use colognes, but prefer the natural odors of clean skin and hair. Also I find men who are in general 'hairy' are those who excite me the most. My husband is 'hairy.' I'm sure I never would have married him if he were not." "A fear of pregnancy has dominated our sex life. Several years ago a vasectomy was performed, but so many years were lost . . ." "Perhaps I am too selective. I would rather go without intercourse for sometime, than have it with a man who is not very appealing. I have often given in to the sexual urge with less than ideal men and found it unrewarding. If I am with a man who is attractive to me, I enjoy the sexual act and contact with his body even when orgasm is not reached." "I am strongly of the opinion that sexual repression and conflicts are a major cause of today's social crimes. I think society has too clearly defined what is 'proper' about sex and what is not. Collective progress toward freedom from these notions will be slow; it depends on individual enlightenment to a large degree. All we can do is spread enlightenment as best we can; drops of water make an ocean. I wish sex were not used so much in advertising. That has done much to lessen the intelligent person's respect for one of God's finest gifts to us." "Too bad you did not ask about anal intercourse. It would be interesting to know how many women engage in this activity and their attitudes toward it. I find it very exciting and enjoyable. Also, too bad you did not ask about experiences with Negro men and white women. . . ." "My husband and I were matched up by an IBM machine. We get along pretty well in most phases except the ones where he lied on the forms he filled out. Where it came to sex, I said I felt it was fairly important, so did he. He really acts as if it is not very important at all. He was ashamed to say otherwise. All in all he is kind, considerate, and thoughtful, so that makes up for a lot." "I really think lots of us are not meant to be monogamous. I have formed several very meaningful relationships with men. They have added considerably to my pleasure and understanding of myself and life in general. I hope and think I have added to theirs . . . I have had several offers of marriage which I have rejected." "Filling out this questionnaire has been sexually exciting. We wonder how you react to reading them." "I have always been a rebel, a nonconformist. Also, I was raised to be an individual and to experiment with life's gifts. . . . I am a strong advocate of wiping all sexually oriented laws from the books of all the states . . . and leaving personal sex and nudist acts to the individual. . . . There should be no stigma on Lesbians. . . . But sex must, at all times, be kept within the confines of a religious belief in the importance of the individual's right of choice, or freedom of enjoyment, of love. I have never had coitus with a man I did not have a love of some kind for. It could never be any other way." "There doesn't have to be sex because one is nude. I have never had sex, been approached sexually, or seen any type of sexual irregularity at any of the nudist camps that I have been to. I have found nudists to be more sexually mature than the nonnudist. Nonnudists are more overconscious of sex and nudity than nudists and talk of sex as 'dirty' and something to be joked about." "I hope this is of some use to you."

"Potential" nudists

"Most girls are hypocrites." "I think what you are doing is very commendable. So many people are in the Dark Ages when it comes to sex. I hope you and the others in your field will be able to bring about a Sexual Renaissance." "I enjoyed doing this [answering the questionnaire]. This also provided a good opportunity for introspection." "I do not think sex is evil. But yet it is not something I play with as some people do. As for cheating husbands and wives, I think they should find another mate—they all do anyway so why make a fuss. As far as my sex life goes . . . I finally found the right partner. I like to experiment with sex. Any position, and going down on him and him on me. Some people think it's digusting, but I feel as long as you both enjoy it there is nothing wrong." "Being a rebel of sorts, I guess I didn't pay much attention to society. I did what *I* felt was right. I don't go down for anyone that comes along. When I go with someone for a while, I become emotionally and sexually involved. To get to know a person completely I feel that you must also know him sexually." "Most girls are hypocrites and have the same tendencies as many men regarding sex (double standard, etc.). It's sad. I have had a very full and rewarding 'sex' life and 'love' life. I am *not* engaged. . . . I am amazingly 'happy' (so I'm told) and secure inside and I feel very alive. I have had extensive sexual experience, which is very 'immoral' according to our society (my mother wouldn't believe all this)—but I have felt no guilt or pressure as I usually trust my 'conscience'." "Sex is an exchanged awareness. . . . Love-making takes tender loving care and preparation. To me, being warm, happy, and ecstatically pleased are all important . . . The quality of the sex reflects how *alive* you are. I like to plan a time for pleasant, uninterrupted, safe sex. I can dominate or be dominated and enjoy either." "Good luck with your study." "[Subject enclosed a number of calendars with her responses.] The calendars are a chart I began keeping when I was —. These are the meanings of the symbols: X first day of period,—masturbation with orgasm,= twice same day or night; V erotic dream,+ erotic dream with orgasm." "You are welcome. All I can say is that I felt perverted until I read this questionnaire—maybe I am perverted but I don't feel that way anymore." "I have a great curiosity to know how other people get along and how they resolve their sexual difficulties. I have never had friends with whom I discussed such things and wonder if other people do. I feel it would be helpful to have such information. Maybe you'll publish something like this sometime." "Intellectually I feel quite free about sex, but as a result of very puritanical training in early childhood by a mother who hated being a woman, I am still very inhibited emotionally." "My husband asked that I not pluck the hairs around my nipples. Says he may cut my pubic hair. He would like me to 'eat' him and swallow it. In time this may happen, but not now." "I hope that in the world my children live in the words sex and fuck will be thrilling words and not dirty as they are considered now. I think until women get adjusted to the word 'fuck' and start fucking, sex will be whispered. I hope you can help us learn to shout!!!—Thank you for *your* time and effort!"

"Potential" nudists (lesbians)

"How long been practicing homosexual activities? Since age 17 yrs. —about 6 yrs. [This subject also reported being 'married' to another female.]" "When I was 17 (a senior in H.S.) I had an experience with a girl eleven months younger than myself. It only involved kissing. I began to have other feelings and thought myself to be the only person with such feelings. I didn't think my friend had such feelings and attributed her behavior to being motherless. I was all ready to call the whole thing off and stop seeing her when my mother, who knew about the situation, tried to 'scare me off,' and told me what it could lead to. This gave me new hope and I went out with renewed vigor. The result was we 'brought each other out'." "I am sorry I've had so little experience. For years I didn't really understand what I was, or would not believe it perhaps. Since moving to California I have been hoping to meet a partner, but so far no luck. I'm very shy in many ways and don't know how to make contacts. I'm proud to be able to take part in your study. Such work needs to be done. Perhaps society will learn to accept us in *some* measure through your work." "Your questions were very clear and complete." "I sincerely hope I have aided you in understanding a female homosexual. I, and most of the homosexuals I know, are not very different from the so-called 'straight' people. We love and hate; get hurt and bleed; try, and fail and succeed in our endeavors. Yet we are constantly on guard because we are not accepted by the 'normal' modes of society. I yearn for a permanent relationship. A husband-figure I can care for—and to care for me as a wife. A home and security and love. It isn't enough to love someone, you have to want and need them. The 'straight' people say we are unstable and flit from one partner to another. Perhaps, if this stigma of social acceptance was lifted—and we were allowed to legally form lasting relationships, i.e. marriage or even common-law standings—we would not be so erratic or under so much tension due to society's persecution. I often wonder how these 'straight' people can beat children, get drunk, hit their wives, run up bad credit accounts and then have the audacity to criticize a homosexual that holds down a good job, lives clean, pays her bills, and doesn't molest or attack anyone. Most homos I know (male and female) say that the biggest Hell of this life is that we cannot have children. So, therefore, we resort to pets for our 'children' images. Are we any worse than the masochists, sadists, necrophiles, pedophiles, peeping Toms, or rapists that walk the streets every night? I think not. . . . What I do in my own home behind closed doors with one (or more) consenting adults or animals, or just myself, is *my* business. As long as I don't hurt or coerce, or endanger, or infringe upon anyone else's rights, I don't see why I should be punished. Many times the 'acts' one performs are illegal, i.e. cunnilingus performed by a man on his wife . . . fellatio performed by a woman on her husband can be punishable by law . . . The law states that any act which cannot result in procreation is illegal and punishable by law, no matter *who* is doing it . . . Who is to say what is the norm and what is acceptable? The majority? But what really constitutes the majority? Which political leader, or judge, or psychoanalytical person has not something in his life to hide? . . . I should not like to bear upon my shoulders the responsibility of pointing my finger at a group of people, saying 'You're normal and you're not normal!' Would you like to bear that responsibility?"

✷✷✷✷✷ 26 ✷✷✷

SUMMARY AND CONCLUSIONS

Sample of Subjects

The sex lives and personality characteristics of 102 female social nudists from twenty-four different states (and Canada), as well as 73 "potential" nudists (some of which were lesbians) from fifteen states (and Canada), were studied through the use of an eight-page detailed questionnaire and Maslow's Security-Insecurity Inventory and Social Personality Inventory for College Women (test for self-esteem). While a major effort was made to obtain a representative sample of female social nudists, it is uncertain that this was accomplished. As in most investigations which deal with sexuality, the subjects who probably were least adequately represented in the present study, were those who may be described as being very conservative, inhibited, and puritanical. Consequently, the results reported and discussed in this book which pertain to the sexual activities and desires of social nudists need to be viewed mainly in terms of the present sample of subjects.

Method of Approach

From time to time, the question is raised relating to the merits of collecting research data by means of the personal interview approach as compared with the use of a questionnaire. This writer having utilized both techniques in sex research would like to offer the following observations.[1] While the personal interview approach enables the interviewer to present his questions in a clear and precise manner and to follow up the participant's responses with requests for clarifica-

---

[1] The personal interview approach was used in collecting the data which was reported in Chapter 5 of my book, *Sexual Behavior and Personality Characteristics.* (New York: Grove Press, 1966).

tion or additional information, the use of a questionnaire provides the subject with the sometimes very vital element of anonymity, which tends to result in the imparting of more intimate and detailed personal information. This seems to be especially true in regard to sex research and those persons who are inhibited. With females who are of high self-esteem and high security feelings (where there also exists a high respect for the interviewer), however, the personal interview technique does not appear to impose any important limitations. The ideal situation would seem to be one in which the investigator could have an opportunity to first go over the nature of his questions with his subjects while they are assembled in a group, and then to have them respond to a questionnaire in an anonymous manner.

Findings

Among the findings, all of which should be evaluated primarily in terms of the present samples of social nudists and "potential" nudists, were the following: 1) Practically all of the nudists and "potential" nudists characterized their attitudes toward sex in positive terms. 2) A majority of both the nudists and "potential" nudists described the strengths of their sexual drives as being either above average, strong, or very strong. Although no significant relationship was noted between the strengths of the sexual drives of the nudists and their levels of self-esteem, a significant relationship was found in regard to their security feelings.[2] 3) An overwhelming majority of both the nudists and "potential" nudists reported having engaged in masturbation, and in the case of the nudists, masturbatory activity was observed to be significantly related to high self-esteem. The primary way in which masturbation was learned by both the nudists and "potential" nudists was through self-discovery. While a variety of masturbatory techniques were utilized by the subjects, the predominant method employed by both the nudists and "potential" nudists involved the use of either the fingers or hand, and some kind of clitoral stimulation. A very great majority of both those nudists and "potential" nudists who had ever masturbated disclosed having experienced an orgasm from this practice, and more than half the females in each group engaged in fantasy at some time during the activity. In reference to the nudists, the experiencing of fantasies during masturbatory activity was found to be significantly related to high self-esteem. The fantasy described most prevalently by both groups of respondents had to do with the subjects

[2] As was stated in Chapter 2, in the case of the "potential" nudists, no correlations were computed between levels of self-esteem and sexual practices.

having sexual relations with a desired male. A very high percentage of both those nudists and "potential" nudists who were married (or had been married) and revealed that masturbatory behavior had been part of their life style indicated that they had done so since being married. The circumstance described most frequently in which masturbation had occurred since marriage was one related to the subject's husband being away. A large majority of the respondents registered an accepting attitude toward masturbation, and in the case of the nudists, a significant relationship was observed between an accepting attitude toward masturbatory behavior and high self-esteem. Finally, the practice of masturbation by the participants tended to have a positive effect on their marital sexual lives. 4) A substantial majority of both the nudists and "potential" nudists had been nonvirgins at the time of marriage or were nonvirgins and single. With respect to the nudists, nonvirginity and high self-esteem and virginity and low self-esteem were found to be significantly related. In regard to both the nudists as well as "potential" nudists, masturbatory activity was found to be related more to nonvirginity than it was to virginity. In reference to both groups of subjects, premarital coitus tended to have a beneficial effect on their marriages. 5) The position used most by both groups of respondents during coitus, as well as the most preferred one, was that in which the female was on the bottom. The second most preferred position was: female on top. With respect to the nudists, a preference for the "on top" position (in some way—including sitting on top), either solely or as one of several described, as compared with a preference for the "bottom," solely or as one of several mentioned, was significantly related to high self-esteem. 6) The practice of fellatio as well as cunnilingus by our two groups of subjects was very widespread; this was especially true in the case of the nudists. Moreover, the experiencing of *both* fellatio and cunnilingus by the nudists was noted to be significantly related to high self-esteem. Hand-genital contact with a male partner was engaged in by well over half the respondents in the two groups of subjects. All of the above sexual acts were viewed in an accepting manner by the overwhelming majority of those nudists and "potential" nudists who had experienced them. 7) A substantial majority of the nudists and well over half of the "potential" nudists reported that they achieved an orgasm from their sexual activities either "always" or "almost always." Although no significant relationship was found to exist between the frequency of orgasm attainment and feelings of self-esteem, when the security levels of those nudists who responded with the words "always" or "almost always" were compared with those who said "sometimes," "seldom," "rarely," or "almost never," while no statistically significant relationship was noted, a definite trend was observed. This trend, however, did not appear in regard to the security ratings of the "potential" nudists. 8) The fantasy experienced most by both groups of respondents during sexual activity (with a mate) involved thoughts of some other male. No significant relationship was observed between either self-esteem or security status and the experiencing of fantasy during sexuality with another person. 9) Many of the nudists and "potential" nudists indicated that they assume an active role in terms of initiating sexual activity, and a large majority of both groups of subjects reported that they are very responsive during the course of love-making. In regard to the nudists, the initiation of sex activity was found to be related strongly to high self-esteem. 10) Although a slow and gentle approach to love-making was the one preferred most by both the nudists and "potential" nudists, many subjects also disclosed that they desired a variety of approaches depending on such factors as their partners, emotional states, etc. In the case of the nudists a preference either solely, or as one of several mentioned, for a sexual approach described by such terms as sweeping, violent, explosive, rough, grabbed, quick, forceful, feeling of being dominated, hot and quick, wild and abandoned, and tantalizing, as compared with a preference for an approach characterized *only* by the words slow and gentle, slow, or gentle, was found to be significantly related to high self-esteem. 11) A substantial majority of the nudists and slightly over half of the "potential" nudists reported that at one time or another they tried to enhance their sexual activity through such innovations as engaging in a "striptease," dancing sexually for mate in the nude or seminude, use of mirrors, music, etc. No significant relationship, however, was observed between either levels of self-esteem or security and the use of such techniques. 12) Over half of both the nudists and "potential" nudists revealed that they verbalized some form of "sexy" talk during their sexual activity. In reference to the nudists, a significant relationship was noted between high self-esteem and the use of "sexy" talk during sexuality. 13) The median (average) number of orgasms experienced by the nudists and "potential" nudists, during a twenty-four hour period, was five and four respectively. With respect to the nudists, the experiencing of five or more orgasms as compared with fewer than five, during a twenty-four hour period (from any form of sexual behavior), was found to be significantly related to high self-esteem. 14) Over one third of the nudists and a little less than one fifth of the "potential" nudists disclosed having participated in group sex activity. Furthermore, more than half of those nudists and "potential" nudists who had experienced such stated that this form of sexual activity appealed to them. While no significant relationship was found between either self-esteem or security status and the experiencing of group sexual behavior, in regard to the nudists, a significant relationship was observed between feelings of high self-esteem and a positive reaction to the *idea* of engaging in group sex activity. 15) Slightly more than half of the nudists and over one third of the "potential" nudists, who were married or had been married, reported having experienced extramarital sexual relations. Extramarital sexual behavior on the part of the nudists was found to be significantly related to high self-esteem. The primary motives noted by the nudists for having engaged in extramarital sexuality fell into two categories: a) unpleasant marital and sexual relations, and b) at husband's suggestion, i.e., wife-swapping and group activity. The motives given by the "potential" nudists for having entered into extramarital sex relations were similar to those of the nudists, except that no mention was made of group activity and a minimum of importance was placed on wife-swapping. In the case of the nudists, the element of high self-esteem was also found to be significantly related to the possibility of engaging in extramarital sexual behavior in the future. Extramarital sexuality on the part of the nudists was experienced significantly more by those females who had had premarital coitus than by those who were virgins at the time of marriage. No such relationship, however, was disclosed in the case of the "potential" nudists. 16) More than one third of the nudists, and almost half of the "potential" nudists, revealed that they had participated in some form of sexual behavior with another female at some period during their life. With respect to the nudists, homosexual activity was observed to be significantly related to high self-esteem. 17) The two primary erogenous zones designated by the nudists and "potential" nudists were: a) the clitoris, and b) the breasts —nipples. In terms of environmental sources of sexual stimulation the one which was mentioned most by both groups of females was: reading. 18) A substantial majority of the nudists and more than half of the "potential" nudists described their reactions to the sight of the penis in a state of erection in positive terms. No meaningful relationship, however, was noted between either the self-esteem levels or security ratings of the participants and a reaction to the sight of the penis in a state of erection. 19) The primary reason given by the respondents for having become social nudists was one which had to do with their *husband's* desire or interest to become such. 20) The nudists as well as the "potential" nudists reported "French" or "deep soul" kissing to be the most sexually exciting and stimulating form of kissing. 21) Some 13 per cent of the nudists and 12 per cent of the "potential" nudists revealed that they had participated in some form of sexual behavior with animals. 22) Thirteen per cent of both groups of participants indicated that they had experienced incestuous relations at some time during their lives. 23) A favorable reaction to the thought of being raped in a nonviolent, but forceful manner was noted by 27 per cent of the nudists and 42 per cent of the "potential" nudists. No significant relationship was observed between either the self-esteem or security levels of the subjects and an approving response to the thought of being raped in a nonviolent, but forceful manner. 24) As described by both the nudists and "potential" nudists, the major mistakes committed by males in their love-making and sexual expression included the following: a) They are too selfish. b) They do not engage in enough sexual foreplay. c) They are too fast. d) They do not make certain that the woman has been satisfied, etc. 25) Included among the suggestions offered by the nudists as well as "potential" nudists for improving love-making techniques, were the following: a) Men should take more time and engage in more extended sexual foreplay. b) Men should educate themselves (through reading) in matters pertaining to love-making. c) Men should be more considerate of the emotional needs and desires of women. 26) Slightly more than three-fourths of the nudists, and half of the "potential" nudists, characterized their marriages as being essentially happy. 27) More than half of the nudists indicated that their husbands were more dominant psychologically than themselves, while only one fifth of these subjects viewed themselves as being (or having been) more dominant. In reference to the "potential" nudists, an equal number (36 per cent) described themselves, and their husbands, as being (or having been) the more dominant person. 28) To a very marked degree the sexual behavior patterns of the nudists were related more to their levels of self-esteem than feelings of security.[3] 29) Because of the changes in sexual attitudes and sexual expression on the part of females in our society which have taken place during the past years, and especially since the highly valuable studies by Kinsey *et al.*, at present there are no established norms for the sexual behavior of females in America. 30) In view of the changes in female sexuality which have occurred over the years, it is essential that males recognize that not only do females have very important sexual desires, drives, and interests which need to be satisfied, but many of them have an inclination, at times,

[3] A similar observation was made in this writer's previous study of females. See: DeMartino, M. F. (ed.), *Sexual Behavior and Personality Characteristics.* (New York: Grove Press, 1966), p. 143.

to assume a very active, aggressive, and dominant role in heterosexual activity. Perhaps, most important, males in our society need to get over equating strong sexual interests and desires on the part of females with "badness" or "immorality." (Such an attitude often prevails at an unconscious level.) Finally, in line with the more liberal attitudes and changing patterns of behavior expressed by females, it is vital from the standpoints of good psychological health and mutual compatibility that males in our society adopt a more accepting and understanding attitude of the needs, preferences, and feelings of females with respect to sexual expression in all of its ramifications.

Social nudism viewed psychologically

Although this writer is not a social nudist and does not have any special desire to become one, nevertheless it is felt that, under appropriate conditions, the practice of social nudism can be very psychotherapeutic in a number of different ways. In addition to providing a wholesome environment in which to raise children, particularly in regard to attitudes pertaining to the human body and heterosexual development, a social nudist setting affords an atmosphere in which adolescents and adults may come to acquire an acceptance of themselves in the truest sense. For if a person is able to feel at ease with himself and others when in a complete state of nudity, a state which tends to make one feel he is without any physical defenses (e.g. clothes) and which also reduces markedly one's psychological defenses, a major step forward is made toward overcoming underlying feelings of self-consciousness, shyness, and unwarranted feelings of embarrassment, shame, and guilt. As Maslow has so colorfully remarked, "I still think that nudism, simply going naked before a lot of other people, is itself a kind of therapy, especially if we can be conscious of it, that is, if there's a skilled person around to direct what's going on, to bring things to consciousness. After all, these training groups are a kind of psychological nudism under careful direction. I wonder, as a matter of fact, what would happen as an experiment if these T-groups remained exactly as they are but added a physical nudism. Suppose all these same people at Lake Arrowhead were required to take all their clothes off for the two weeks that they were here.[4] I suspect that the results would be even faster, more startling, and more beneficial. People would go away from there an awful lot

[4] Maslow is referring here to his visit to the Lake Arrowhead Conference Center of the University of California (Los Angeles) which involved a series of unstructured training groups.

freer, a lot more spontaneous, less guarded, less defensive, not only about the shape of their behinds or whether their bellies were hanging or not, but freer and more innocent about their minds as well. If I can learn not to be conscious about the fact that my ass is hanging, or that my belly sticks out too much, if I can throw off this fear, this defense, maybe this act of freedom will enable me thereby to throw off a lot of other defenses—maybe the defense of looking ignorant, or uncontrolled, or something like that."[5]

GENERAL CONCLUSIONS

As a group, our sample of female social nudists seemed to be of relatively sound psychological health and tended to be oriented rather strongly toward sexuality. This tendency was exemplified by the high percentage of strong (very strong, above average) sexual drives and desires, and high prevalency of masturbatory behavior, nonvirginity, fellatio, cunnilingus, group sex activity, extramarital relations, homosexuality, sexual contacts with animals, etc., on the part of the subjects. As was reported previously by Maslow, a number of sexual practices and desires were found to be significantly related to feelings of self-esteem. While no broad generalizations pertaining to the sexual activities of all female nudists may be drawn from the present, somewhat select, sample of social nudists, it would appear from the results obtained, that among *other reasons*, a liking for, and an interest in, social nudism, is to a fairly large extent related to an *interest* in sensuality.[6] In all likelihood, for many social nudists this sensuous interest exists mainly at an unconscious or subconscious level of awareness.

[5] Reprinted with permission from A. H. Maslow, *Eupsychian Management: A Journal*. (Homewood, Illinois: R. D. Irwin, Inc., 1965), p. 160.

[6] See also: a) Ilfeld, F. Jr., and Lauer, R., *Social Nudism in America*. (New Haven, Connecticut: College and University Press, 1964), especially pp. 174–85. b) Dennis, Gail, "Nudism, Sun or Sex," *Sexology*, 1964, September, 80–83.

BIBLIOGRAPHY

1. Allport, G. W. "The Trend in Motivational Theory," *The American Journal of Orthopsychiatry*, 1953, *23*, 107–119.
2. Bass-Hass, R. "The Lesbian Dyad," *Journal of Sex Research*, 1968, *4*, 108–26.
3. Beach, F. A. (ed.) *Sex and Behavior*. New York: John Wiley and Sons, 1965.
4. Beigel, H. G. (ed.) *Advances in Sex Research*. New York: Harper & Row, 1963.
5. Bell, R. R. *Premarital Sex in a Changing Society*. Englewood Cliffs, N.J., Prentice-Hall.
6. Benjamin, H. *The Transsexual Phenomenon*. New York: The Julian Press, 1966.
7. Benson, R. O. D. *In Defense of Homosexuality*. New York: The Julian Press, 1965.
8. Bieber, T. "The Lesbian Patient," *Medical Aspects of Human Sexuality*, 1969, *3*, 6–12.
9. Bindum, P. "A Report on a Marathon: The Effect of Physical Nudity Upon the Practice of Interaction in the Marathon Group," *Psychotherapy Theory, Research and Practice*, September, 1968.
10. Blake, R. *The American Dictionary of Sexual Terms*. Hollywood, California: Century Pub. Co., 1965.
11. Blank, L. *Nudity and Sexuality: Studies in Voyeurism and Exhibitionism*. Chicago: Aldine Pub. Co., 1966.
12. Blank, S. *Life in a Nudist Camp*. Girard, Kansas: Haldeman-Julius, 1948.
13. Bonaparte, M. *Female Sexuality*. New York: International Universities Press, 1953.
14. Boone, I. *Joys of Nudism*. New York: Greenberg, 1934.
15. Brecher, R., and Brecher, E. (eds.) *An Analysis of Human Sexual Response*. New York: New American Library, 1966.
16. Breedlove, W., and Breedlove, J. *Swap Clubs*. Los Angeles: Sherbourne Press, 1964.
17. Burgess, E. W., and Wallin, P. *Engagement and Marriage*. Philadelphia: J. B. Lippincott Co., 1953.
18. Calderone, M. S. *Release From Sexual Tensions*. New York: Random House, 1960.
19. Casler, L. "Some Sociopsychological Observations in a Nudist Camp: A Preliminary Study," *Journal of Social Psychology*, 1964, *64*, 307–23.

20. Chapman, J. D. *The Feminine Mind and Body*. New York: Philosophical Library, 1967.
21. Christensen, H. T. "Cultural Relativism and Premarital Sex Norms," *American Sociological Review*, 1960, 25, 31–39.
22. Cox, B. *Sexual Techniques During Prescribed Continence*. New York: Medical Press of N.Y., 1968.
23. Cuber, J. F., and Harroff, P. B. *The Significant Americans, A Study of Sexual Behavior Among the Affluent*. New York: Appleton-Century, 1965.
24. Davis, M. *The Sexual Responsibility of Women*. New York: Dial Press, 1956.
25. DeMartino, M.F. (ed.) *Sexual Behavior and Personality Characteristics*. New York: Grove Press, 1966.
26. Dennis, A. *Taboo, Sex and Morality Around The World*. New York: G. P. Putnam's Sons, 1967.
27. Dennis, G. "Nudism, Sun or Sex," *Sexology*, 1964, September, 80–83.
28. Dickinson, R. L., and Beam, L. *The Single Woman*. Baltimore: Williams and Wilkins, 1934.
29. Edwardes, A. *The Jewel in the Lotus*. New York: The Julian Press, 1960.
30. Ellis, A. *American Sexual Tragedy*. New York: Twayne Publishers, 1954.
31. Ellis, A. *Suppressed*. New York: New Classics House, 1965.
32. Ellis, A. *If This Be Sexual Heresy*. New York: Tower Publications, 1966.
33. Ellis, A. "Homosexuality: The Right to be Wrong," *Journal of Sex Research*, 1968, 4, 51–56.
34. Ellis, A., and Abarbanel, A. (eds.) *Encyclopedia of Sexual Behavior*. New York: Hawthorne Books, 1961.
35. Ellis, A., and Conway, R. *The Art of Erotic Seduction*. New York: Lyle Stuart, 1967.
36. Ellis, A., and Sagarin, E. *Nymphomania*. New York: Macfadden-Barten, 1965.
37. Ellis, A. *The Art and Science of Love*. New York: Dell, 1965.
38. Fisher, S., and Osofsky, H. "Sexual Responsiveness in Women," *Archives of General Psychiatry*, 1967, 17, 214–26.
39. Ford, C. S., and Beach, F. A. *Patterns of Sexual Behavior*. New York: Harper and Bros., 1951.
40. Freeman, M. G. "The Sexual Behavior of American College Women: An Empirical Study and an Historical Survey," *Merrill-Palmer Quarterly of Behavior and Development*, 1965, 11, 33–48.
41. Fromm, E., Suzuki, D. T., and DeMartino, R. *Zen Buddhism and Psychoanalysis*. New York: Grove Press, 1963.
42. Gay, J. *On Going Naked*. New York: Garden City Publishing Co., 1932.
43. Gebhard, P. H. "Factors in Marital Orgasm," *Journal of Social Issues*, 1966, 22, 88–95.

44. Goldberg, M., Brill, N.Q., Chez, R.A., Gallant, D.M., Laidlow, R.W. "What Do You Tell Patients Who Ask About Coital Positions?" *Medical Aspects of Human Sexuality*, 1968, *2*, 43–48.

45. Graham, S. R. "The Effects of Psychoanalytically Oriented Psychotherapy on Levels of Frequency and Satisfaction in Sexual Activity," *Journal of Clinical Psychology*, 1960, *16*, 94–98.

46. Greene, G. *Sex and The College Girl*. New York: Dell Pub. Co., 1964.

47. Hartman, W. E., and Fithian, M. *Nudism in America: A Social Psychological Study*. to be published.

48. Hartogs, R., and Fantel, H. *Four Letter Word Games, The Psychology of Obscenity*. New York: Evans and Co., 1967.

49. Hettlinger, R. F. *Living With Sex: The Student's Dilemma*. New York: The Seaburg Press, 1966.

50. Hollender, M. H. "Women's Fantasies During Sexual Intercourse," *Archives of General Psychiatry*, 1963, 8, 86–90.

51. Ilfeld, F. Jr., and Laner, R. *Social Nudism in America*. New Haven, Connecticut: College and University Press, 1964.

52. Johnson, D. *The Nudists*. New York: Duell, Sloan and Pearce, 1959.

53. Johnson, D. *Nudist Primer*. Spokane, Washington: Mervin Mounce, Pub., 1960.

54. Johnson, E. W. *Love and Sex in Plain Language. For Boys and Girls and Their Parents*. Philadelphia: J. B. Lippincott Co., 1965.

55. Kinsey, A. C., Pomeroy, W. B., Martin, C. E., and Gebhard, P. H. *Sexual Behavior in the Human Female*. Philadelphia: Saunders Co., 1953.

56. Kirkendall, L. *Premarital Intercourse and Interpersonal Relationships*. New York: The Julian Press, 1961.

57. Klausner, S. Z. "Inferential Visibility and Sex Norms in the Middle East," *Journal of Sex Research*, 1965, *1*, 201–20.

58. Kleegman, S. J., and Sherwin, A. K. *Infertility In Women*. Philadelphia: F. A. Davis Co., 1966.

59. Knight, R. P., and Wright, T. *Sexual Symbolism: A History of Phallic Worship*. New York: The Julian Press, 1957.

60. Konopka, G. *The Adolescent Girl in Conflict*. Englewood Cliffs, N.J.: Prentice-Hall, 1966.

61. Kronhausen, P., and Kronhausen, E. *The Sexually Responsive Woman*. New York: Ballantine Books, 1965.

62. Levitt, E. E., and Brady, J. P. "Sexual Preferences in Young Adult Males and Some Correlates," *Journal of Clinical Psychology*, 1965, *21*, 347–54.

63. Levitt, E. E., and Hinesley, R. K. "Some Factors in the Valences of Erotic Visual Stimuli," *Journal of Sex Research*, 1967, *3*, 63–68.

64. Lief, H. I. "Changing Sexual Patterns and Their Impact on Clinical Practice," *Medical Opinion and Review*, 1965, *1*, 10–14.

65. Lipton, L. *The Erotic Revolution*. Los Angeles: Sherbourne Press, 1965.

66. Lorand, S. "The Psychology of Nudism," *Psychoanalytical Review*, April, 1933.
67. Lowen, A. "In Defense of Modesty," *Journal of Sex Research*, 1968, *4*, 51-56.
68. Lowen, A. *Love and Orgasm*. New York: The Macmillan Co., 1965.
69. Mace, D. R. "The Present Status of Marriage in the United States," *Medical Aspects of Human Sexuality*, 1968, *2*, 14–26.
70. Mann, W. E. "Sexual Standards and Trends in Sweden," *Journal of Sex Research*, 1967, *3*, 191–200.
71. Maslow, A. H. "Self-esteem (Dominance-Feeling) and Sexuality in Women," *Journal of Social Psychology*, 1942, *16*, 259–94.
72. Maslow, A. H. "The Dynamics of Psychological Security-Insecurity," *Character and Personality*, 1942, *10*, 331–344.
73. Maslow, A. H. *Motivation and Personality*. New York: Harper and Bros., 1954.
74. Maslow, A. H. *Religions, Values and Peak-Experiences*. Columbus: Ohio State Univ. Press, 1964.
75. Maslow, A. H. *The Psychology of Science. A Reconnaissance*. New York: Harper & Row, 1966.
76. Maslow, A. H. *Toward a Psychology of Being*. Revised Edition. Princeton, N.J.: D. Van Nostrand Co., 1968.
77. Maslow, A. H., Rand, H. and Newman, S. "Some Parallels Between the Dominance and Sexual Behavior of Monkeys and the Fantasies of Psychoanalytic Patients," *Journal of Nervous and Mental Disease*, 1960, *131*, 202–12.
78. Masters, R. E. L. *Cradle of Erotica*. New York: The Julian Press, 1963.
79. Masters, W. H., and Johnson, V. E. *Human Sexual Response*. Boston: Little, Brown & Co., 1966.
80. McCary, J. L. *Human Sexuality*. Princeton, New Jersey: Van Nostrand-Rheinhold Co., 1967.
81. Merril, F. and Merril, M. *Among the Nudists*. New York: Alfred A. Knopf, 1931.
82. Merril, F. and Merril, M. *Nudism Comes to America*. New York: Alfred A. Knopf, 1932.
83. Money, J. (ed.) *Sex Research, New Developments*. New York: Holt, Rinehart and Winston, 1965.
84. Moskin, J. R. "The New Contraceptive Society," *Look Magazine*, February 4, 1969, 50–53.
85. Mosse, H. L. "The Influence of Mass Media on the Sex Problems of Teenagers," *Journal of Sex Research*, 1966, *2*, 27–35.
86. Oliven, J. F. *Sexual Hygiene and Pathology. A Manual for the Physician and the Professors*. Second Edition. Philadelphia: J. B. Lippincott, 1965.
87. Opler, M. K. "Cross-Cultural Aspects of Kissing," *Medical Aspects of Human Sexuality*, 1969, *3*, 11–21.
88. Packard, V. *The Sexual Wilderness*. New York: David McKay Co., 1968.

89. Pomeroy, W. B. "Some Aspects of Prostitution," *Journal of Sex Research*, 1965, *1*, 177–87.
90. Reiss, I. L. *Premarital Sexual Standards in America*. Glencoe, Ill.: The Free Press, 1960.
91. Reiss, I. L. *The Social Context of Premarital Sexual Permissiveness*. New York: Holt, Rinehart and Winston, 1967.
92. Rubin, I. *Sexual Life After Sixty*. New York: The New American Library, 1967.
93. Ruitenbeek, H. M. (ed.) *Psychoanalysis and Female Sexuality*. New Haven, Connecticut: College and University Press, 1966.
94. Schofield, M. *The Sexual Behavior of Young People*. London: Longmans, Green and Co., 1965.
95. Schur, E. M. (ed.) *The Family and the Sexual Revolution*. Bloomington, Indiana: Indiana University Press, 1964.
96. Shope, D. F. "The Orgastic Responsiveness of Selected College Females," *Journal of Sex Research*, 1968, *4*, 206–19.
97. Shor, J. "Female Sexuality: Aspects and Prospects," *Psychoanalysis*, 1954, *2*, 47–76.
98. Silverman, H. L. (ed.) *Marital Counseling*. Springfield, Ill.: C. C. Thomas, 1967.
99. Sprague, W. D. *Sexual Behavior of American Nurses*. New York: Lancer Books, 1964.
100. Stacey, C. L., and DeMartino, M. F. (eds.) *Understanding Human Motivation*. Revised Edition. Cleveland: World Publishing Co., 1963.
101. Stokes, W. R. "Inadequacy of Female Orgasm as a Problem in Marriage Counseling," *Journal of Sex Research*, 1968, *4*, 225–30.
102. Strachstein, A. *Sunbathing and Nudism*. Girard, Kansas: Haldeman-Julius, 1949.
103. Walin, P. "A Study of Orgasm as a Condition of Woman's Enjoyment of Intercourse," *Journal of Social Psychology*, 1960, *51*, 191–98.
104. Warren, H. C. "Social Nudism and the Body Taboo," *Psychological Review*, 1933, *40*, p. 178.
105. Weinberg, M. S. "Sexual Modesty, Social Meanings, and the Nudist Camp," *Social Problems*, 1965, *12*.
106. Weinberg, M. S. "Becoming a Nudist," *Psychiatry*, 1966, *29*, 15–24.
107. Weinberg, M. S. "The Nudist Camp: Way of Life and Social Structure," *Human Organization*, 1967, *26*, 15–24.
108. Williams, C. E. *The Psychology of Nudism*. Mays Landing, N.J.: Sunshine Publishing Co., 1941.
109. Wilson, T. J. B., and Meyers, E. *Wife Swapping*. New York: Counterpoint, Inc., 1966.

SUBJECT INDEX

Animals, sexual contacts with, 183–185, 223
  and relationship to feelings of self-esteem and security, 184
  prevalence of, 183
Approach to study, plan of, and sources of data, 11–12
Attitudes of subjects toward sex, 20–25, 219
  and relationship to feelings of self-esteem and security, 20

Changing sexual attitudes of females, 19
Coitus, locations in which occurred, 61–66
Comments, additional, by subjects concerning nudism, nudists, nudist camps, their reactions to study, etc., 211–217
Cunnilingus (mouth-genital contact), 74–83, 179, 180, 181, 182, 183, 220
  acceptance of, 74–75, 76–83
  definition of, 74
  prevalence of, 74, 75

Daughters of Bilitis, IX, 11, 12, 144

Educational levels of subjects, 13–14
Erogenous zones of subjects, 155–158, 222
Extramarital and premarital coitus, relationship between, 141, 222
Extramarital sexual relations, 133–143, 222
  and motives for having engaged in, 134–140, 222
  and possibility of engaging in such, in the future, 140–143
  and relationship to feelings of self-esteem and security, 133–134, 140–141, 222
  prevalence of, 133

Fantasies experienced during sexuality, 87–90, 221

and relationship to feelings of self-esteem and security, 88, 221
  prevalence of, 87
Fellatio (mouth-genital contact), 74–83, 180, 220
  acceptance of, 74–75, 76–83
  definition of, 74
  prevalence of, 74, 75
Fellatio and cunnilingus, practice of *both*, and relationship to feelings of self-esteem and security, 75, 220

Geographic locations of subjects, 15
Group sexual behavior, 127–132
  and relationship to feelings of self-esteem and security, 128, 222
  prevalence of, 127, 128, 222

Hand-genital contact (masturbation) with partner, 75–83
  acceptance of, 76–83
  prevalence of, 76
Historical background of social nudism, 1–2

Incestuous behavior, 185–187
  effect of, on overall sexual life, 185–186
  prevalence of, 185, 223
Initiation of sex activity, and relationship to feelings of self-esteem and security, 92–221
Initiator of sexuality, and degree of participation during activity, 91–96

Janus society, 144

Kissing, kind of, found most exciting sexually, 179–182, 222–223

Lesbians, nature of sample, 11
Love-making by self-actualizing persons, 92
Love-making, mistakes made by males in, 192–199, 223

AUTHOR INDEX

ABOUT THE AUTHOR

Previous to his present position of Associate Professor of Psychology at the Onondaga Community College in Syracuse, N.Y., Mr. DeMartino taught at Syracuse University and Auburn University in Alabama. A Member of the American Psychological Association, the Society for the Scientific Study of Sex, and the American Association for Humanistic Psychology, Mr. DeMartino, who is a certified psychologist, has been engaged in private clinical practice since 1956. Books published by Mr. DeMartino include: *Dreams and Personality Dynamics* (editor and contributor), *Counseling and Psychotherapy with the Mentally Retarded* (co-editor and contributor), *Understanding Human Motivation* (co-editor), and *Sexual Behavior and Personality Characteristics* (editor and contributor). He has also had research articles published in such psychological and psychiatric journals as the *American Psychologist*, the *Journal of Clinical Psychology*, and the *Psychiatric Quarterly Supplement*.